Youth
Ministry
in Modern
America

Youth Ministry in Modern America

1930 to the Present

JON PAHL

© 2000 by Hendrickson Publishers, Inc.
P. O. Box 3473
Peabody, Massachusetts 01961–3473

ISBN 1–56563–467–5

Printed in the United States of America

First printing — September 2000

Library of Congress Cataloging in Publication Data

Pahl, Jon, 1958–
    Youth ministry in modern America: 1930 to the present /
Jon Pahl.
        p. cm.
    Includes bibliographical references and index.
    ISBN 1–56563–467–5
    1. Church work with youth—United States—History.
    2. United States—Church history—20th century.   I. Title.

BV4447.P24   2000
259'.23'09730904—dc21

                                                    00–037007

To the young people of:

St. Mark's Lutheran Church
Medaryville, Indiana

First Christian Church
Valparaiso, Indiana

and

Camp Arcadia
Arcadia, Michigan

December 28, 1999

Table of Contents

Foreword

Barely a century has passed since "adolescence" was first identified as a distinct stage within a human life. During that century, brief by historians' reckoning, teenagers and young adults have made their presence felt in every corner of American society. They have also caught the attention of the world, as performers and protesters, athletes and trend setters, criminals and consumers. Even so, sometimes they seem to be barely visible, keeping to themselves on the margins of church, state, or family life—or being relegated to the margins by adults who are uncomfortable with their questions and their energy.

Historians and other scholars of American religious life have been among those who relegate young people to the margins. Even though youth have been involved in every denomination and religious movement, they rarely appear in books about American Christianity. As a result, our understanding of faith and culture is less complete than it should be. Moreover, in overlooking youth we miss an especially important and dynamic aspect of the story, for their questions and energy characteristically press at the boundaries of church and society. Looking to the margins on which young people dwell we are likely to see traditions undergoing challenge and believers exploring new paths.

Modern American Youth Ministry begins to redress the invisibility of youth in books about American Christianity. In early chapters, portraits of young people in four twentieth-century denominational settings shine a spotlight on a set of representative stories. This part of the book should encourage additional scholars to explore how young people have been involved in other aspects of American religion. Later chapters set forth more general concerns and make some provocative proposals about youth, their vulnerability, their hopes, and adult accountability to and for them. Here the book becomes a summons to Christian adults to take young people and their participation in church and culture as a matter of crucial importance.

The young people in this book are not the mere recipients of youth programs initiated by adults. Rather, they make choices and stretch limits. They are historical agents involved in creative ways in some of the central social and spiritual dramas of their time; and so are the young people of today.

Conventional wisdom affirms that the future belongs to young people. For this reason, it is said, they deserve the best insights and most attentive presence we adults can offer. Fair enough. Less conventional and more important, however, is the idea that they deserve such wise and attentive companionship as we can offer because they are already, today, precious beyond price, beloved of God. Both insights have inspired some of our forebears. May they also inspire us as we accompany today's youth in their passage from childhood into adult life-paths that are good for them, for others, for creation, and attuned to the presence of God.

DOROTHY C. BASS
Valparaiso University

Acknowledgments

This book began in 1994 when my colleague Dorothy C. Bass asked me to write a chapter for a collaborative work she envisioned on "Christian education and spiritual formation in modern America." More specifically, Dorothy asked me to compare mainline Protestant, Roman Catholic, Evangelical, and African-American youth ministry from 1930 to the present, including not only descriptions of youth ministry in these four streams of the Christian tradition but also normative judgments across the traditions in light of the "central argument" of Christianity. It was a daunting assignment; so daunting that what began as a chapter has now become this rather lengthy book. Dorothy was a steady guide throughout my research and writing. I'm grateful to her, and, through her, to the Lilly Endowment, for financial support of this project.

Scott Appleby and other members of the original team also provided editorial and substantive support. Margaret Bendroth, Virginia Brereton, David Daniels, E. Brooks Holifield, Martin Marty, and John McGreevy read and provided comments on an early draft, and their criticisms and insights were helpful to me. Members of my class on "Christianity in America," Theology 353,

Spring, 1999 also read the chapter drafts and provided me with considerable stylistic and substantive help. Other colleagues also read parts of the manuscript, or provided conversational support or friendship that advanced it, notably Nandini Bhattacharya, Michael Caldwell, members of the Colloquium on Violence and Religion, Betty DeBerg, Rick and Sarah DeMaris, and the ever-changing members of the Valparaiso NBA (that would be the Noon-Hour Basketball Association—they know who they are). The Valparaiso University Gospel Choir—and especially the director, Ms. Judith Erwin-Neville, has provided me a "balm in Gilead" at a time when I needed it.

My family—wife Lisa, sons Justin and Nathan, and daughter Rheanne—know more than anyone that the life of a scholar does not always translate into constant domestic relations. I love them all in ways I sometimes find hard to put into words (not usually a problem for me). I also hope they know that our shared moments of laughter *and* tears bring a depth to life that, even if I too often take for granted, also gives me glimmers of that grace which surpasses human understanding.

Librarians and archivists at the Concordia Historical Institute, the University of Notre Dame, the Billy Graham Center at Wheaton College, and Valparaiso University saved me countless hours and many steps. Members of Bethel African Methodist Episcopal Church in Baltimore and notably Rev. David DeVaux welcomed me to their congregation for a week of research and gave me access to literature I normally would not have had. I am thankful for all of them and appreciated the professional support and personal courtesies they extended to me. Yvonne Hale and Lara Urban of the Huegli Hall Support Staff helped me with many administrative matters, and Jan Rubsam expertly turned my footnotes into the bibliography, and prevented me many embarrassing mistakes along the way.

The folks at Hendrickson Publishers have been very pleasant to work with. Dave Zagunis contacted me early to convey his shared interest in youth ministry, and Shirley A. Decker-Lucke was a careful and thorough copy editor of the manuscript. I'm grateful especially to Patrick Alexander—who, with an introduction and some encouragement by J. J. Johnson Leese, took a leap-of-faith on a book in a relatively new area of research.

Finally, I have had the benefit of participation in several Christian communities while I worked on this manuscript. For two years I was the Deacon at a small rural church—St. Mark's Lutheran

Church in Medaryville, Indiana. For another two years I served as youth minister at First Christian Church in Valparaiso. Finally, for nearly three summers I was part of the community at Camp Arcadia, a Christian family resort in Northern Michigan. In all three places, I worked with and learned from young people who were in one way or another striving to live out their Christian pilgrimage in modern America. I am grateful to them for letting me walk with them for a while on our journeys through life and hope that despite my failures they learned from me that which is in the end the deepest message of this book: that for Christians purity doesn't entail perfection, but when put into practice love is stronger than death. It is to these young people that I dedicate this book.

Abbreviations

JOURNALS AND MAGAZINES

ChrCent	*Christian Century*
CurTM	*Currents in Theology and Mission*
JAAR	*Journal of the American Academy of Religion*
ThTo	*Theology Today*
USCathHist	*U.S. Catholic Historian*
WLM	*Walther League Messenger*
WQ	*Workers Quarterly*
YFC	*Youth for Christ*

ORGANIZATIONS

A.M.E.	African Methodist Episcopal
CYO	Catholic Youth Organization
NAE	National Association of Evangelicals
NCC	National Council of Churches
WCC	World Council of Churches
YCW	Young Christian Workers
YFC	Youth for Christ

| YMCA | Young Men's Christian Association |
| YWCA | Young Women's Christian Association |

OTHER

ca.	circa
cf.	compare
ch(s).	chapter(s)
ed(s).	editor(s), edited by
e.g.	*exempli gratia,* for example
esp.	especially
et al.	*et alii,* and others
n.	note
no.	number
vol(s).	volume(s)

Introduction

Do not say, "I am only a youth." . . . Do not be afraid . . . ,
for I am with you to deliver you.

—Jeremiah 1:7–8

Apparently Jeremiah was a young man when he sensed the call of the Lord to undertake his vocation as a prophet. "Now the word of the LORD came to me," Jeremiah recalled, "saying, 'Before I formed you in the womb I knew you, and before you were born I consecrated you; I appointed you a prophet to the nations. . . . to pluck up and to pull down, to destroy and to overthrow, to build and to plant.'" Young as he was, Jeremiah knew that this talk of plucking up and pulling down nations not only sounded arrogant but was likely to land him in trouble with the authorities. So, like many prophets before and after him, Jeremiah tried to evade his calling: "I am only a youth," he excused himself to the Lord; "I do not know how to speak." God responded with a promise—the epigraph to this book—to be with Jeremiah and to deliver him from danger. Jeremiah took the promise to heart. His book indicts injustice in Israel's southern kingdom (called Judah) yet also offers the same solace and deliverance to Judah that he experienced in God's promise. Indeed, Jeremiah's book ends with the prospect of a renewed Judah, now faithful to the Lord.

Today, I hear variants on Jeremiah's lament, "I am only a youth," almost every day from students in my college classrooms and from the teenagers with whom I work.[1] The young people who utter these spoken or unspoken complaints are generally middle class or above, yet they have experienced in their lives substance abuse, violent crime, family instability, racism, rape, and more. Many of them bear scars from psychological trauma. They are aware of injustice and corruption in church, state, and business. They know their government and economy are heavily invested in war or the preparation for war. Like Jeremiah, America's youth have plenty to fear and plenty from which they will need deliverance. They are vulnerable, and they know it.[2]

At the same time, the youth and young adults with whom I work and teach sometimes surprise me with a Jeremiah-like sense of justice and courage. For all they have to fear, some of them possess little sense of danger, and a few even share Jeremiah's confidence in God's presence. At their most unguarded moments, they reveal to me that they expect to re-create the future, just as Jeremiah sought to re-create Judah.[3] Even more, we count on them to do so. Thus, America's churches, recognizing the potential of youth, have developed countless agencies, organizations, programs, and institutions to educate, form, and serve them.[4] Youth groups and organizations are among the most notable twentieth-century examples of the institutional creativity of Christianity in the United States.[5]

If so many programs have developed for U.S. children and youth, why are they still vulnerable? Study after study has documented the dangers facing them. The homicide rate for teens aged fifteen through nineteen nearly doubled between 1970 and 1994. Young men were especially vulnerable to gun violence; firearms accounted for 87 percent of youth deaths by homicide in 1994.[6] Young women were especially vulnerable to the trauma of rape: one in four young women reports being a victim of sexual assault by the senior year in high school, and 30 percent of girls report having thought seriously about suicide by age eighteen.[7] Even schools and families are not safe havens; one in four high schoolers reports being hit by a parent, and recent shootings in Jonesboro, Arkansas, and Littleton, Colorado, highlight the threats faced by teens across the United States.[8] On a typical day in America in the 1990s, twenty-three young people died from gunshot wounds, fourteen thousand were victimized by theft, and over eight thousand were raped, stabbed, beaten, or abused.[9] Little wonder that the suicide rate for all adolescents tripled between 1960 and 1990 and that private psychiatric beds for teenagers "became the fastest growing segment of the hospital industry."[10] These numbers are numbing, but they highlight the fact that "by the time they reach adolescence, many children already have experienced a level of violence that only combat soldiers used to know."[11]

That youth are so vulnerable despite the intense institutional attention paid to them is one of the great ironies of twentieth-century American history. In the following pages I will untangle the twisted strands of this irony. I will draw and analyze four portraits of Christian youth and the efforts of their churches to educate and form them in faith during the late twentieth century. Why study *Christian* youth? In part, the answer is obvious: most youth throughout American history have been Christians of one variety or another, and their histories and the histories of the institutions that have served them have not been told. Sociological and psychological studies of youth abound, but few historians have (until recently) documented the lives of youth.[12] So, writing the history of Christian youth and the history of the organizations to which they belonged will uncover a neglected facet of historical change and innovation, not only illuminating the narrow history of Christian youth ministry but also suggesting new angles of vision on the broad sweep of twentieth-century American social and cultural history.[13]

From among the wide variety of Christian youth ministries in the late twentieth century, I have drawn portraits of four: the Walther League (Lutheran), the Young Christian Workers (YCW, Catholic), Youth for Christ (YFC, Evangelical), and African-American congregational youth ministries (Methodist, Baptist, and United Church of Christ). Why study these four cases?[14] They represent what are probably the most significant groups of Christian believers in the second half of the twentieth century. Lutheran youth who joined the Walther League did so in part because it gave them passage into the mainline of Christianity and American culture. When Lutheranism, the earliest of the sixteenth-century Protestant reform movements in Europe, was transplanted to the United States, it took the form of numerous ethnically based sects. In the twentieth century, however, Lutherans in the United States increasingly adopted the status and style of mainline Protestants

with a long history of influence in America, such as the Presbyterians, the Episcopalians, and the Methodists. Similarly, Catholic
youth who joined the YCW movement did so as members of
an ancient faith traceable to the founding of Christianity. In the
twentieth century, however, Catholics became the largest single
group of Christian believers in the United States. The young
people of YFC were part of the Evangelical resurgence of revival-
based religion, whose leaders (most notably Billy Graham) gained
prominence across American culture in the late twentieth century.
Finally, African Americans developed in local congregations—if
not in national youth organizations—distinct styles of worship,
theology, and youth ministry that deserve distinct attention. Perhaps no movement transformed twentieth-century American culture more dramatically than the civil rights movement, which itself
is not understandable apart from African American congregations
and youth.

Each of the first four chapters, then, draws a historical portrait
of the distinct genius and development of one youth organization
during the years from 1930 to 1999. Each chapter traces the contours and changes in what I call the "life-path" of each youth ministry. Leaders in all four settings of youth ministry intended to
transmit Christianity across generations: the idea of a life-path is
designed to convey that each organization directed youth toward a
particular goal, identity, or way of life. Youth ministries communicated these ideal life-paths to youth through many means: study,
worship, social service, and formal and informal rites of passage.
This idea of a life-path is a construct. Life-paths are often shaped
unconsciously, by extrinsic cultural factors as much as by intentional programs or prescriptions. But agents of history are not
without understanding of their motives and actions, and they leave
evidence of their intent in the historical record. Just as there have
been distinct (if changing) streams of the Christian tradition in
America, so, too, distinct (if changing) normative Christian life-
paths have been communicated to America's youth in the twentieth century.[15]

In chapter 1 the Walther League's life-path of "Christian Knowledge, Christian Service" is an example of a movement within
mainline Protestantism that sought to educate knowledgeable
Christians who were motivated to serve society. If this sounds like a
platitude, it is testimony to how mainline the Walther League was
during this period. In downtown Chicago, the Walther League
leaders operated an office out of which they coordinated a wide

array of youth-serving programs and institutions. Educational opportunities, social programs, and rites of passage all sought to
nurture faith in the Walther Leaguers, who were organized into
regional districts which networked youth groups from Lutheran
congregations (primarily but not exclusively in the Lutheran
Church–Missouri Synod) across the United States. Through their
participation in this youth organization, Walther Leaguers learned
to be Lutherans, but through their links with a mainline denominational structure they also learned plenty of lessons about being
American and Protestant. The genius of the Walther League was its
effort to nurture young Christians who embraced a paradox that
held in tension Christian knowledge (or "inwardness") with Christian service to society (or "outwardness"). Over time (most dramatically in the sixties), the balance in this paradox tilted toward
the side of social service—a trend we shall find shared widely by
youth ministries during this time. This shift within the Walther
League's life-path—from purity to practices—was not popular
among conservative Lutherans, and by 1977 the Walther League
had disbanded. The history of the Walther League foreshadowed
both a greater ecumenical and mainline future for Lutheranism in
America and a schism within the Lutheran Church–Missouri Synod
that turned the denomination in a quasi-fundamentalist direction.
Money from the sale of the Walther League office building went to
two social service agencies—the Lutheran Volunteer Corps and the
Wheat Ridge Foundation. In the absence of a centralized national
organization for young people, Lutherans increasingly went local
with youth ministry in the late twentieth century.[16]

Chapter 2 describes Young Christian Workers, a movement
to educate and form "lay apostles" within the Roman Catholic
Church. Like Lutherans, Catholics in the United States were initially divided into distinct ethnic groups upon arrival in the New
World. During the nineteenth century, however, the hierarchy of
the church—pope, cardinals, archbishops, bishops, priests—and
the laity effected a degree of centralization in American parishes.
The genius of the YCW movement was that it took what had often
been considered a clergy prerogative—apostolicity—and offered it .
to young laypeople. The YCW was one of many reform movements
to empower laypeople in mid-twentieth-century Catholicism. Like
the Walther League, it constituted a paradox: the life-path of a lay
apostle included spiritual formation by the beliefs and rites of passage that made a person a Catholic individual, but Catholics were
also to express their faith collectively in social practices that held

universal significance, as the word *catholic* implies. Over time, cleri-
cally appointed YCW leaders shifted the movement toward the traditional Christian education of individuals, and the movement
lost its collective focus. Young people were interested in *practical*
Christianity, and by 1968 YCW had folded. By failing to embrace
relevant practices for youth, YCW leaders were left with a pure
ideal but no movement. Still, youth ministry among Catholics
continues today in a wide variety of other organizations and agencies as well as in local parishes.

Chapter 3 is a historical portrait of Youth For Christ, an Evangelical movement, led in its early years by Billy Graham, that
sought to nurture in young people a life-path of witness for Christ.
The roots of YFC can be traced to the history of revivalism in
America. Youth for Christ began in the 1940s with spectacular revivals in auditoriums filled with young people, who were urged to
commit themselves to a personal relationship with Jesus Christ. At
these revivals, and through ongoing YFC programs in the fifties
and sixties, converts were also encouraged to be patriotic Americans who lived lives of personal moral purity. Witnesses for Christ
could also be warriors for the American way. Evangelical movements not only have been culturally confirming but also have
linked personal conversion with efforts to reform American society. Youth for Christ was no exception. Especially in recent years,
YFC and other Evangelical organizations for young people have
deepened the meaning of witness beyond patriotism and moral
purity to include explicit social and political reforms and stances.
The movement's normative life-path has shifted somewhat from
purity to practices.

Chapter 4 narrates how African-American Christian congregations forged among their young people a life-path of freedom. In
churches such as the Bethel African Methodist Episcopal (A.M.E.)
Church in Baltimore and through programs that extended congregational walls beyond sacred confines into secular problems,
African-American youth ministries translated purity teaching into
practices that forged freedom. Again, a paradox appears. On the
one hand, African-American churches taught youth an inward-
looking theology that stressed doctrines and teachings designed to
promote individual purity—heaven, holiness, and devotion to a
personal God. On the other hand, these churches also taught
youth to take the freedom they experienced in church as a template
against which to judge the relative justice of the world. The world
American blacks inhabited during the twentieth century did not

fare well in that judgment, and as a result, young people in African-American congregations were encouraged to change the world through prophetic social activism and political involvement. The life-path of freedom referred, in short, to both internal spiritual freedom and external political freedom. This paradox of purity translated into practices endures in the teachings and rites of passage in black churches today.

Chapters 5–8 analyze and explain details provided by these four portraits. Chapter 5 compares and contrasts the four groups. The metaphor of life-path helps us to see how each group sought to lead youth toward a particular way of life whose content and contours were determined by the character of the tradition at the core of the movement. Lutherans, Catholics, Evangelicals, and African Americans all drew upon deep wells of tradition to shape rites of passage and life-paths for young people. Leaders of all four groups were able to introduce youth to intellectual traditions and social practices with long lineages and well-articulated rationalizations. There were thus key differences between these four youth ministries even as they sought to engage young people in solving common problems.

Four of these problems will be highlighted. First, all of the groups sought to relate private (inward) piety to public (outward) life; I discuss in this context especially the difficulty youth ministries had in addressing the escalation of violence in modern America. Second, the groups were voluntary programs; youth *chose* to participate but then were involved in a *normative* program. This tension between choice and obligation gave the movements depth but also made them fragile. Third, the groups struggled to reconcile individualism and group identity; they had to both encourage individual "becoming" and ensure group "belonging." Finally, the groups oscillated between purity and practices. *Purity* here means primarily the effort of churches to keep youth safe and secure, especially by keeping them innocent of cultural problems and by helping them to avoid precocious "adult" behaviors. *Practices* means the effort of churches to engage young people in active experiments and risks with adult roles and responsibilities. Over the past seventy years, youth ministries generally emphasized practices over purity in their teaching to youth; otherwise, they saw their youth ministry programs wither. In some cases, purity and practices were kept in balance; the four groups treated here struggled to accomplish this. Knowing when to protect youth and when to encourage them has been a central dilemma for youth ministries throughout this period.[17]

Chapters 6–8 analyze more deeply the reasons for the gradual shift from purity to practices in modern American youth ministry. Chapter 6 considers how changes in the international role of the United States and in U.S. domestic policies and practices affected Christian teaching to young people. The world shrank, America developed an empire, and youth programs had to adapt. As America grew into an international superpower, American Christian youth were enlisted in a variety of practices that drew them out of purity-based enclaves and into common national life. Domestically, the centralization of federal programs in the wake of the New Deal also had an impact on youth ministries. Youth ministries increasingly faced competition from the secular state and markets in the education and nurture of youth. These revolutionary changes in American society were exogenous factors—causes from outside the Christian tradition—propelling youth into practices to which youth ministries had to respond.

Chapter 7 considers how changes within America's churches—endogenous factors—modified the Christian traditions of youth ministry over the past seventy years. As the first half of the chapter title, "Convergences and Choices," indicates, Christians in America actively converged in many ways over the past seventy years. They cooperated in unprecedented fashion, converged on a modern understanding of Christian missions, and produced together (often through debate) a virtual renaissance of biblical study, new worship forms, and various agencies to promote Christian social activism. Converging, activist churches produced converging, activist youth ministries. As the second half of the chapter title suggests, churches also gave people unprecedented choices in the last decades of the twentieth century. Christians met people where they were to offer them meaningful paths through life, they built into their ecclesiastical structures increased pluralism and public roles for women, and they imaginatively reconceived central aspects of the Christian tradition in light of specific social contexts of modern life. Choices for Christian adults also meant choices for Christian youth. Together these convergences and choices also helped move youth ministry from purity to practices.

Chapter 8 examines how the choices and activities of youth themselves caused the shift from purity to practices. Many youth over the past seventy years have sensed hypocrisy in Christian purity preaching. Consequently, some of them created for themselves rites of passage in American popular culture—including "sex, drugs, and rock 'n' roll"—that directly contradicted narrowly conceived and negative preaching of purity. These rites of passage proved remarkably durable in teenage cultures even when these symbolic tests of "adult" status proved to have violent consequences for youth. At the same time, young people and youth ministries also "re-created America" in some perhaps surprising ways over the past seventy years. Christian youth ministries involved millions of youth—among them some who were making love, drinking beer, and listening to rock music—in practices that helped produce dramatic changes in American culture. Youth joined international and national service agencies, attended educational institutions, and promoted practices that produced new cultural forms and, in some ways, a new America. Christian young people and youth ministries contributed to the end of what Yale historian Sidney Ahlstrom called "the Great Puritan Epoch" in American religious history.[18]

This volume concludes with an extended essay drawing together the threads of the argument and offering theoretical and practical suggestions for Christian youth ministry in twenty-first-century America. Using insights from anthropologists Victor Turner, Mary Douglas, and René Girard, it recommends that Christian youth ministry focus on creating (or reviving) meaningful rites of passage for young people. The contours and character of these rites can be diverse, but Turner shows that they must indicate to young people a separation from their childhood, challenge them with meaningful tests of adult responsibility, and definitively incorporate them into adulthood with a clear mark of their new status.[19] The ways Christian churches can do this are many. Douglas demonstrates that these rites of passage must avoid the temptation to impose upon youth a purity system that controls and orders the dangers they face. The move from purity to practices in modern youth ministry has been a good one, but it also can be grounded more coherently in the Christian tradition than it has been in the past. We have often sold youth short intellectually. Youth ministry in the new millennium needs to challenge young people intellectually with the depths and dilemmas of modern Christian thought and practice.[20] This essentially theological task can be accomplished in many ways. Finally, from Girard we can learn to teach youth nonviolence. For Girard, this is what Christianity means: Christ came to save us from violence by exposing its sway over us and by showing us a better way. Christians affirm that on the cross

God incarnate was crucified by legitimized violence. This event means that no one is immune; all share responsibility for the desires to dominate and for the scapegoating at the root of violence. The cross means further that God identifies with those who suffer and who are victimized by violence. Through the cross comes the Christian affirmation of the resurrection. The resurrection means that love is stronger than death. Violence fails; love prevails.[21] This affirmation of Easter is not an idealist or romantic project. It is historical truth, grounded in the ongoing teaching and practices of the church, where individuals are incorporated as the body of Christ so as to renounce evil and practice compassion. Of course, any one Christian individual or organization only approximates this truth. In the new millennium, churches face the challenge of focusing their rites of passage so as to teach the faith to young people as the practice of nonviolence.

The last half of this book points out that the rapid pace of social change in the twentieth century bred uncertainty on the part of many American Christians in their attempts to communicate faith across generations. Violence escalated as technology improved. The state and the marketplace competed with churches to educate and form youth. Institutional unification among Christians eroded group boundaries. Life-paths blurred in a multitude of marketed choices. Rites of passage were scattered across several sites. Many Christians therefore perceive a decline in youth ministry. Diffusion, or differentiation, however, is a better metaphor. Christian youth ministry has mirrored, as it has also helped to create, the specialization and differentiation characteristic of late-twentieth-century American culture. The end of the Great Puritan Epoch in American history thus offers a particularly pregnant moment for Christian youth ministry. We are beginning to see how neither purity nor practices alone can prepare youth to accept responsibly the challenges of contemporary American culture. Shielding youth through purity alone leaves them unprepared; simply giving them autonomy through practices puts them at risk. The movement in Christian youth ministry must be from childlike purity (a secure sense of presence and promise like what Jeremiah experienced) to adult practices of compassion (courageous confrontation of injustice, violence, and oppression wherever it is manifest). Any other movement, although it may make youth ministries popular or even "successful," will make them less than fully Christian.[22]

Assumptions and arguments such as these are embedded throughout this book, and since it is not likely that all (or even most) readers will share my assumptions, it is worthwhile to fore-shadow them as fully as possible here. First, no historical descrip-tion is ever simple, objective, or unbiased. Every history is written from, and influenced by, the author's point of view. Authors choose which facts to include and how to arrange them. Often the assumptions driving these choices are left undisclosed to the reader (and, in some cases, are unconscious to the author). It is most important for the reader to understand that I write as a Chris-tian. In the portraits of youth ministry organizations, I am doing more than simply arranging facts so as to narrate biographies, events, and historical outcomes. To be sure, I will describe key indi-viduals, events, and outcomes in their contexts, but I also seek to assess where the various programs in youth ministry succeeded or failed to educate and form youth as Christians in the United States.

To write explicitly as a Christian is not to erode historical stan-dards. On the contrary, the more you acknowledge where you stand, the more you can recognize how your point of view influ-ences what you see, and thereby the more likely you are to produce a work that is both fair and accurate. On the matter of accuracy, the criteria by which to judge this book are the same as for any history—are the characters clear, facts straight, texts and contexts reasonably interpreted? On the matter of fairness, I will use the un-derstanding of Christianity within each stream of the tradition to define its contours; that is, I will see each movement "from the in-side." This is a difficult task. The anthropologist who works with living subjects may appear to have an edge over the historian, who has the distinct disadvantage of subjects who are usually dead. Nevertheless, both social sciences demand creative reconstruction through language of complex phenomena, and the historian has the benefit, perhaps, of knowing how the story ends in a way the anthropologist cannot. In any case, fairness as a goal of historical writing is hardly a radical notion.

Beyond both accuracy and fairness, however, is the question of truth. Authentic Christianity embraces neither the absolutism of "facts alone" positivism nor the absolutism of "everything is rela-tive" deconstructionism. Christianity embraces a paradox in which the Absolute is incarnated in a particular time and place. Christian historiography, similarly, must not only be grounded in the his-torical contingencies of a particular time and place but also seek to comprehend more than mere random events in the flow of time. Any one Christian does not know the end of history, but a Chris-tian historian is also not opposed to the prospect that history does have a purpose or goal. Historical truth is thus a matter of probable verifiability and falsifiability: a history is more or less true insofar as it incarnates the meaning of events within the flow of time so that these events are depicted in their complexity and specificity in a way that a reader can comprehend, verify or falsify, and benefit from. In short, truth is in the telling—in the fruits of history as much as in its roots, Christian or otherwise.

For the purpose of this book, the fact that I seek to convey not only details but their meaning implies that I cannot simply leave the relative norms of each particular stream of Christianity to be the sole criteria by which to determine its place in history. Rather, insofar as youth face problems in common and insofar as Christianity has normative boundaries, I will make normative judgments across traditions. I am tempted at times to issue my own version of Jeremiah's complaint when faced with this task: "I am only a historian!" Nevertheless, to understand how Christian youth ministry developed in American culture, we must critically assess not only the distinct teachings and practices of different streams or subcultures but also assess how these teachings and practices connected with the broader culture in which they were set. In other words, this is a *critical* history of Christian ministry with youth in the years 1930–1999, written from the perspective of a Christian who recognizes that each historic manifestation of Christianity is a partial approximation of the larger tradition. I recognize that my own appropriation of Christianity is partial as well, but this is a matter for theologians to discern and historians to puzzle over. I am confident that this approach to history loses nothing—certainly not "the facts"—but, rather, gains the reader insight into their meaning from the perspective of a Christian who loves the tradition but also seeks to evaluate critically its role in culture.[23]

A second key assumption in this study is that violence is badly understood by many people in America. I accept throughout this book what scholars call a "maximalist" definition of violence because I believe that violence includes far more than the street crime, aggression, and physical force against persons to which the term refers in popular usage.[24] Violence is also institutional and cultural; as I explain my use of the term to students, violence is like an iceberg. We see only the tip—instances of criminal violence—but the deepest levels of violence are the institutional systems and cultural habits that lead us to depend upon force to solve problems and that often inspire more violence in reaction. We focus on the tip of the iceberg—for instance, street crime—because it appears to be susceptible to simple solutions. Kill and be killed, runs the logic.

As the example of capital punishment illustrates, however, we live in a society that produces violence through institutions as well as in person-to-person encounters. Police forces, prison systems, and the military are all institutions in which violence is consciously legitimized. Institutional violence also occurs when people are systematically excluded from quality education, housing, health care, or economic opportunity. Usually these exclusions are unconscious—they are no one person's fault—but they nevertheless inflict real damage on individuals, families, and entire subcultures, as our history makes amply evident. On one level, it should be obvious, then, that institutions can be violent. On another level, however, we tend to overlook institutional violence because it is troubling to recall that we have enough military might to destroy the entire planet or that we need to build prisons to house alienated citizens. It is also notoriously difficult to change institutions. We avoid facing problems of institutional violence such as nuclear proliferation, poverty housing, and economic inequity because they demand the type of social change, at the level of policy and law, that runs counter to a dominant myth of American individual opportunity and responsibility. No Lone Ranger is likely to rid the world of nuclear weapons by taking personal responsibility for them. Institutional violence paralyzes us because we depend upon it for our own security, because we cannot see how to avoid it, and because, somewhere deep in the recesses of our being, we *desire* vengeance.

This last fact leads us to the most troubling and basic form of violence. I call it cultural violence, but the Christian tradition has usually called it evil, or original sin. Herein fall patterns of collective belief and practice that stem from hatred and desire and that seek to produce domination, destruction, and survival of the self at all costs. Victims of cultural violence invariably face despair. Cultural violence can be expressed in works of art, social conventions, even languages. Racism is a good example. Racism is a blend of prejudice and power. It expresses itself in the threat (or reality) of physical harm, organized through institutions or groups that can effect such harm, and stems from a prejudicial desire to inflict harm or assert dominance (even if indirectly by not including others in common human benefits or by trying to "take care of one's own" at the expense of others). Racism is thus a cultural system that can be expressed in physical action, through an organization (such as the Ku Klux Klan), or even through a simple word. Our history makes obvious how the cultural system of racism violates— from the institutional violence of slavery down to the subtler forms of exclusion still in place today. Sexism is another good example of cultural violence. Very few overt "male chauvinist pigs" will admit their problem in polite company, but women still earn seventy-four cents to a man's dollar, suffer through the violence of rape at a rate well beyond that endured by males, and find it hard to locate a church where the explicit teaching of Genesis 1:27, with its image of God being male *and* female, is understood and practiced. Violence, then, is like an iceberg, encompassing acts of physical force, institutions that consciously or unconsciously exclude, and languages and cultural attitudes that desire domination and destruction and produce despair. Unless we recognize these deepest levels of the violence iceberg, from which crime and the use of force usually spring, the iceberg will likely sink the *Titanic*.

A third assumption of this book is that the violence of American culture over the past seventy years has made it difficult to grow up in the United States. Of course, growing up has never been easy, but the facts point to new challenges over the past seventy years. Significant segments of every generation of youth in the United States since 1930 never had the chance to grow up. Millions have been lost physically or emotionally through war—in Europe, in the Pacific, in Korea, in Vietnam, in the Persian Gulf, and elsewhere. Many youth who did not succumb to war have been lost to the violence of crime or to systems of institutional violence, such as prisons or poor educational systems.[25] Still other twentieth-century American youth have been kept from realizing their full potential through forms of cultural violence that sap their will to live, such as racism or sexism. Finally, many of the youth who survived war, economic injustice, racism, or sexism have been lost into adult life-paths of work and consumption that practically enslave them to the market and from which, more than perhaps even Jeremiah could have foreseen, they need deliverance.[26] As the bumper sticker puts this gospel: "The boy with the most toys at the end, wins."

It has been difficult to grow up in the United States during this century. And it has been especially difficult to grow up Christian. Christian teaching to youth in the United States has grown confused in the context of escalating institutional and cultural violence. Christians have taught youth to depend upon, defend, and consume the very systems that violate them. The reason for this is easy enough to understand: we want our youth to be safe, rather than victims. Much of Christian teaching and formation for youth has focused on shielding youth from violence by teaching them to be individually and morally "pure." Youth organizations began, in most cases, as Victorian-era purity programs designed to keep youth Lutheran or Catholic or German or Irish and, in all cases, to keep young people away from individual sin or vice, which usually meant to keep them virgins until they married a suitable spouse of the same faith.[27] Now, in itself, to teach moral and individual purity is both salutary and necessary; but when purity was communicated to mean, negatively, avoiding "sins of passion," or avoiding "strangers" (who were usually depicted as unusually passionate sorts), the message being communicated to youth was no longer the message to Jeremiah—"I am with you to deliver you"—but, rather, "You are only a youth; beware of 'them.' " Thus, America's churches, with all good intentions, disconnected Christian purity from practices of courage, justice, and compassion in their teaching to youth.[28]

Nevertheless, youth sometimes saw through the attempts to isolate them into purity. Furthermore, churches have often been critical of the manifestations of institutional and cultural violence in America. Especially during the Vietnam conflict and the civil rights movement, but also before and after, churches (and parachurch ministries) formed and educated young people not only by segregating them into Victorian-like purity programs but also by offering them opportunities to form their faith through nonviolent study, rites of passage, and practices of compassion. The life-paths that flowed out of Christian youth ministries have varied widely, from traditional evangelical witnessing to radical community organizing, but through them young people have in fact grown up as Christians over the past seventy years.[29] The four portraits will, I believe, reveal some of the institutional creativity, and perhaps some of the theological integrity, of diverse expressions of Christianity in America.

At the same time, I hope readers will see that America's ministries for youth have often failed to communicate what I take to be the long argument of Christianity, extending back to Jesus and before him to Jeremiah, that purity—a secure sense of the presence of God—is paradoxically the source of courage and compassion to engage the social and political dangers of the world, not a reason to flee from and fear the world. The vulnerability of youth has been highlighted in the United States by the demise of many purity-based youth programs, but a proper Christian response to this development will not seek nostalgically to shield youth (negatively) from adult problems but, rather, prepare young people to cope with adult problems by incarnating God's presence with youth as they come of age.[30] This problem is at the core of Christian theology: we will probably always struggle to understand how to relate personal purity and practices of compassion, just as we struggle to understand a God who is both divine and human, without sacrificing either.

Clearly, Americans, in part through the institutional creativity of their churches, have constructed and supported a life stage called "youth" that involves young people in a long, dangerous liminality or transition.[31] The sheer length of this transition in America—from as early as age eleven to as late as thirty-five—is undoubtedly an innovation explainable as a social accommodation to the need for specialized workers in a technological economy.[32] For Christians, however, there must be more to it than that. People are not simply cogs to be fitted and shaped for a market machine. And here the ancient complaint of Jeremiah and the answer he recorded still rings true: what youth lack is the power—symbolically offered to them through meaningful rites of passage—to articulate and choose a life-path that truly will deliver them from violence and evil. What youth need is a pure sense of presence—conveyed to them in relevant and coherent symbols—that will give them courage to act in ways that will fill their lives with a passion for justice and compassion for others. America's churches have, for many reasons, failed to teach youth both purity and compassion, but youth themselves have also led churches into institutional creativity that is ongoing and with wide-ranging cultural significance. Indeed, Christian youth have re-created America and its churches time and again. Whether (or rather how) they will continue to do so may depend, to a large degree, on what we teach youth about violence.

chapter 1

"Christian Knowledge, Christian Service"

THE WALTHER LEAGUE, 1930–1977

On May 23, 1934, the Executive Secretary of the Walther League, Otto Paul Kretzmann (known as "O.P." to all), introduced what would become a favorite rite of passage for the Leaguers: a solemn candlelight ceremony. As the lights were dimmed in a Chicago church basement, Kretzmann lit a small candle and turned and lit another held by his brother, Adelbert Raphael ("Bert" even to himself), the pastor of the Chicago church. Gradually around the room, fifty or so candles began to glow, reflecting up on the earnest faces of the young men and women, aged fifteen to twenty-five, assembled for the evening banquet. It was the forty-first birthday of the Walther League, and the Leaguers were both celebrating their past and committing themselves to a future.[1]

Kretzmann spoke quietly but with passion, to explain the significance of this night to the Leaguers:

> One of the world's most crying needs today is a new consciousness of the oneness of humanity. . . . For the birthday of the Walther League in 1934 . . . from coast to coast . . . the entire body of young people belonging to the Walther League will meet in their respective rooms . . . [and] will . . . light a candle in order to bring to the minds of all present the purpose of these

> meetings. . . . To a world torn by hate and fear and to a Christen-
> dom split by strife and confusion the united testimony of thou-
> sands of young people in behalf of their Church can become a
> voice in the wilderness which will not be stilled.[2]

The banquet had ample potential to draw out the worst in American sentimentality. A darkened room, candle glow, and young men
and women created a dangerous combination. But the sublima-
tion effected by Kretzmann made the event more than a flirtation
with the sexual oneness of humanity: the event became an annual
rite of passage that challenged young Lutherans to unite as a voice
of knowing service in the world. When five thousand Walther
Leaguers gathered for a reunion in Chicago in 1993, fifteen years
after the organization had ended, the Lutherans who were now
fifty years old and older included a "birthday banquet" in the fes-
tivities and recalled Kretzmann's words as a challenge with continuing relevance.

LUTHERANS JOIN THE MAINLINE

The history of the Walther League is, in part, the history of the
maturation of Lutheranism into the mainline of American Christianity. Lutherans were present from the very earliest European
settlement of North America, and some of them, mostly on the
East Coast in Pennsylvania, New York, and New England, were
comfortable with English and were largely Americanized by the
middle of the nineteenth century. But the vast majority of Lutherans emigrated from Germanic or Scandinavian countries in several
waves during the later nineteenth century, and when they settled,
mostly in the Midwest, they formed churches to perpetuate their
ethnic and theological distinctiveness. By the turn of the century,
there were nearly as many synods of Lutherans as there had been
waves of immigrants: Ohio, Buffalo, Missouri, Wisconsin, and
Iowa all hosted their own Lutheran church bodies. The story of
Lutheranism in the twentieth century, then, is the story of the con-
solidation of these many ethnically and geographically based sects
into primarily two American denominations with national scope:
The Lutheran Church–Missouri Synod and the Evangelical Lutheran Church in America.[3]

World War I especially "pushed Lutherans into a new era," in
the words of historian Fred Meuser. At the outset of the war, when
the United States was officially neutral, many German Lutherans

outspokenly favored the German side of the conflict with France. Consequently, when the United States entered the war against Germany, some of their fellow citizens looked suspiciously at Lutherans. German books were banned and burned in cities across the United States, and Lutheran church buildings and schools were vandalized and torched. Largely in response to this persecution, the Americanization of Lutheranism (which some had been advocating well before the war) proceeded rapidly. All of the major Lutheran bodies at the time sponsored well-publicized "soldiers' and sailors' welfare campaigns." And the official language of many Lutheran publications and business changed, in some cases overnight, from German to English.[4]

The Walther League was a catalyst in the process whereby Lutherans accommodated themselves to American culture. Founded in 1893 with twelve societies and named after the founder of The Lutheran Church–Missouri Synod, by 1929 the league had expanded to 1607 societies (by 1960 the number was over five thousand) and eighteen regional districts across the United States and Canada (by 1960, thirty-four), with a central headquarters in Chicago.[5] Each local society was based in a local congregation. Without congregational support there was no Walther League society (a key organizational decision that contributed to the demise of the league in the late sixties). The regional districts held rallies, published study programs and newsletters, and coordinated big-ticket events that a local society alone could not organize. It was the league's "international" headquarters in downtown Chicago, however, that identified these Lutherans with the business-like mainline.

In 1943 the league built its own modern two-story office building in Chicago's Loop, near the Newberry Library. Out of this office the league produced four major publications and organized a host of programs and educational opportunities. The *Walther League Messenger* was the banner publication. Published eleven times per year from 1892 to 1963, it included fifty pages of news, feature articles, opinion, and correspondence. The *Messenger* was recognized in 1951 and 1961 by the Associated Church Press for journalistic excellence.[6] It had originated in 1892 under the title *Der Vereinsbote* ("The Society Messenger"), but the name was abruptly changed in 1918. The other three Walther League publications were the *Bible Student* (detailed, line-by-line exegetical helps), the *Concordia Junior Messenger* (for youth under sixteen), and *Workers Quarterly* (a collection of practical suggestions for local groups). The league headquarters also coordinated a wide range of events: an annual convention, held in a U.S. city; oratory, choir, and sporting contests; a network of "hospices" (boarding houses) for Lutheran youth in major urban areas; and many more. Finally, the league founded in 1904 and administered from 1923 a sanitarium for sufferers of tuberculosis (a disease often afflicting youth) in Wheatridge, Colorado.

Throughout its history the Walther League had sought to nurture in youth both knowledge and service, but when O. P. Kretzmann was appointed executive secretary in 1930, he reorganized the league to focus explicitly on these two key facets of the Christian life.[7] He explained,

> These two departments recognize sharply the two sides of the individual Christian life—the knowing and the doing. . . . The Lutheran Church . . . has not succumbed to sectarian influences by emphasizing blind, aimless doing . . . [and] it has not followed those who reduce Christianity to . . . ice-bound acceptance of eternal verities with no sign of their practical, inspired results in life. In adopting these two departments the Walther League has therefore presented to its members a definite and vital challenge to recognize the final purpose of the Eternal in their individual lives.[8]

From 1930 until its lingering demise between 1968 and 1977, the Walther League formed and educated young Christians in a life-path of knowing and serving that was distinctively Lutheran, but it also assisted them in becoming members of an American mainline church.

CHRISTIAN KNOWLEDGE

Most of the Walther League's spiritual formation and education occurred at local churches. Leaguers joined the league sometime after Confirmation, a rite of passage that usually took place for Lutherans in the eighth grade and was preceded by several years of catechesis or instruction. Bible study was a constant in all of the societies. *Workers Quarterly*, the monthly "program guide" for local groups, had at least one Bible study outline in each issue, and for more in-depth study, the *Bible Student* (and after 1938 the *Junior Bible Student*) was available. These outlines stressed traditional Lutheran interpretation of Scripture. The Lutheran theme of justification by grace through faith came through in most of them. One 1950s study of Jonah, for example, focused not only on the historical details of the text and its literary genre but on the way in which Jonah was "a type of Jesus, that Obedient and Perfect Servant of Jehovah." The outline concluded with a quote from Paul, where Jesus is described as one "delivered for our offenses, and raised again for our justification" (Romans 4:25).[9] This was typical Lutheran exegesis of the neo-orthodox style. God acted in history in Christ, and in types or representations of Christ throughout time, to redeem fallen humanity.[10]

Leaguers heard the core message and appropriated it. Elizabeth Zoller, a seventeen-year-old member of the Regina, Saskatchewan, Walther League Society, was asked to give a homily at one Holy Week service in the late fifties. Her topic was Jesus' sentence on the cross "Father, into Thy Hands I commend my Spirit" (Luke 23:46). Zoller focused on the agony of the cross but also on its effect in the individual believer: "Because Jesus loved me and washed me from my sins in His own blood, I am now at-one with God and have the privilege of walking and talking with Him. . . . I have free access to God . . . [and] need not fear His righteous anger any longer."[11] Zoller's classic Lutheran interpretation of the "theology of the cross," she reflected years later, came from her education in the league. "The 'messages' in the Walther League were always Christ-centered," she wrote. " There was the common bond of faith which bound us so closely together, and . . . our one goal was to serve Jesus Christ."[12]

For a young woman to preach a homily in 1950s North America was a daunting rite of passage into "Christian knowledge." The Leaguers could, then, challenge middle-class and ecclesiastical conventions with their understanding of this knowledge. They had voted in 1900, against the advice of seminary experts and church leaders, to include women as voting delegates of their annual international convention. Throughout its history, the league provided women with leadership opportunities. Marilyn (Rook) Bernthal, active in the league in Frankenmuth, Michigan, in the 1950s, recalled, "The home society was the place . . . we had the chance to lead, to figure out our own finances . . . to dream and to [do things] ourselves."[13] A pro-and-con piece in the *Messenger* in 1951, "Should Girls Go to College," received a firestorm of support for the pro argument from women throughout the league. No one went in print to support the con.[14] The league helped dispel stereotypical gender roles for youth in the fifties and sixties.

Not all of the education into Christian knowledge at local league meetings focused on Bible study, theology, or ecclesiastical leadership. An "ideal" league meeting from the 1950s had five components: "Worship, Education, Fellowship, Service, and Recreation."[15] The recreational and fellowship activities of the Leaguers varied widely from place to place. Officially, for instance, Lutherans were not supposed to dance. The party line was articulated well by Concordia Seminary professor P. E. Kretzmann in a 1940 speech he delivered on a circuit of local league gatherings. The speech was entitled "That Vexing Question of Dancing." Its thesis was a somewhat grudging admission that "the sex passions of the adolescent are easily aroused." Consequently,

> there is no essential difference between the embrace of "petting" which is so generally indulged in by frivolous young people in our days, and the embrace of the modern dance. . . . Our young "neckers" and "petters" are doing something that almost deserves the word "unnatural act." . . . Any physical contact, in fact, any form of communication by word, or glance, or picture, or gesture, or posture, which is apt to arouse or to strengthen carnal desires, whether that be in the home, in an auto, in a boat, on the dance-floor, or anywhere else, is sinful. . . . Any girl who permits a man to dance with her, is in fact only a *demi-vierge*, only half a virgin, youth half of her virginity is gone.[16]

The virginity of the male was apparently not affected.

Despite official prohibitions, however, the youth of the Walther League found ways to learn this important lesson about modern American culture. They danced, under the code word "playparty games." The Iowa District reported to the *Messenger*, "Playparty games and squares are a common sight in our district. As informal mixers they are tops. . . . All you have to do is mention the word 'playparty' and the toes begin to twitch."[17] Even the toes of Leaguers in Grand Forks, North Dakota, thawed out enough in 1953 to twitch their way through games of "Patty Cake Polka," danced to the tune of "Little Brown Jug." "A few rounds of this," explained Pastor Walter M. Wangerin Sr., "and we are ready to go back to a slower game again."[18] Local Leaguers in Mt. Rainier, Maryland, even went beyond dancing to stage a "Roman Banquet," later immortalized as the fraternity toga party. "Everyone, of course," the correspondent to the *Messenger* pointed out, "wore white sheets to resemble Roman togas. . . . The meal was eaten in a reclining position. At intervals guests were given the opportunity to clean their hands in a community finger bowl passed around by a slave."[19] Not all of the education at local league meetings, in short, focused on spirituality and theology. Much of it was also designed to accommodate Lutheran youth to middle-class American youth culture.

Even the simplest matters of etiquette came into the purview of the league's educators. One article, simply entitled "Church Manners," commented, "Many a pastor is dismayed as he faces a congregation of gumchewers. One pastor said, 'When I see those jaws moving in such solemn rhythm, I'm reminded of my father's pet herd of Guernseys. I tell you it's disconcerting.'" More substantively, the league tried to teach Lutheran youth middle-class standards of behavior and demeanor: don't be late, don't put on makeup in church, don't make appointments during the service. Even apparel was recommended: "Shorts and dungarees are fine for the picnic, but not for church. Remember? The church is the house of God. Our dress and our entire behavior in church reflects our reverence for God."[20]

Away from church, Lutheran youth could relax a little. Over the centuries, Christians created many institutions to transmit knowledge across generations, from monasteries and convents to Sunday schools and universities. In the modern era, Christians created a new institution to form youth in Christian faith—the summer camp. Like other mainline Protestant groups, the Walther League sponsored camps across the United States throughout the middle decades of the twentieth century. These were often week-long rentals of a YMCA or other denominational camp, but by 1949 the list of camping experiences directly sponsored by the league had expanded to thirty-nine sites across the United States. A few of the camps were entirely owned and operated by the league or by regional district offices. The best-known and most enduring of these camps is Camp Arcadia, on the northeastern shores of Lake Michigan. Nestled in a tranquil valley an hour south of Traverse City, Michigan, the beachfront and acreage for Arcadia was donated to the league by the region's lumber baron in 1922. Between 1922 and 1968 Arcadia served as the "international" camp to train league leaders. A private group of Lutheran investors purchased the property in 1968 when the league began to falter as an organization, and it continues to operate today as a "family retreat center."

In 1938 camper Bernice Baker reported in the *Messenger* on the ethos and program at Arcadia: "Out of a deep sleep . . . to awaken to the sound of a bugle call, somewhere in the distance, muffled by the continuous rolling in and out of the lake. . . . To breathe deeply. . . . What joyous and blessed feeling of freedom and ecstasy!"[21] In fact, the program to train league leaders was rather regimented—as the morning bugle call suggests. The director of the camp from its founding until his death in 1964 was W. F. "Chief" Weihermann. Weihermann used a military model for the organization of the camp—including children's dormitories appropriately dubbed "Army," "Navy," and "Cadets," to go along with a rustic inn with space for 150 guests per week. Family-style meals were eaten on a strict schedule in a large dining hall, and the playing of taps ended each evening's activities. The combination of Christian and military "knowledge" communicated to campers at Arcadia was made even more explicit in the songs they sang around the campfire: "Onward Walther Leaguers" was one, set to the tune of "Onward Christian Soldiers." The God of these Lutheran youth was militant and aggressive and needed soldiers.

As the decades passed, however, the military metaphors mellowed up at Camp Arcadia, and the regimentation receded. New forms of Christian knowledge less linked to Lutheran (or national) dogma were communicated to the youth who attended the camp. The camp features a beautiful beach, acres of old-growth forest, and big dunes that provide splendid vistas of Lake Michigan's vast expanse. The natural beauty did not escape the theological reflection of the Leaguers. One author commented that at Arcadia "nature and God present an ever changing panorama of beauty: a storm tossed lake in driving rain, the friendly silence of a lonesome wood . . . the beauty scattered with such profusion that one need only open his eyes to see it everywhere."[22] The lake, especially, drew together God and nature for Leaguers. "By a Lake, We Come to Know Him" was the title of the hymn commissioned in 1997 to celebrate Arcadia's seventy-fifth anniversary, with lyrics that recalled the role of water in the life of Jesus and in the Christian life.[23]

Along with appreciation for nature, leisure and recreation became increasingly significant concerns for the young people who attended Arcadia from an emerging Lutheran middle class. Games, festivals, and hikes filled the afternoons and evenings at the camp. One visitor, Hilda Jass, recalled the options: "Tom likes tennis, volleyball, and loves the water; Ken is a devotee of shuffleboard, softball and golf in the woods; Marian likes volleyball and the beach, Hans still dashes around . . . and I am now just a rootin' spectator at all of these sports."[24] Even dancing made its way up to Arcadia. By the seventies Lutheran youth were shaking their booties to the "Amos Moses" on Arcadia's tennis courts at a weekly dance.

In short, the content of Christian knowledge shifted over the years at Arcadia, from traditional Lutheran dogma and piety, with a dose of American military regimen, to patterns of accommodation with American middle-class values and behavior. The shift brought with it a willingness to experiment theologically and socially. To a degree, the remote setting of the camp had lent itself to theological and practical experimentation right from the start. Worship was held twice a week, on Sunday and Wednesday evenings, but an outdoor chapel and vespers on the beach patio of the camp diffused the location of the sacred in young Lutheran minds beyond the usual church setting. A two-hour lecture/discussion in a large assembly hall followed breakfast Monday through Friday; there young Lutherans explored new paths of Christian knowledge with a Lutheran leader chosen for his or her expertise in Bible, theology, or ethics. Bernice Baker reported, "[The lectures] begin on familiar ground and carry you along paths you never dared venture before. . . . There is stimulus for thought and emotion all the day . . . and conversation that buzzes here and there continually."[25] At Arcadia and the dozens of other Walther League camps begun in the thirties around the country, middle-class conventions of leisure and recreation, Christian appreciation for nature, and new pathways of Christian knowledge coalesced in an example of Christian institutional innovation that continues to form young minds and lives even today.[26]

Walther Leaguers supported Christian knowledge through more than just local societies and camps. Many of them developed their leadership skills and Christian understanding by attending a new Lutheran university in northwest Indiana. Valparaiso University was founded in 1859 but was purchased nearly bankrupt by a group of Lutheran laity in 1925. It was, according to O. C. Kreinheder, first Lutheran president of the university, "an institution of higher learning for preparing [the young people of our church] for secular positions in life."[27] "Valpo" was the first Lutheran University specifically designed to educate and form laypeople for secular professions (other Lutheran colleges had been teachers' or seminary prep schools, or had general liberal arts programs). Leaguers flocked to Valpo in the forties and fifties, especially after O. P. Kretzmann resigned as Executive Secretary of the Walther League to become Valparaiso's third president in 1940.[28]

As at Arcadia, the content and form of Christian knowledge communicated to youth at Valparaiso has changed over the years. Daily mandatory chapel has been replaced by required courses in academic theology and religious studies for all students. The curriculum in theology has grown from a church-related emphasis on the Bible and Lutheran dogma to a culturally and historically informed understanding of Christianity and world religions. The student body, once almost completely Lutheran, has diversified to include nearly one-third Roman Catholics, along with Sikhs, Jews, Muslims, Buddhists, and most of the religions represented in the United States. The faculty, also once almost completely Lutheran, now is hired as much for academic credentials as denominational loyalty, although "sympathy" to the Christian tradition remains a clause in all contracts. Perhaps the most successful of the university's colleges, the Christ College Honors Program in the Humanities, regularly sends students to the most prestigious graduate schools in the country and recently has taken the lead in coordinating an ecumenical network of church-related institutions of higher education, the Lilly Fellows Network. In short, the content of Christian knowledge communicated to youth at Valparaiso has changed considerably from its days as a place to train young Lutherans "for positions in secular life."

Another venture in Christian knowledge grew out of the Walther League when Kretzmann started in 1937 a new league publication, *The Cresset: A Review of Literature, the Arts, and Public Affairs* (it continues today under the sponsorship of Valparaiso University). Intended to offer a corrective to "the insidious departmentalizing of the individual Christian life," the *Cresset* quickly became a vehicle for progressive Lutheran writing and a venue for many young Lutheran writers (such as myself) to break into print. The goal of the publication was to extend Lutheran awareness of Christian knowledge into public life, and this goal often took the publication onto controversial terrain. For instance, when Hitler came to power in Germany, many German-American Lutherans were favorably inclined toward "the new Germany." One of them happened to be the editor of the *Walther League Messenger*, Rev. Walter A. Maier, who was also a Concordia Seminary professor and internationally known speaker on *The Lutheran Hour* radio program. Maier penned editorials in the early thirties with titles such as "Hitler Shows the Way" and "The Credit Side of the Hitler Ledger," arguing that Hitler was "cleaning up" Germany's "decadence" and that reports of violence against Jews were "propaganda."[29] The *Cresset*, in contrast, offered some of the earliest and best-informed Christian critiques of the violence of Nazi anti-Semitism published in the United States. On the night after Kristallnacht (November

10–11, 1938), Kretzmann, drawing on German radio and news-paper sources, wrote, "The photographs of burning synagogues . . . [and] of broken plate-glass windows are glimpses of a hell of racial and religious persecution . . . [which] is against God, against Christ, against the entire Christian philosophy of life. . . . We must protest because we cannot remain unaffected."[30] Similar columns on a wide variety of topics awakened young Lutherans to a Chris-tian knowledge of literature, the arts, and public affairs, about which they had previously been little informed.

Lutheran youth were readers, and the primary publication of the Walther League—the *Walther League Messenger*—changed dra-matically over the decades in ways that document the shift from purity to practices in the content of Christian knowledge as com-municated by Walther Leaguers. Maier edited the *Messenger* be-tween 1930 and 1945. He was a pietist, and the *Messenger* reflected this strand of Christian theology. Each issue featured a devotional article, along with articles promoting Bible study, foreign mis-sions, and personal purity. Articles with titles such as "The Sin in Syncopation" (opposing dancing) and "Keep Clean!" (encourag-ing marital fidelity and sexual restraint during courting) were com-mon.[31] Maier was also a political writer, and his commentaries on topics of the day, collected in a monthly column, "The Watch Tower," and in feature articles, reflected a conservative Lutheran point of view.

In 1946, after Maier resigned when the league leaders sug-gested he tone down an anticommunist essay he had written, Al-fred P. Klausler took over as editor of the publication. Klausler was not a pietist, and the *Messenger* began to emphasize a Christian knowledge formed less by personal purity and more by social prac-tices. For instance, movie reviews began to appear. This caused some controversy among league youth, who wrote letters to the ed-itor arguing for and against this new practice. Some found the re-view page inappropriate. "The page of movie review . . . is out of place," offered Albert E. Carlson of Clifton, Kansas, "[and] I sin-cerely hope that you will see fit to eliminate [it], and use the space for something more befitting a Lutheran publication." Christina Santee of Olympia, Washington, spoke even more clearly for Lu-theran purists. "Picture theaters are so wholly 'sold out' to sin that no Christian should ever attend one," she argued. "Too many of our present day Christians, like the people of Sodom, have set their affection on things of the earth. . . . They will perish with the world, if they do not repent and receive a change of heart and mind." This seemed too harsh to Helen Gillett of Coyle, Wyoming, who understood that the reviews intended to filter Hollywood offerings through lenses informed by Lutheran knowledge: "I enjoy movies very much, and only attend movies listed in the *Messenger*. . . . Please continue your movie review. It is really a big help to most teenagers."[32] The reviews continued.

Klausler continued to shift the emphasis of the *Messenger* from knowledge about personal piety to knowledge about social practices. He stressed especially labor and race relations. For instance, he landed an editorial coup with an exclusive 1948 interview with Walter Reuther, president of the United Auto Workers and a member of the Missouri Synod. "We are opposed to a small group controlling our economic life and wealth," Reuther stated, making the case of labor against management. "Christ said it was easier for a camel to go through the eye of a needle than for a rich man to enter the gates of heaven. And, you know, we're not nearly that rough with [management]. The basic philosophy of the labor movement reflects the ethical and moral standards of Christianity."[33] Klausler also raised Lutheran consciousness about race problems, beginning with a proclamation in 1946 that "the *Messenger* hopes to hit, and hit hard, any manifestations of racial discrimination in the Christian church."[34]

By the late fifties, questions of personal purity were no longer answered in the *Messenger* with the absolute prohibitions that had once characterized league writing. For instance, one tormented young Lutheran wrote in 1956 looking for advice regarding a practice known to begin around puberty: "I habitually commit one of the most horrid sins on earth," the youth began. "I have prayed and cried over it," the Leaguer lamented, "but apparently the Lord hasn't seen my tears or heard my prayers." Paul G. Hansen, the ordained clergyman who edited the *Messenger*'s advice column, responded with tact:

> You asked me not to print your question, but it is such a common one that I am sure it would never be recognized. . . . There is nothing in Scripture which forbids masturbation. . . . There is nothing physically harmful about masturbation. . . . More harm is usually done by false ideas about what the practice can do to the mind and body. People whose guilty consciences make them fear all kinds of consequences may suffer ill effects just because of their worries. . . . Use the Word of God faithfully, and I am sure the Lord will hear your prayers. "He will not suffer you to be tempted above what you are able."[35]

By 1967, the executive director of the league, Elmer Witt, could pen a piece entitled "Life Can Be Sexual—Now!"[36]

Over the decades, then, the leaders of the Walther League had shifted the content and form of the Christian knowledge they conveyed to Lutheran youth. In the thirties, the league communicated to youth teachings based upon traditional Lutheran piety and dogma, and moral lessons encouraging personal purity. By the sixties, both content and form had diffused, focused less on personal piety and purity and more on ecumenism, social justice, and international understanding. Lutherans were moving from an ethnic enclave into the mainstream of American Christian culture. Their youth organizations led the way. The goal remained the same—a knowledgeable Christian—but the means to the goal had changed dramatically over a few decades in both content and form.

CHRISTIAN SERVICE

If the Walther League sought throughout its history to teach young Lutherans to be knowledgeable Christians, it also aimed to form in youth practices of Christian compassion, or "service." One of the earliest examples was the "hospice" program run by the league up through 1945. Loosely modeled on the YMCA and YWCA program of boarding houses, the league hospices provided temporary housing for young Lutherans who sought to move into new areas. Generally located in big cities, the homes provided employment services, room and board, and other services of hospitality to Lutheran youth. In 1929, twelve hundred cities across the United States had a listing in the league's *Hospice Directory*. (This was a bit deceptive; the league owned only sixteen homes—the others were private residences managed by "hospice secretaries.")

During an era when Lutherans were migrating from farms to the cities and were often separated from mainstream culture by language, the hospices provided a real service. Ruth Erdman, who stayed at the St. Louis hospice in the late twenties, recalls that "it would have been a lonely time for many girls" if they didn't have this place to stay. "It was anything but lonely there. We had fun together." The women attended church as a group, ate common meals, had a Bible study every Tuesday night, and sponsored "socials" in the large living room. "We had crystal chandeliers," Erdman recalled.[37] But as Lutherans entered the mainstream of American culture, the need for the hospices seemed to wane. As early as 1933, "A Tale of Hospice Work" from the Central Illinois District narrated how "the Hospice Committee in 'X' failed because 'John' and 'Sylvia' agreed to be elected to the committee only because they liked one another, and then did no work." It was seldom so simple. The Depression took its toll on many of the hospices, and the growing tendency of Lutherans to seek out college, rather than a working-class lifestyle, eroded the need. By 1940, all of the houses but six had closed.[38]

The Leaguers continued to support Wheat Ridge Sanitarium in Colorado. The sanitarium had been funded by the league from its inception in 1904 as a place for young Lutherans affected with tuberculosis to receive the "air treatment" (this medical theory maintained that fresh, especially mountain, air was beneficial in relieving TB symptoms). Borrowing an idea initially developed by the Red Cross, Leaguers annually mailed "Christmas Seals," or small adhesive stamps, to church members in exchange for donations to the Wheat Ridge cause. The national program raised hundreds of thousands of dollars over the years—$319,000 in 1949 alone.[39] Following the development of penicillin, the sanitarium incorporated as a hospital, and the Leaguers shifted their support to the Wheat Ridge Foundation—now Wheat Ridge Ministries, a broad-based social-service agency to seed ministries of health and hope around the globe. "Support from all, service to all" is how the executive secretary of the league in the forties and fifties, O. H. "Frenchy" Theiss, explained the Wheat Ridge cause to Leaguers throughout the country.[40]

In 1935, the Walther Leaguers initiated a new venture in service, in keeping with traditional Lutheran offerings to public life, when 650 young voices joined together in a St. Louis amphitheater for what was called "Choral Union." "It was marvelous" to hear 650 voices join in "A Mighty Fortress," one youth participant noted. Another added, "I was moved to tears." Annually up through the midsixties, a public Choral Union concert was a part of every national Walther League convention and many regional and district meetings.[41] By 1950, nine thousand gathered in Denver's Red Rocks Amphitheatre to hear 500 Lutheran youth, accompanied by the Denver Symphony Orchestra, perform fugues, preludes, and chorales. "Bach in the Rockies," advertised the *Messenger*, while a young Leaguer named Martin Marty propagandized: "Can Bach still be listened to?" he asked. The answer was, of course, affirmative: "Bach leads heavenward. . . . We lift our heads and open our hearts rather than merely tap our feet."[42] As with the candle-lit

"Birthday Banquet," a Choral Union was featured in the 1993 Walther League reunion; Lutheran youth had learned for a lifetime to serve the church and the public with their voices.

During the forties and fifties "Wartime Service" occupied local Leaguers. Various local and national initiatives had grown by 1942 into the "Walther League 30 Point Program for Army and Navy Service." Leaguers were encouraged to hold farewell services for departing servicemen and servicewomen (one estimate put the number of Leaguers who enlisted at twenty-five thousand), to keep an "Honor Roll" listing men and women in the armed forces from their church, and to correspond with those overseas and send them gift packages. The program also emphasized ways for Leaguers to serve military families and urged Leaguers to cooperate with United Service Organizations, the Red Cross, and government agencies "in any way possible." Finally, the league began a Wartime Service Fund, to which Lutheran youth contributed over $120,000 by war's end.[43] Young Lutherans were learning to serve as both citizens and church members.

After the league moved into its new Chicago headquarters in 1943, the staff ran an expanding range of other service programs. In 1944, for instance, the league first sponsored Lutheran Service Volunteer Schools. These intensive, weeklong leadership training institutes around the country stressed "learning by doing." For instance, youth had to prepare brief talks (for the "volunteer hour") on topics of significance to them. "My Baptismal Vow," "Seeing God in Things Beautiful," "Glorifying God While at My Job," and "Glorifying God in My Play" give an idea of the range of topics. A participant commented, "Practice in the volunteer hour . . . gave me a chance at self-expression of my thoughts and helped me to gain confidence in myself."[44] By 1949, eighteen different Lutheran Service Volunteer camps welcomed over three thousand Leaguers. The schools continued well into the sixties, when they were taken over by the Missouri Synod's denominational youth board under a different name. Walther League "Christian service" meant becoming a person who could articulate the faith in connection with the concerns of everyday life.

As the fifties' years of "organization men" and atomic fear set in, a countercultural agenda to form youth less in purity than in practices of compassion spread throughout the league. Beginning in 1954, carefully screened youth were sent as "Foreign Mission Builders" to serve as construction crews at various overseas sites. In Mambisanda, New Guinea, for instance, Leaguer Bob Marquardt helped build a hospital, school, hydroelectric power station, doctor's and nurse's residence, and bathroom and laundry facilities during a two-year stint. "Our living conditions here are very poor," Marquardt wrote back to readers of the *Messenger*, but "work is coming along fine." Purity was not on the agenda of the Leaguers—"Our shower is just a 5-gallon bucket located up on a rope," Marquardt remembered—but practicing the faith was.[45]

Leaguers also traveled to international ecumenical assemblies, such as meetings of the Lutheran World Federation. These young ecumenists returned from their international service with a new sensitivity to practicing the faith in a global setting. For instance, Linda (Gerling) Schroeder reported in the *Messenger* that her experience at the European Ecumenical Youth Conference in 1960 had taught her about "the pain of disunity. . . . At home it's so easy. We just sit in our snug little church pews and never have to . . . face up to the facts of spiritual unity and theological disunity and make judgments for ourselves. We don't really know where we stand because all we've been doing is sitting."[46] Here the league had formed a Christian with a critical, courageous conscience (Schroeder today runs a St. Louis program to integrate ex-convicts into local communities).

Moving youth from passively sitting to compassionately standing became a primary goal of the Walther League headquarters in the sixties. The national study program in 1960, for instance, was called Inasmuch, from Matthew 25:40: "Inasmuch as ye have shown love to the least of these my people, ye have done it unto me." It was a classic passage of the "social gospel" movement—one of the leading examples of a Christian social activism that stressed practicing the faith over purity. To promote Inasmuch, League staffers produced devotions, Bible studies, topic discussions, and project suggestions, along with filmstrips, tracts, and a "district manual." On the local level, Leaguers began holding "Inasmuch" retreats, or "Inasmuch Canvass for Christ" nights.[47]

Nationally, Youth Work Camps were the first phase of the Inasmuch program. Eight such camps were started in 1964. Elmer Witt, executive secretary of the league from 1953 to 1967, was the dean (with his wife, Ginny) of the 1964 Inasmuch Work Camp at Lutheran Hospital in Baltimore. He observed that at this camp the Leaguers

> plunged into the background, basis and moment-by-moment story of the ministry of healing. They learned hospital lingo, watched nurses, doctors, and technicians. . . . [They] conducted

devotions for personnel and patients broadcast over the hospital sound system. They visited patients and talked of home and hope and God. They found time to tour, to swim, to talk (the wee hours of the morning), to play and sing ("O my Darling, O my Darling Turpentine"). . . . In word and deed the Savior moved within, transforming scared Leaguers into ready witnesses. . . . Through the unifying love of God, 12 Work Campers and their deans became a living, working, worshiping demonstration of the Body of Jesus Christ.[48]

Today Lutheran youth around the country regularly participate in similar "servant events," sponsored by the denominations and local youth groups. Youth and their leaders have been changed by these events, from scared youth to ready Christians; and these events have changed the Lutheran Church from a denomination largely focused on Lutheran purity or accommodation to American power to one also focused on practicing the faith through compassion.[49]

In 1965 the Inasmuch program took on a more permanent cast as Prince of Peace Volunteers spent a year or more in various front-line social ministries. Patterned after the successful Peace Corps program of the federal government, the Prince of Peace Volunteers program recruited hundreds of young Lutherans. One Prince of Peace Volunteers participant reported on her experience in a Chicago African-American community in 1967: "We were changed in attitude toward the community's dreams and yearnings. Open housing marches compelled some of the volunteers to express [a] new sympathy. . . . Epithets of hecklers, stones, and bricks hurled their way showed the crying need for redemption and change."[50] Walther Leaguers were hardly the leaders of the civil rights movement, but through their work as Prince of Peace Volunteers and through their "new sympathy" with the hopes and dreams of a community very different from the typical Lutheran one, some of them learned how to practice their faith in a changing social world.

From the thirties through the fifties, therefore, Walther Leaguers had been educated and formed in a life-path that stressed both Christian knowledge and service. Through camping ministry, a Lutheran university, local societies, Wheatridge, Wartime Service, Mission Builders, and more, Lutheran youth had been taught that Christianity involves both knowledge and service. Along with the specifically Christian, and Lutheran, slant to their formation, however, had come a significant dose of accommodation to mainstream American culture. In the sixties, this accommodation came back to haunt the league, which came apart as the culture itself split over a variety of divisive issues.[51]

ACCOMMODATION TO VIOLENCE: THE DEMISE OF THE WALTHER LEAGUE

For many young Lutherans and their parents, the primary function of the Walther League had been to preserve youthful purity. Up through the fifties the Leaguers themselves called their organization "a Lutheran marriage bureau," and with good reason. The *Messenger* and local league publications had routinely included a "Cupid's Corner" to report on the engagements and marriages of loyal Lutherans to each other. Leaguers had learned through articles and lectures about the dangers of interfaith marriage, the "harm in a kiss," and the "sin in syncopation." Like many youth organizations begun during Victorian America, the league was intended to keep Lutheran youth pure.

The issue was deeper than just sexual purity. A main function of the league had been to educate and train Lutheran youth not only to become knowledgeable Christian servants but also to become American citizens. Thus, the chief event sponsored by the league each year was its convention, complete with banners of the state delegations, parliamentary procedures, long ponderous speeches, elections, and other trappings of American democratic life. For the earliest Leaguers, these events were clearly training in democracy. For later Leaguers, they were all but redundant: one Leaguer from the fifties recalled that "the primary order of business every year seemed to be where we were going to have next year's convention."[52] The league was part of the process by means of which young Lutherans in the United States became accepted members of a national church. But in the sixties, the nation, and its churches, came apart.[53] Conflicts erupted over sexuality, civil rights, and the Vietnam War. Youth were often at the center of the conflicts, and in time a generation gap emerged between those who had served the nation without question during World War II and a new generation of youth.[54]

Confessional Lutheranism had always stressed a paradox between the "two kingdoms," whereby a Christian both transcended and submitted to worldly authority. But in the minds of a generation trained in patriotism, the two realms had blurred. Consequently, as the movement for "peace and love" swept across

American youth culture in the sixties, some came to fear that the purity of youth was being swept away with it. A few critics had cited the league for "worldliness" in the early fifties. "In the home congregations the young people are warned against the sinful dances," one offended pastor wrote to the league headquarters, but "when these young folks return from the conventions, they report what a wonderful time they had . . . 'dancing to beat the band.' "[55]

Again, however, more than sexual purity was at issue. Civil rights became the first flash point. Letters of protest began to stream into the league office when African-American entertainer and activist Dick Gregory lectured before five thousand young Leaguers at the 1963 convention. Gregory made clear that the problem of racism in America was a problem for the churches as well as for society. "It would have been a great thing had the church stepped forward with leadership to free a great many of the oppressed people in America," he argued, "[but] the church has failed."[56] League leaders tried to put the best spin on the controversy aroused by Gregory's presence: "The Walther League was criticized in some quarters for bringing such a controversial figure as Dick Gregory to its convention. . . . By and large, however, the Walther League received the approval of thoughtful churchmen, lay and cleric, for helping youth face a troublesome problem."[57] The spin didn't work.

A second set of angry letters appeared when a 1965 article in the *Messenger*'s inter-Lutheran continuation, *Arena,* encouraged Lutheran-Jewish dialogue. "It is high time that Christians, especially Lutherans, reevaluate their attitudes toward the Jews," wrote editor Klausler. "Lutherans . . . have given at least tacit consent to various forms of anti-Semitism," he explained to a generation in danger of forgetting that even Walter A. Maier had once supported the Nazi cause.[58] The judgment from some Lutheran leaders was swift and violent. The article was accused of being "false doctrine," one that "tore down the faith of our young people" and "denied plain Scriptural truth." Several overtures to the 1965 Missouri Synod convention called for the dismissal of Klausler.[59] They failed, but the end of the Walther League was imminent in a culture that was coming apart.

The final straw for many was when the league office invited folksinger Pete Seeger to provide music for the league's 1965 convention, held in Squaw Valley, California. Seeger had once been indicted by the House Un-American Activities Committee, before whom he refused to answer questions. Conservative Lutherans were incensed. One mother wrote to a league official, "Of all the Great outstanding American Christian men who would be glad to speak to our youth, you insist on this (Commie low down lier[sic]). . . . Why don't you get out of the Lutheran church? Yes, better yet why not get out of America and go to Rusia [sic]."[60]

The new spirit eventually led the league to "reorganize" as a "youth-led, issue-oriented" movement in 1968. The national convention that year—held at Purdue University—was still attended by over three thousand young Lutherans, but by 1971 a convention in Rose Bud, South Dakota, featured only three hundred fifty Leaguers sleeping in tents. By then, funds for the national office had nearly dried up, as pastors and parents refused to allow their youth to participate in the "new" Walther League and as the synod in convention offered resolutions condemning the league and withdrawing financial support. Local societies that did endure (largely in urban centers) sponsored "hunger hikes" and "coffeehouse ministries" where "happenings" were held. The league journal, no longer either the *Messenger* or *Arena*, but *Edge*, offered strident essays on racism, the draft, and women's rights. *Edge* drew some criticism: "Your God-awful mess is a disgrace to the Lutheran Church. Don't look further if you want to know why more money isn't coming in. Stop corrupting our youth and blessing it with the Lutheran label. Fold up and die nice!!!"[61] The violent rhetoric matched well the violence of the late sixties. And die the league did, after surviving in some venues until 1977 on a trust fund left from the sale of the headquarters building in 1972. The funds remaining were eventually passed along, appropriately, to two Lutheran social service agencies: the Wheat Ridge Foundation and the Lutheran Volunteer Corps. Wheat Ridge, located in Chicago, had transformed the mission of the old TB sanitarium into a variety of grant-making programs for churches engaged in ministries of "healing and hope."[62] The Lutheran Volunteer Corps, located in Washington, D.C., enlisted young Lutherans for service in frontline social ministries.[63] After the demise of the Walther League, Lutheran congregations were largely forced to go local with ministries for young people when the Missouri Synod dramatically reduced spending on youth causes in the seventies.[64]

What had happened? As American culture spun into violence in 1968, the Walther Leaguers and their parents and leaders mimicked the polarization that beset the entire nation. League board member Charles Sauer observed,

The care of our young had become an issue. . . . People, young
and old, assumed poses and postures. . . . These were [Lutheran]
youth . . . and not a splinter group of "Weathermen." . . . [And
all] adults were . . . not co-conspirators of the Military-Industrial-
Complex out to destroy the youth of the nation. . . . We were all
held hostage by our own ignorance, sparring with shadows while
our substance wasted away. But how could we know? Our history
was lined with a thousand mirrors.[65]

Many of them reflected the culture.

At their best, the young Lutherans of the Walther League and
their leaders had learned that Christian faith meant not only purity
but practices: they had learned to incorporate a Christian identity
formed by both knowledge and service. Margaret Hartmeister, a
Leaguer from St. Louis active in the forties, recalled that "through
[the league] the Lord produced good strong lay leadership for the
Church. . . . You can't cut the ties—we are members of the Body,
Jesus Christ Himself."[66] At their worst, young and old Lutherans
alike had learned to mirror the polarized posturing of America's
left and right, and scapegoated each other with violent rhetoric
and exclusionary politics. The adults, of course—and increasingly
those within the Missouri Synod concerned with purity—had the
power. For having learned through their faith to identify compassionately with some of the key problems in American culture and
for having formed the courage to point out cultural contradictions,
Lutheran youth and their leaders were blamed for the problems of
America. Sacrificed in this process was an organization that had
once empowered many young Lutherans to realize their hopes and
dreams around the life-path of Christian knowledge and Christian
service.

chapter 2

Forming Lay Apostles

THE YOUNG CHRISTIAN WORKERS, 1938–1968

In 1957, Frank Ardito, president of the YCW section of St. Bartholomew's parish in Chicago, made a pilgrimage to Rome. Gathered in St. Peter's Square with thirty thousand other YCW workers from eighty countries, Ardito heard Pope Pius XII encourage the youth to be

> young working men and women . . . [who] wish to live an intense, authentically Christian life, not only in the secret depths of your conscience but also openly—in your families, in the neighborhood, in the factory, the workshop, or the office, thus showing that you belong fully and sincerely to Christ and to the Church. Your strong organization; your method . . . [of] See, Judge, Act; your activities . . . all these enable you to contribute towards the extension of God's Kingdom in modern society.[1]

For Ardito, hearing the pope's words, seeing the "real joy upon [his] face as he made his way among us, showering us with blessings and greetings," and experiencing the camaraderie of meeting thirty thousand fellow Christian workers was "an overwhelming emotional experience of joy and spiritual exhilaration at feeling myself a part of the great, living, active Body of Christ."[2] Long felt to be the preserve of ordained priests alone, the life-path of an apostle was now opening before laity such as Frank Ardito.

At another Chicago parish, St. Urban's, an eighteen-year-old garage worker named Red was the president of his new eight-member YCW section in 1959. The chaplain was Rev. John Hill. Red initially rejected the "inquiry method" of "Observe, Judge, and Act," telling Chaplain Hill that "we're not interested in helping others, Father, we just want to have a good time." When Hill suggested inviting a young Puerto Rican from among the working people of their parish to a section meeting, Red laughingly rebuffed the idea: "The guys at work don't like the Puerto Ricans. They say they are loud, they dress cheap, and they are greasy." Still, Rev. Hill persisted and eventually was able to persuade them to hold one meeting at a Puerto Rican home. Red bounced a one-year-old boy on his knee and concluded after the meeting that he now knew a Puerto Rican family that wasn't greasy.

That November, the section planned a canned-food drive for the poor in the parish, and since many of the poor were Puerto Rican, Red found himself learning about these neighbors of his. Over the next year, Red began to study Spanish. One night, working along with Mary, the section vice-president (who had also begun to study Spanish), he organized a meeting devoted to the dilemmas of Latino workers in Chicago. The young Catholics studied Scripture and contemporary American society, offered judgments about how the gospel related to Latino workers, and decided upon three actions. They began an English class for native Spanish-speaking people, offered free of charge at the parish by a teacher arranged through the board of education. They organized welcoming committees to meet newly arrived immigrants from Cuba and Puerto Rico at Midway Airport (the section also prepared a pamphlet in Spanish to list basic services in the Chicago area for immigrants). And the youth organized a religion class for Spanish-speaking young men, to prepare them to become certified catechists. When the last action failed, these Spanish-speaking men were simply invited to join YCW. The other programs endured for five years, until the YCW section at St. Urban's disbanded.[3]

Between these two stories, some of the scope, detail, and limitation of the YCW movement becomes clear. The YCW had its roots in the larger program of Catholic Action, which was a movement for lay Catholics to encourage practical applications of the faith in everyday life.[4] Like its Catholic Action counterparts, the Christian Family Movement (for married couples), and the Young

Christian Students (for those in school at any level), YCW applied to the situations of young laborers and clerical workers the Catholic Action inquiry method of "Observe, Judge, and Act" designed by Belgian canon Joseph Cardijn.[5] Never intended to be a mass movement, YCW over its thirty-year history involved more than twenty thousand U.S. Catholics. In 1958, the high point of numerical involvement in the movement, fifty-two small-group sections existed in the city of Chicago alone.[6] Drawing on the church's social teachings and an emerging theology of the laity, YCW engaged young lay workers in practices of spiritual formation that demonstrated their status as full members of the Mystical Body of Christ—the church. The YCW formed young workers such as Frank Ardito and Red to "participate in the apostolate of the hierarchy," or to walk on the life-path of a lay apostle.[7]

CATHOLICISM IN AMERICA: FROM ENCLAVES INTO THE MAINSTREAM

The history of Catholicism in America that led to the founding of YCW is a remarkable story of adaptation. In Europe, from which most Catholics immigrants came in the early twentieth century, the Catholic Church was often established by law. Centuries of Catholic presence, along with a well-developed system of economic support through taxes and wealthy patrons, made Catholicism an intrinsic part of most European cultures. Entire nations—Italy, Ireland, and Austria—and entire provinces, as in Germany, among others, were Catholic by law and custom. When immigrants from these countries came to the United States, however, they discovered a very different situation.

Aside from the Vikings, Catholics were the first Europeans to discover North America, and traces of their arrival can be found across the continent at places such as St. Augustine, Florida, named for the fourth-century Catholic theologian, and San Francisco, California, named for the thirteenth-century Catholic monastic reformer. But these early Catholic presences came in the context of a number of complicating factors. By 1700, the majority of immigrants to the New World were Protestants, and Protestants—some of them with lingering memories of Europe's religious wars and persecutions—were, at best, suspicious of Catholics and, at worst, overtly hostile and violent toward their non-Protestant neighbors.[8] By 1786, Catholics could at least take refuge in the First Amendment's guarantee of the free exercise of religion, but the same amendment that guaranteed Catholics a right to worship also posed for them an obstacle: how could people accustomed to being part of an established church in their own countries continue to practice their faith when the amendment specifically prohibited any "establishment of religion"? Furthermore, Catholics were ethnically diverse. Although united in worship by the common Latin language used in the Mass, in daily life Catholics were separated by language, custom, and, eventually, geography. Irish settled among the Irish and established Irish parishes. Italians, Poles, and Germans all did the same. Consequently, the Catholic Church in the United States has only in recent years begun to emerge out of ethnic enclaves where the purity of the Catholic faith was preserved in a variety of distinctive forms.

Catholics moved out of their enclaves at the impetus, to a significant degree, of laypeople and lay movements such as YCW. On the early American frontier, lay Catholics often had to assume the responsibilities of carrying on the faith in the absence of priests. In the nineteenth century, laypeople assisted "bricks and mortar" priests in building thousands of Catholic institutions across the country—churches, schools, hospitals, colleges, and universities. In the late nineteenth century, national organizations of Catholic laity began to emerge. The most significant—the Knights of Columbus—was founded in 1882 and continues as a Catholic fraternal association and insurance agency.[9] Many of these organizations—such as the aptly named Knights of Labor—were tailored to meet the needs of the large Catholic working class in the United States. Especially after a series of papal encyclicals seemed to give them sanction, lay organizations for workers came to play a key role in the move of Catholics out of their enclaves and into the American national scene.

The most significant of these papal encyclicals was undoubtedly *Rerum Novarum: On the Condition of the Working Classes*, issued by Pope Leo XIII in 1891. *Rerum Novarum* was, in the words of one historian, "a document of prophetic and bold statements." The pope wrote,

> Some opportune remedy must be found quickly for the misery and wretchedness pressing so unjustly on the majority of the working class. . . . By degrees it has come to pass that working-men have been surrendered, isolated and made helpless to the hard-heartedness of employers and the greed of unchecked competition. . . . To this end must be added that the hiring of labor

and the conduct of trade are concentrated in the hands of the
comparatively few; so that a small number of very rich men have
been able to lay upon the teeming masses of the laboring poor a
yoke little better than that of slavery itself.[10]

Rerum Novarum carved out a Catholic economic strategy between
capitalism and socialism, based upon three principles: "The church
must seek popular rather than princely support for its actions; the
church must work for and assist in the maintenance of industrial
peace; and . . . Catholics must usher in a new organization of society based upon a concept of equality."[11] These principles were,
in fact, also well suited for the American nonestablishment of
religion.

Catholics in the United States—laity and priests—answered
the pope's call. Rev. John A. Ryan, a faculty member at Catholic
University in Washington, D.C., developed in 1906 many of the
ideas of *Rerum Novarum* in a book called *A Living Wage*, and Ryan
later served as an advisor on the New Deal programs of President
Franklin D. Roosevelt.[12] Lay groups such as Dorothy Day's Catholic
Worker movement emerged in the 1920s and 1930s, and lay-edited
journals such as *Commonweal* (1924) provided a forum for discussion of the issues pressing upon Catholics in America.[13] By the
1950s and 1960s, Catholic intellectuals such as Yves Congar[14] and
Daniel Callahan[15] had developed a clear theology and history of
the laity, and writers such as the Jesuit John Courtney Murray had
articulated ways that Catholicism was compatible with American
pluralism and nonestablishment of religion.[16] In this context, lay
movements such as YCW flourished. Historian Patrick Carey explains, "The overall objective of these lay movements was to unite
religion and life . . . [and thereby resist] the individualism and secularism . . . characteristic of the modern age. But, resistance alone
was insufficient. The more positive side of these movements was
transformative . . . to put Christian love into action."[17] When
Catholic John F. Kennedy was elected to the presidency in 1960,
it was apparent that Catholicism in America had moved from the
inward-looking purity of its ethnic enclaves into the practice of
faith in everyday and national life.

This move was not, however, without its ironies. By moving
into the mainstream, Catholics in America were caught up in national trends and cultural conventions, many of which had little to
do with the faith. Catholic lay activism, furthermore, was not motivated solely by altruism. Historian Florence Henderson Davis suggests, "This was a highly upwardly mobile community. The initial

energy that made them immigrants in the first place was now turned toward bettering their situation. There are numerous stories [in U.S. Catholic history] of maiden aunts working . . . [to pay] for the college education of the nieces and nephews who went on to become lawyers, doctors, college professors, and successful politicians."[18] Catholic sociologist Andrew Greeley puts a slightly different spin on the irony by pointing out that over the course of the twentieth century the Catholic Church in the United States became "a church for immigrants who are no longer immigrants, a church for the poor who are no longer poor, a church for the uneducated who are now well educated."[19] Catholics fought alongside their Protestant neighbors during World War II, and those who survived returned to take advantage of the free college education provided by the G.I. Bill and then to buy the burgeoning number of consumer goods a prosperous American economy offered. In such an upwardly mobile community, it is perhaps not surprising that a movement to form *young* Catholic *workers* in the practices of their faith would be short-lived.[20] The very success of Catholics in the United States eventually seemed to erode the need for the life-path of a lay apostle, as formed in youth through their participation in YCW.

THE LIFE-PATH OF A LAY APOSTLE: "OBSERVE, JUDGE, AND ACT"

The YCW was a European—specifically a Belgian—import to the United States. The movement began when Canon Joseph Cardijn pledged on his father's deathbed—or so the story goes—in 1903 to dedicate his life to improving the quality of life for Christian workers like his dad—who died of "overwork" at age forty-three. It was an ambitious pledge. Drawn by Marxism and repelled by the church's indifference to, or complicity with, their plight, young Belgian workers—like workers across Europe—were leaving the churches in droves. Cardijn's first assignment as a parish priest was in Laecken, Belgium, in 1912. There he began gathering small groups of young workers to discuss their lives and faith. Out of these meetings Cardijn developed the threefold method of small-group action for which YCW and the other Catholic Action programs became known: "Observe, Judge, and Act."[21]

Cardijn himself was modest about the origins of YCW and Catholic Action. Near the end of his life, he wrote simply that the problems of workers had "attracted" him since his adolescence. He admitted, however, that this problem became an "obsession," and he had few limits on his hope for how lay apostles could transform the world. "The older I get," wrote the priest when he was eighty, "the more I am convinced that the . . . lay apostolate is a decisive factor in the future of the world and the salvation of humanity." One person at a time, YCW would return the church to the people, and return the people to the church, starting with young workers. "I never tired," Cardijn wrote, "of repeating to the young people of the YCW 'Each young worker, each working girl has a divine destiny and a divine mission, beginning not after death, but from today, in the conditions of everyday life, where they are the first and immediate apostles of God in their environment and among their comrades.' " The YCW was officially recognized by Rome in 1925, and rapidly spread in Europe thereafter. As the movement grew, it often took on intense political significance. A group of young workers who were motivated to assert their rights on the basis of Catholic faith was surely a challenge to the standard Marxist line that religion was the "opiate of the masses." Cardijn admitted that YCW was a "reply to the Marxist dialectic," and this undoubtedly contributed to its growth, but the priest was also insistent that the movement was "part of the very essence of Christianity." That it flourished around the globe was due, in no small part, to Cardijn's charisma. As he put it, his life was "a long spiritual journey: an idea which has been put into practice and lived. . . . After fifty years, 'Seek' . . . is still my motto."[22]

The "Observe, Judge, and Act" method developed by Cardijn to mobilize small groups was a life-path as much as a means to organize meetings. The threefold process was called the "Social Inquiry." At a typical YCW meeting, it came after a brief "Gospel Inquiry" and a "Reporting" of the previous week's events. The Social Inquiry was the longest part of any meeting. Each step had its own integrity. The "Observe" step was a time to gather data; to investigate and diagnose a situation. Workers shared what they had seen over the past week on a topic assigned at the previous meeting. Members were encouraged to share specific details of their situations, based on "objective" reporting of "who, how, what, when, where," and so forth. The idea was to "awaken" workers, through discussion, to the practices, language, and situations in which they worked and lived. Topics could range from family life to capitalism versus socialism. Just about any aspect of human association was likely to fall under the Catholic Action rubric "Observe."

The second step in the Social Inquiry process was "Judge." Here, young workers were encouraged to relate their Catholic faith to the situations they had observed. Catholic youth had usually been taught the faith through study of the catechism and had re-affirmed their baptism through the sacramental rite of passage of Confirmation, but these were general activities not specifically re-lated to the lives of workers. In YCW, young workers were formed in practices of discerning judgment that challenged them to relate the gospel and the teachings of the church to the situations of their everyday lives. "Is this Christian?" was the guiding question for the judgment phase of the inquiry. Was what the young workers had observed over the past week compatible with the church's teaching or not? As they observed their situations, workers were challenged to locate the sources of misery, greed, isolation, and injustice iden-tified in *Rerum Novarum* and other social teachings of the church as characteristic problems besetting modern workers.

Finally, Cardijn was convinced that study alone was not enough; thus, the "Act" step. The Social Inquiry had as its purpose the formation of youth through action, through specific practices that responded to their observation and judgment and sought to transform injustice into justice, inequity into equality. In the meet-ing itself, members decided upon what actions were required and who among them could carry them out. Then, over the course of the next week (or longer), members were responsible to put in practice the actions they had agreed upon. These could be individual ac-tions, such as improvement in moral behavior or attitude, or col-lective actions, such as attendance at Mass or organizing a strike. The range of potential action was intentionally left broad, although Cardijn's initial impulse for YCW was to make it a sort of "junior labor union" with a Christian foundation. In fact, it became much more than that.[23] The Social Inquiry became a rite of passage for young Catholic workers. It awakened them to observe their world as adults. It challenged them to judge social problems on the basis of reason and faith. It incorporated them as adults able to act on faith. Indeed, for young people deeply steeped in YCW, the Social Inquiry became their life-path, a way of life as a lay apostle.

The theoretical foundation for YCW was in the sacramental theology of the church. Fr. Louis J. Putz, the chaplain of YCW at the University of Notre Dame, articulated it well:

> Through the sacrament of the Eucharist the recipient commits himself to live a community life that mirrors the Mystical Body of Christ; through marriage the couple commit themselves to a

life of selfless love, and devotion to offspring. Through the sacrament of Confirmation we accept the responsibilities of the apostolate. This apostolate may be one of Christian witness or one of Christian influence or one of total dedication. Whichever we undertake, we are assured of the grace, the power of the Holy Spirit. But grace does not dispense with the human effort of learning to be apostolic, of acquiring the habit of dealing with our fellowmen, of learning the spiritual and material needs of mankind in this day and age.[24]

As confirmed members of the Mystical Body of Christ, young Catholic workers formed "cells" of the body—and that is what their small groups were called.

YOUNG CHRISTIAN WORKERS IN AMERICA

The first cells of YCW were established in Brooklyn, New York, after a series of lectures on Catholic Action there in 1938 and 1939 by Paul McGuire, an Australian Catholic activist invited to America by the Knights of Columbus. Brooklyn layman John Berkery heard McGuire speak, consulted with local priests, and began to meet with a small group of other laity to form a YCW cell. Others quickly followed, in Brooklyn and wherever McGuire spoke. A report on these early meetings indicated typical topics treated by the first American cells. Groups discussed "the working environment, dancing, dress, dates and preparation for marriage, movies, family life." At each meeting, "members were expected to bring in facts about a specific topic chosen ahead of time." After discussion of these observed facts, "the group would make a judgment. Did the facts indicate a problem? Should something be done? What?" Early actions by the Brooklyn cells included campaigns for decent movies, getting fellow workers to return to the sacraments, and trying to create a more Christian celebration of Christmas by placing displays in stores and encouraging the use of religious cards.[25] The Brooklyn cells called themselves "American Jocists" (Jocism was an acronym from the French name for YCW: Jeunesse Ouvrière Chrétienne).

The movement did not grow without difficulties. Some local YCW cells had trouble translating the theology of the Mystical Body into action. One evening in 1939, for instance, a young women's cell in Chicago—men and women did not meet together in the early years—studied Matthew 22:35–46. In this story, Jesus describes for Pharisees the greatest commandments, to love God and one's neighbor. After observing and judging on the basis of this text, the Young Christian Workers concluded, "As Christ was able to answer the Pharisees in such a way that they could find no fault or reason for contention, so we should try to grow in knowledge and faith so we too could find satisfactory answers."[26] This abstract quest for answers was not exactly what Catholic Action intended. A different but related problem arose when some newly awakened laity took the idea of the Mystical Body of Christ with scrupulous seriousness. "I got so I couldn't even sit on my way to work on the bus," recalled one South Bend YCW worker. "Observe, Judge, and Act. Acts of service. See Christ in others," she reiterated the slogans of her formation into the movement. "Crowded buses, and just when I got comfortably seated, there was Christ standing beside me and He needed a seat."[27] After decades of guidance by priests, a group of more or less autonomous laity had to struggle to interpret and apply the faith.[28]

Along with lay timidity or scrupulosity, overt opposition sometimes stymied YCW's effort to form lay apostles. In the early years, part of the problem was a refusal by YCW leaders to affiliate with other recognized Catholic youth programs such as the Catholic Youth Organization (CYO), founded in 1930 by Chicago bishop Bernard J. Sheil.[29] Although invited, for example, to associate with the National Catholic Youth Council (an officially recognized bureau of the National Catholic Welfare Conference), YCW leaders "agreed . . . that we were different from other youth organizations which were primarily concerned with the personal and religious behavior of Catholics. . . . We were convinced that we must be concerned with the problems of social justice."[30] Without official affiliation with a national Catholic agency, the success or failure of YCW in any given locale depended upon the largesse of the bishop or the political savvy and charisma of the local YCW chaplain, usually a parish priest appointed to the task. In some cases, local priests were denied permission to start YCW programs.[31] Even in Chicago, where Catholic Action pioneer Msgr. Reynold Hillenbrand served as YCW national chaplain, Cardinals Mundelein and Stritch emphasized a low-key approach, with little publicity or attention to mass causes.

Another early barrier to YCW success was the tinge of radicalism associated with Catholic Action generally, workers in particular, and the young especially. Aside from YCW's associations with labor, which grew into clear alliances, the lifestyle of YCW organizers troubled some. A key issue for YCW men was finding new

leaders. "Few were to be found around the parish church," one participant remembered. "Where did the fellows hang out? Often, it
was the neighborhood bar. Bar hopping became a common tactic
for YCW organizers. Over the years beer-drinking became an identifying mark of many a Young Christian Worker."[32] A movement of
young beer-drinking "workers," even if baptized with the name
"Christian," became an obvious target not only for anti-Catholic
stereotyping but also for conservatives within the church who mis-
trusted or wanted to control youth. And increasingly both the elite
of the church and the youth themselves accommodated YCW to
the individualism and capitalism that were all but unquestioned
American cultural conventions. Anticommunism especially became so deeply entrenched in the American ethos that any workers'
movement was suspect. The YCW rhetoric therefore sought to distance the movement from communism, and in fact the leaders offered YCW as an effective deterrent to communist influence.[33]
Indirectly, this Americanization undermined the movement's potential to form lay apostles who walked the life-path that observed,
judged, and acted as Young Christian Workers. Over the years,
YCW diffused its focus from a young workers' to a generic youth
movement, and then from a grass-roots, practices-based movement of spiritual formation to an educationally based movement
with top-down direction. The Mystical Body of Christ became little
more than a metaphor for the American middle class.

RESISTANCE AND ACCOMMODATION: A PRACTICES-BASED MOVEMENT OF YOUNG WORKERS

It was perhaps inevitable that the leaders of YCW in the United
States would adapt the European-inspired Jocist model to American culture. In Europe, YCW had to persuade a large, relatively permanent and alienated working class to return to an established
Church and then put their faith into action. In U.S. Catholicism,
the boundaries and allegiances of the working class were fluid, and
the church was one more voluntary organization in the market
economy. From the outset, the U.S. version of YCW stressed less
the mass and class appeal of YCW than the benefits to individuals
of participating in small groups of like-to-like service. "In a small
group the members gradually build a spirit of friendliness and
common purpose," explained one U.S. YCW manual. "They feel
what psychologists call a 'sense of belonging,' since the small group

belongs to its members—and they belong to it—in a way that rarely is possible in a larger organization."[34] The YCW in the United States sought less to convert the alienated masses than to educate already Catholic "workers" into the social teachings of the church and to form through practices lay apostles. Of course, conversion remained a goal, but it was secondary to practices of service. Louis Putz argued that "we will not convert others by preaching or telling others of our religion; we will do it by our service."[35] In its early years, YCW stressed that practices were the means to conversion, not conversion the path to practices. This accorded well with the developing American tendency to stress practices over purity in youth ministries, but it also significantly altered the internal dynamic of YCW from its European character.

Another significant adaptation of the YCW program to the American context came in 1954, when the national leaders of YCW decided to break with the European pattern of separate men's and women's cells. Fr. William Schackmuth, the chaplain of active YCW sections at St. Andrew parish in Chicago, observed that ten groups of male and female leaders met separately each Thursday evening in his parish hall, after which they adjourned to the back room of a local tavern to dance and talk together. Encouraged in consultations with lay leaders, Schackmuth approached YCW national chaplain Reynold Hillenbrand with the idea of mixed groups. Hillenbrand was initially opposed. "That is not the Jocist way," he responded. During the 1954 Summer School of Catholic Action (an annual weeklong retreat and training session for YCW national leaders), however, Hillenbrand was persuaded. He wrote, "We have clung too closely to what was done in Europe. . . . The primary interest of the young people in the age group with which we work is marriage. By keeping our sections separate, we . . . are not capitalizing on the natural tendencies which exist."[36] That this was good Thomist theology—St. Thomas taught that grace fulfilled nature—made the cultural adaptation that much easier. Practices built on "natural tendencies" could override a precedent of gender separation for the purposes of sexual purity.

Mixed groups thus became standard across the United States after 1955. The results included a favorable jump in recruitment, but the internal dynamic of the cells again changed. Mary Irene Zotti, a former member and a historian of the movement, notes that "the women learned to play dumb at meetings so the less experienced men could appear to be in control." Nancy Lee Conrad, sent to New Orleans as an organizer in 1960, was cautioned to stay "one step behind" the male leader of the organizing team. "She tried hard, but it wasn't easy. . . . Most of the male leaders in those days took it for granted that they should be in charge. One young man in the days following the changeover remembers how long it took him to get used to young women who voiced their opinions frankly and freely."[37] Many women feel that the gender dynamics in YCW stemming from this adaption to American mores contributed to its demise: "The YCW really missed the boat on women in modern society," offered one former member.[38]

At the same time, YCW also clearly enabled young laywomen to articulate and practice their faith in ways previously not possible in the church. Americanization had its upside. For instance, Dodie Marino, a young worker at an electrical factory in Milwaukee, joined YCW and learned to "Observe, Judge, and Act" on her job. This meant "getting a cup of coffee for a gal or lending money to someone who needs it. . . . Service is the life of the YCW." Marino also observed a lack of safety measures at her factory and acted by becoming a union leader and by taking a trip to Madison to support legislation to improve working conditions. Finally, Marino published about her YCW experience. Her essay "YCW in Our Factory" was widely reprinted; another, "YCW Joins a Picket Line," documented her involvement in a labor dispute with Kohler plumbing manufacturing in Sheboygan.[39]

Women's concerns found their way into YCW publications and local activities in a variety of ways. For instance, *AIM,* the national YCW publication printed between 1957 and 1959, issued in March 1958 a "Special Report": "U.S. Girls' Biggest Problem: Loneliness." The title was a bit misleading. The authors of the article—identified only as the "YCW girls' staff"—defined the problem of loneliness to include the fact that "although women workers are one-third of the labor force, they get only one-fifth of the nation's wages and salaries." *AIM* also proposed a solution to "loneliness": "A reform of economic life will assist in the position of women in this country. . . . The forty-one million unorganized workers in this country must be organized . . . [so that] equal pay for equal work" can be realized.[40] Thus, despite suffering through unmistakable subordination, women also were awakened in key ways through YCW involvement.

In its early years, then, YCW was a practices-based movement of young workers that both accommodated Catholic youth to, and encouraged them to resist, American culture. For example, YCW directed the attention of young Catholic men and women to the difficult problem of race. *AIM* reported in 1958 that the YCW section at Holy Cross parish in Omaha discussed "Discrimination and the Law" at a weekly meeting in June. Observing that "Nebraska has a law prohibiting discrimination in restaurants" and judging that "the law was badly kept," members acted to survey local restaurants and publish a list of those establishments willing to provide equal service to blacks. Less than half of the seventy-six restaurants surveyed made the list. In a published release, YCW members claimed this "was not a survey just to determine statistics about discrimination, but also a means of determining where, how, and when we personally could Christianize and educate our fine All-American City."[41] In American culture, where anti-Catholicism and racism were often linked (the Ku Klux Klan is the most notorious example), it was important to couch cultural resistance in patriotic rhetoric.

In short, the adaptation and development of YCW in America formed youth in practices of both accommodation and resistance. The example of music—a key area of concern to youth—might illustrate the tension. In April 1959, *AIM*'s editor, Bernard Lyons, offered an opinion piece under the title "Ain't Gonna Rock 'n' Roll No More." "Rock 'n' roll, now that it has about run the course of most fads, is coming in for some pretty strong criticism," the piece began. "Call me a pessimist, but . . . I despair of much being done in a positive way about such forms of music . . . unless [we] get at the roots of the specific problem—our false concepts of leisure . . . our economic injustices . . . and other symptoms of the bankrupt Christianity of our selves and our society." Music "suitable to the dignity of man" that "pictures him as a child of God rather than an economic digit" was preferable for YCW members.[42] The Mystical Body of Christ had little room for the "sensuality" and "lack of modesty" of rock. Aside from being a poor prophet of musical trends, Lyons probably offered his opinion so forcefully because it was less than universally shared among the YCW rank and file. Catholic youth, like American youth generally, found ways to make their Christian faith compatible with the practice of rock 'n' roll, even as some of their peers resisted.

FROM A WORKERS' MOVEMENT TO A YOUTH MOVEMENT

The most telling way YCW was adapted to the American context over the years was a lessened focus on "workers." By 1957, 77

percent of the youth involved in YCW were white-collar employ-
ees, and only 15 percent were blue-collar workers.[43] *AIM* and the
other publications tried hard to keep the focus of the movement
clear. *AIM* published columns with titles such as the monthly feature "Shop Talk" to report on local activities, and articles and in-
quiries on joblessness, worker safety, and sexual harassment, but a
tension between being an American youth movement and a Catholic workers' movement proved difficult to resolve.[44] A candid critique of the movement on this point came in 1958 from Fr. Keith
Kennedy, a YCW leader among Mexican workers in California.
Kennedy appealed for YCW to throw off "dilettante apostolicity"
and truly focus on "genuine love and 'guts' Christianity. If [YCW] is
merely to be a youth movement, even an apostolic youth movement, it is doomed, I fear, to superficiality." Rejecting the claim
that there were not specific workers' problems in the United States,
Kennedy listed low-cost housing, insurance, workers' compensa-
tion, right-to-work legislation, displacement of migrant workers,
materialism, and other issues as problems needing to be "seen,
and touched, and felt, and smelled in the individual lives of workers and their families—of human personalities made in the image
and likeness of God."[45] Kennedy felt that belonging to the Mystical
Body of Christ needed to be more than a metaphor for joining
America's middle class.

But the adaptation of YCW to U.S. mores proceeded. Jean Pew,
a full-time YCW staffer between 1953 and 1959, recalled that "the
'worker' idea was discussed in gradually lessening degrees. It was
felt that it could keep people out of the movement." Even Hillenbrand, long a holdout for the pure Jocist way, concurred at the
1957 national meeting: "We need *growth*," he emphasized.[46] By
1962, a survey of YCW chaplains in Chicago concluded that "every
priest interviewed saw the YCW as a youth movement. . . . The
priests did not consider YCW a 'workers' movement in the European sense of the phrase."[47] By 1964, the move away from workers
was made explicit when the name of the organization was changed
to the Young Christian Movement.[48]

Despite these adaptations, the intent to form young workers in
a life-path as lay apostles endured in many ways. Between 1955
and 1966 one-month leadership training courses were held several
times a year in Chicago for national YCW workers. As many as
twenty-five leaders from across the country took a month off from
work (and paid several hundred dollars) to live with national staffers or Chicago leaders and undergo an intense process of educa-

tion, formation, and practice. Sessions on the apostolic spirit of the movement, its techniques and methodology, running meetings, participating actively in the Mass, and labor and international issues were common. National chaplain Hillenbrand regularly offered classes on the social teachings of the church.

Russ Tershy, who ran the program from 1955 to 1962, recalls, "We did intense training. . . . We even took some of [the visitors] to picket lines when a strike was going on." A participant remembers, "The national training course . . . had superb resources, experts, and was highly organized. . . . This one-month-long communal life was exhilarating and dynamic and, most of all, conveyed an understanding of what we were: people serving people. It provided the opportunity to live the YCW techniques and ideology in depth. It was the pinnacle of one's formation.[49] The "intense training course" also demonstrated a shift in focus from YCW as a local grassroots movement to a more nationally directed program. As this shift continued, YCW's days were numbered: young people in the sixties clamored for practices of local relevance in everyday life.

FROM A YOUTH MOVEMENT TO AN EDUCATIONAL MOVEMENT

The top-down approach dominated the last years of YCW. Under the leadership of Msgr. Hillenbrand, lessons prepared by the Chicago office focused upon "Seven Areas of Life" that were to be discussed and acted upon in a three-year cycle. They were (1) work and economic life, (2) marriage and family life, (3) political life and citizenship, (4) leisure, (5) international relations, (6) race relations, and (7) parish life. The broad program met with resistance in local societies. As early as 1961, one St. Paul leader argued that YCW "is becoming an educational movement." By this, the author meant that the movement was taking young people away from the problems they faced in everyday life. In the same year, the New York federations of YCW issued a joint statement that made this complaint explicit. It read, in part, "The national program has been of an educative nature and [is] not really dealing with the needs of young people in a way that they may grow, develop, and seek answers to the problems that relate to their daily lives."[50] Youth wanted practices. The YCW gave them a program. As Notre Dame historian Scott Appleby writes, "Catholic Action [in America] sought to empower lay people, but [too often] their newfound apostolic energy was derived, rather than self-generated."[51]

No cataclysmic end signaled the demise of YCW. National and local YCW sections throughout the sixties worked effectively with a wide range of agencies, among them the AFL-CIO, the National Committee on Agricultural Labor (migrant workers), the President's Committee on Children and Youth, the NAACP, and CORE. In a few cities, some sections continued to meet until 1978, but as early as 1968 no cells remained active in Chicago (this was also the last year of the influential Summer School of Catholic Action). The diffuse "Seven Areas" program, changes in the social setting of young Catholics in America, and Vatican II rendered many of the emphases of the program moot. Catholics continued to form and educate lay apostles among young workers but in a less focused way than through YCW. Catholic attention to youth was diffused through various institutions, such as Catholic schools; strengthened programs in the Confraternity of Christian Doctrine; voluntary agencies, such as the CYO or the Jesuit Volunteer Corps; special events, such as World Youth Day; and the development of professional parish religious educators.[52] In the years after 1968, a diffuse but inclusive "theology of God's people" replaced the Mystical Body of Christ as a rallying cry for Catholic social action.[53] It was not specifically a theology of the laity, much less a theology of youth, but it suited its time as well as the idea of the Mystical Body had fit its own.

Still, as Zotti explains, in the days before Vatican II the YCW movement

> had a sureness of purpose and a Christian vision for the world. Its method and organizational style brought the social teachings of the Church into the lives of ordinary people. Its realistic method—Observe, Judge, Act—deeply ingrained its members with a Christian social conscience and a habit of service that has remained with them. Its organizational style, based on the small group, gave support to the individual man or woman trying to bring Christian values to the world. Moreover, its stress on a lay spirituality, based on the Gospels and active participation in Eucharistic worship, made God and religion more meaningful to thousands of young men and women. Its leadership training motivated those who chose it to become more than they might otherwise have dreamed of.[54]

Zotti's own biography demonstrates her point. She began with YCW as a worker in a Chicago parish. Within two years, she represented the national headquarters at an international YCW meeting in Europe; upon return, she undertook full-time work on behalf of the movement. In 1990 she published the only full history of the organization—*A Time of Awakening.*

For the thirty years of its history, YCW in the United States developed a distinctly American version of the Jocist program. As one choice among a growing number of ways for young lay Catholics to be formed and educated in faith, YCW transformed both the church and (in discrete individuals and instances) the culture by helping Catholic youth move from the purity of ethnic enclaves to practices of the faith in everyday and national life. Thoroughly grounded in Catholic theology but also reaching out to the problems of American society, YCW taught select Catholic youth to understand themselves as part of the Mystical Body of Christ and practice this apostolic calling in face-to-face and collective practices of compassion. That many Catholic youth were formed indelibly by this life-path of a lay apostle is undeniable; they stayed Catholics and became deeper Catholics than before their involvement in YCW. They were, furthermore, generally well prepared for the changes of Vatican II. At the same time, YCW was also an American youth movement that enabled many Catholics to move into mainstream, middle-class American culture with confidence. This contribution of the YCW movement was no small part of its success.

chapter 3

Becoming Witnesses

YOUTH FOR CHRIST, 1945–PRESENT

In 1963 Melanie Garrett, a member of the Jackson, Mississippi, YFC club, wrote to *Youth for Christ Magazine* to describe her experience as a "witness" for Christ.[1] "During a recent choir trip," she began, "on the Saturday night before a Sunday service, my roommate and I went down to talk to some girls. It was about 2:30 when we got to talking about salvation. My girlfriend and I both told them how we had received Christ as our personal Savior. By the time I went to bed at 3:30 a.m., I felt so good I just couldn't explain it—I'm so glad the Lord gave us a chance to witness to others." Jim Sundholm of the Greater Seattle YFC also became a witness. One summer night he and some buddies went out to a local drive-in theater. One of the boys pulled out a pack of cigarettes and offered one to Jim. Jim refused. "Before I knew it, the guy who brought the cigarettes put his out and threw the rest away. The other boys also put out theirs. After a moment of silence, one of the guys said, 'Ya know Sundholm, if Christ means this much to you, there must be something to Christianity. You may not realize it, but by your Christian stand you've gained respect instead of losing it.' "[2]

To become this sort of witness—where a person through conversation and moral example displayed Christian faith—was the primary life-path encouraged by YFC in its earliest years. Recently, YFC's emphasis on individual witnessing has been deepened by youth ministries that also challenge youth through practices consistent with the classical Evangelical concern for social justice. The shift from purity to practices in modern youth ministry has been subtle but clear in YFC and other Evangelical youth organizations.[3]

THE "NEW EVANGELICALS" AND THE RISE OF YOUTH FOR CHRIST: PURITY AND PATRIOTISM

Youth for Christ, International, is one of the many significant phenomena to flow from the revivalist tradition in American religious history. In the 1730s and 1740s, evangelists George Whitefield, Jonathan Edwards, and others sparked a series of dramatic conversions to Christianity. This Great Awakening, as it came to be called, at the least provided Protestants in colonial America with something to argue about; at most, it provided them a common culture that laid a foundation for the revolution against Britain.[4] In the early 1800s, another series of revivals spread across the United States, led most notably by lawyer-turned-preacher Charles Grandison Finney. This Second Great Awakening burned hottest in New York State but traveled quickly west and south. Through it Christians were not only converted or revitalized but also motivated to contribute to a variety of social reforms, including the Christian antislavery movement.[5] Finally, some scholars point to a third wave of revivals in the years from 1890 to 1920, centered largely in America's cities and led by evangelists such as Dwight L. Moody and Billy Sunday.[6] These urban awakenings also contributed to social reform—most notably the passage of the Eighteenth Amendment in 1917 prohibiting the sale and consumption of alcoholic beverages.[7]

Shortly after 1920, however, the revivalist tradition in America unraveled as the unofficial Protestant establishment in America came apart in the face of modern historical criticism, science, and the growing pluralism of American culture.[8] Protestantism splintered into two parties—the modernists, who liked or at least accommodated criticism, science, and pluralism, and the fundamentalists, who did not. Those with conservative affinities splintered further into a variety of often hostile camps—Holiness, Pentecostal, Fundamentalist, Four-Square Gospel, and many more.[9] Through the writing of cultural elite such as journalist H. L. Mencken and novelist Sinclair Lewis, fundamentalists were depicted as ignorant, superstitious, small-minded bigots, and Evangelicals (not all of whom were fundamentalists) felt the sting.[10] Once part of the Protestant establishment, Evangelicals now felt like outsiders. A significant number of them expected the imminent return of Christ to rescue the few pure Christians from the many decadent modernists.[11] Still, despite their millennial anticipation, Evangelicals continued to build colleges, Bible camps, Christian academies, and churches. They also, of course, continued to hold revivals, and held out some fragile hope that Americans, whose moral practices seemed to have spun completely out of control, might someday "return to purity."[12] In the rise of YFC, Evangelicals began to see that hope realized as a coalition of new Evangelicals emerged to attract favorable public attention.

Youth for Christ was one of three Evangelical nondenominational youth organizations founded during World War II (the others were Young Life and InterVarsity Christian Fellowship). Between them, these three organizations drew thousands of young people to rallies, small-group meetings, and Bible studies throughout the forties and fifties. Youth for Christ was organized in 1944 during a conference at Winona Lake, Indiana, under the leadership of Evangelicals Lloyd Bryant, Percy Crawford, Jack Wyrtzen, and Torrey Johnson. The group was funded in part by Chicago businessman Herbert J. Taylor. In 1945 the organizers chose Billy Graham—at the time a pastor in the Chicago suburb of Western Springs—to be YFC's first full-time staff person as traveling evangelist.[13]

Youth for Christ had roots on the East Coast, but it grew most rapidly in the Midwest. Johnson, pastor of the Midwest Bible Church, scheduled rallies at Orchestra Hall in Chicago for twenty-one consecutive Saturday nights in 1944 and booked half-hour spots on radio station WCFL to coincide. Graham preached the first sermon at the first rally. At the conclusion of the twenty-one weeks, a "Victory Rally" to support the Allied cause in World War II drew more than twenty-eight thousand people to the Chicago Stadium. A year later, fifty thousand young people converged on Chicago's Soldier Field for a YFC rally. After these successful revivals, Chicago became the organizing center for YFC, and the pattern of radio broadcast and rallies became YFC's signature.[14] The public began to take notice.

Harold E. Fey, a writer for the mainline journal *Christian Century*, attended the Soldier Field rally and penned a report. The tone of Fey's article indicates the disdain with which Evangelicals were held by some in the mainline. "Is this a revival or a racket?" Fey asked. He admitted that the answer to his question depended on the "point of view of the answerer." Fey's point of view compressed the message of the revival to this description:

> Give your heart to Christ. Conversion is not explained but is made to seem very urgent, absolutely necessary. At a given time in every meeting a person is asked to raise his hand or to stand. Later he is given a copy of the Gospel of John and asked to read it. There are vague suggestions that he should join a church if he can find one which is "true to the Book." . . . He is told that he should continue to attend YFC meetings and that he should "witness for Christ." This witness consists in getting other people to attend meetings or inviting the person next to him to "give his heart to Christ."[15]

Fey admitted that "revivalism has a long history in American religious life" and that it "has a good side." He struggled to find it.

Fey did notice that, in addition to the call to conversion, the Soldier Field rally also included an "all-out emphasis on national pride." "In all Youth for Christ assemblies," he generalized, "the war is presented as a holy crusade, the service of Christ and the military service of country are equated, and soldiers, sailors, marines and members of the women's auxiliaries are singled out for special honor . . . in a 'smooth blend of religion and patriotism.' "[16] Evangelicals were hardly the only Christians to support the war effort—almost all of the mainline denominations had their War-time Service Boards. But Fey sensed in YFC a kind of hyperpatriotism that grew out of the religious impulses in the movement. When the service of Christ and military service were equated, the result was a crusade, and the Crusades had not been a pretty part of the historic Christian witness.[17]

The choice of Graham as YFC's leader was instrumental in the growth of the movement. Graham became model and epitome of the witness to be formed through participation in YFC. Every sermon called youth to convert: "Your choice can be one of two decisions—accept Christ and believe Him, or die without Him and suffer judgment at the Great White Throne of Judgment."[18] And every message linked conversion to "America's Hope," as the title of a chapter in his first book, *Calling Youth to Christ*, had it: "America, I present to you a spiritual call to arms. 'Come, and let us return unto the Lord.' . . . America cannot organize her way out [of decadence]. She must *pray* her way out."[19] Indeed, Graham was an "admirable, clean-cut young man" who "seemed to many to embody American virtue, and his utterances comported well with the conventions of American folkpiety."[20] Graham's call to arms was intended to be spiritual, to make witnesses for Christ; but it also prepared warriors for the American way.[21]

Rallies continued throughout the forties and fifties, reaching their height perhaps in 1957, when Graham had a falling-out with fundamentalists. Youth for Christ rallies followed a consistent pattern of "Saturday night in a big auditorium, lively gospel music, personal testimonies from athletes, civic leaders or military heroes, and a brief sermon, climaxing with a gospel invitation to receive Jesus as personal Savior."[22] Historian Joel Carpenter develops the portrait further: "Rally evangelists hammered at the sins of youthful desire, while creating an atmosphere of wholesome entertainment, patriotic affirmation, and religious commitment. [Early YFC] meetings featured carefully orchestrated visions of innocence, heroism, and loyalty . . . all wrapped in a contemporary idiom borrowed from radio variety shows and patriotic musical revues."[23]

Converts talked of being cleansed by the rallies. One soldier testified, "I was a sinner, but now, praise the Lord, I am clean, through Christ."[24] Language baptizing America's military success with Christian purity was common. Well into the fifties, YFC leaders spoke of forming "invasion teams" to establish "beachheads" of missionaries around the world, and leader Torrey Johnson proclaimed, "Who knows but what we've got an army of occupation for the purpose of establishing Youth for Christ."[25] Even during the Vietnam conflict, Evangelicals generally remained resolute in their support for the American anticommunist cause.[26] In short, YFC originated to form American youth into witnesses for purity and patriotism.

THE LIFE-PATH OF A WITNESS: THE BIBLE, BELIEF, AND BELONGING

To form youth into such witnesses for Christ, YFC encouraged a number of practices. First of all, youth were encouraged to develop the habit of reading their Bibles. A *Youth for Christ Magazine* symposium in 1951, for example, "challenged" its readers with examples of diligent study. Pauline H. Barkhuff wrote, "I come expectantly to my Bible in the morning, knowing there will be something new and fresh because I am meeting a person, God Himself. . . . I know God will transform me as I obey . . . the commands and standards of Christian living." Hubert Mitchell, YFC international vice president for India, also favored morning study; "As Much as Possible before Breakfast" was the title of his piece. "I like to read the whole Bible through several times a year. In this manner your Bible becomes its own commentary. . . . Memory work is one of the best ways of study. . . . The actual words of Scripture are thus engraved on the mind and heart."[27] What this method had in quantity it lacked in quality. Youth for Christ publications routinely ignored modern, academic methods of biblical study.[28] Such individualized study reinforced both the strengths and the weaknesses of the "passion for the total authority and infallibility of the Bible" among Evangelicals.[29]

The infallibility of the (English) words of Scripture was the linchpin in the system of beliefs supported by YFC. The doctrinal statement of YFC coincided intentionally with that of the National Association of Evangelicals (NAE), also organized in 1944. Every issue of *Youth for Christ Magazine*—the national publication begun in 1946 and continuing since 1965 as *Campus Life*—included a "Statement of Faith" in which YFC members were reminded of their basic beliefs: the infallibility of the Bible; the trinity; the deity and miracles of Jesus; salvation through regeneration by the Holy Spirit; the command to "live a godly life"; resurrection of both the saved and the lost; and the "spiritual unity of believers in Christ." In its policy statement, drafted by 1950, YFC sought to chart a course that was "inter-church, non-political, and non-sectarian." Rallies were to "avoid any conflict with . . . established worship services," and local leaders were encouraged to cooperate with international missionary societies.[30]

After Bible study and belief, YFC encouraged young Christians to belong to one of the growing number of Evangelical organizations and institutions. Their names were legion: Miracle Book Clubs, High School Born-Againers, Singspiration, New Life Boys Ranch, and Word of Life Fellowship had all emerged around the same time as YFC and drew positive attention from movement leaders.[31] Among the more enduring was Young Life, founded by Texas evangelist Jim Rayburn in 1941. Young Life featured a Bible club pattern of youth ministry, with meetings in the homes, schools, or hangouts of youth for skits, jokes, and singing.[32] The close connection between these movements became clear when in the fifties YFC shifted its primary focus from rallies to small-group meetings. "The rally idea is sound," President Bob Cook explained, "but in most places the . . . rally is just the show window. Let's get something on the counters the rest of the week." Youth for Christ Bible clubs made up of high schoolers fit the bill. Youth for Christ counted 1,956 Bible clubs meeting around the country by 1955.[33]

These various Evangelical clubs often met in local high schools, and this highlighted the beginning of a shift from purity to practices in the movement. Youth for Christ members were encouraged to think of themselves as "leaven" in an atmosphere they perceived as generally un-Christian, but by taking the witness beyond the confines of the church, the character of the witness was bound to change. Youth for Christ staffer Jack Hamilton made the intention clear in a 1950 essay entitled "Are High Schools Pagan?" The answer was yes. Hamilton followed up his critique with a more positive article, entitled "Missionaries Are Made in High School." "I have observed," Hamilton offered, "that . . . God has witnesses in almost every school. Of course," he continued with a commercial for YFC Bible clubs, the witness "is strongest and most effective, when these kids are bound together in a club and with a common purpose—that of making Christ known to those around them."[34]

Beyond high school, participation in YFC became a stepping-stone for many youth to attend one of the Evangelical Bible colleges that flourished in the middle of the century. Fifteen pages of them were profiled in the 1965 "College Issue" of *Youth for Christ Magazine;* this became an annual feature.[35] In college, Evangelical youth could join a club similar to YFC or Young Life, such as InterVarsity Christian Fellowship or Campus Crusade for Christ. The latter was begun by Bill Bright in 1951; the former had roots in British Evangelicalism in the nineteenth century but came to the United States in 1939.[36] These Evangelical clubs and colleges were alternatives to secular or modernist schools, and they attracted young Evangelicals (and their parents) primarily by presenting themselves as bastions of personal purity. But the Evangelical schools and clubs also harbored potential to develop into politically active communities from which Evangelicals could challenge American culture. The seeds of the shift from purity to practices in Evangelical youth ministry were first planted in clubs and schools.

The practices encouraged in the early years of YFC were, however, by and large, practices of individual piety and purity. Not surprisingly, YFC taught youth to pray. Graham routinely credited the success of his revival preaching to "the prayer of God's people." "How would you feel," he asked readers in his report on the pivotal 1949 revival in Los Angeles, "if you started preaching in a campaign which had had **regular** prayer meetings in its behalf for a full nine months before it started?"[37] Torrey Johnson suggested, "The first, second, and third things to do in getting [YFC] started are, in order of their importance: 1. Pray. 2. Pray. 3. Pray."[38] Finally, YFC youth regularly reported on the power of prayer in their daily lives. Jim Nyholm, for instance, "student body president of Washburn High School, Minneapolis" in 1960 and "a hockey star," testified that "before every game I put my trust in the Lord and claim His promise, 'I can do all things through Christ which strengtheneth me.'"[39] Prayer in YFC was both an individual and a collective witness; it bound Evangelicals together as a community and created solidarity between the individual and the transcendent. Whether that transcendent was victory at hockey, success in a revival, or the living God was not always clear.

Constructing a narrative of conversion—which usually meant describing how an individual was saved from sin and for pure living—was another key practice by which witness was made through YFC. A 1949 article, in *Youth for Christ Magazine*, for instance, "God Works in San Francisco," reported on the conversion of Harley Poslethwaite, a "scrawny" fifteen-year-old "skid row hoodlum" and gang member who "smoked and drank and was handy with a knife in street brawls." Upon attending a YFC rally one Saturday night in 1949, Harley reported, "when the invitation was given, [I] went forward and in a private prayer room a Christian businessman patiently explained the way of salvation. . . . When I left the room . . . I knew Christ in a way that has completely changed [my life]." "Today," the article concluded with editorial commentary, "young Harley Poslethwaite is president of the local YFC youth council, plays in the orchestra, teaches Sunday-school, and is active in his high school Bible club."[40] Everything was possible through Christ, who would change America one witness at a time.

Implicit in a story such as Harley's was a subtheme of conversion from a "scrawny kid" to a man. When YFC formed witnesses through its rite of passage of revivalist conversion, these witnesses usually testified as much to American middle-class gender conventions as to Christ. An essay penned in 1947 by a young woman in YFC demonstrates the pattern. "Becoming a Christian does place certain restrictions upon a girl's conduct," offered Dorothy Haskins. A Christian girl "does not wear clothes obviously styled as 'man-bait.' She conforms more closely to the rules of good conduct." Addressing the issue of sexual conduct, particularly the question "Why doesn't the Christian girl pet?" Haskins concluded, "Girls are like jewelry. Cheap, imitation jewelry in the dime store may be picked up and handled by anyone. At exclusive shops, however, the jewels are kept in a glass case. You may look, but only the owner may possess them."[41] It would be difficult to find a clearer analogy to legitimize midcentury American patriarchal conventions.[42] Youth for Christ leaders, like most Christian youth ministers, did not feel called upon to point out that many "jewels" were mishandled by their "owners."

If the YFC woman was thus to save herself for her "owner," the YFC man was ideally to become an athlete who exhibited control of his passions (and presumably thereby his "jewelry") through religious practice. "Make prayer a sizable part of your romantic endeavors," suggested YFC member Don Jacobs. "Be definite in your dating. Don't say, 'What are you doing Saturday night?' Say, instead, 'How would you like to go to Youth for Christ with me Saturday night?' " Jacobs also recommended that "active sports are good for dates. The more strenuous the better as long as she can take it." In summary, "Be a committee of one to see to it that your relationship with the gals is going to be on the up and up always."[43] That this emphasis on control and domination by "a committee of one" excluded women as subjects in a relationship of two was again not part of the teaching of individual purity favored in the early years of YFC.

In short, YFC in its early years formed individuals through Bible study and belief, and by encouraging them to belong to an Evangelical organization. On the one hand, Evangelicals sought to preserve or create among youth devotion to Christ. The very name of the organization made this much clear. On the other hand, this life-path was communicated through the idioms, conventions, and institutions of middle-class America: radio and gospel music, individualism, college, clear gender roles, and increasing political power in America. The line between Evangelical faith and what Evangelical historian Joel Carpenter has called "American civic faith" was thin.[44]

It is difficult to find anything critical of American culture in the early years of YFC publications. To be sure, YFC critiqued individual moral standards—they were universally thought to have slipped badly. The perils of premarital sex were a frequent target, as highlighted in a 1964 article that began, "Read this girl's tragic letter before you say you could never ruin your life through sex."[45] Youth for Christ leaders found plenty of ways for individual youths to ruin their lives, but saving them was simple: accept Jesus as an individual, and accept American social norms and national policies. The example of race illustrates the pattern. As late as 1964, YFC published an article, "Prejudice and the Christian Teenager," that reduced the problem of racism to a matter of "opinion." The tag line for the article summarized the whole: "Fear, hate, distrust, pull at the seams of society. How can you stop them from destroying your world—and you?"[46] The article said nothing about racism as a system, or segregationist schooling, or unjust laws. In fact, it all but made the victims of racism out to be the Evangelical youth who read YFC publications. Attention to matters of individual purity shielded Evangelical youth from attending to the systematic causes of cultural problems in America.[47]

Part of this shielding was intentional. The educational practices endorsed by YFC were intentionally out of touch with modern social-scientific scholarship. Evangelical historian George Marsden notes that "anti-intellectualism was a feature of American revivalism, and fundamentalists were not free from this tendency." Marsden shows further how fundamentalists came to depend upon a naive version of "common sense." This system of thought once had a distinguished Scottish philosophical pedigree, but over the course of the twentieth century it became little more than a cover for the increasingly truncated, extreme, and defensive versions of Christianity fundamentalists and Evangelicals came to support.[48] Christianity had, with some crucial exceptions, been closely aligned with the best intellectual currents of European cultures for centuries. In America, and especially in revivalist traditions, the heart took sway over the head, and the heart is notoriously subject to the prevailing political winds. As Marsden concludes, fundamentalists and Evangelicals drew deeply "from the stockpile of American assumptions and concepts."[49] Youth for Christ was no exception.

Belonging to America, then, was perhaps the deepest yearning of Evangelicals in the early days of YFC.[50] Consequently, when YFC was noticed favorably by the secular press, these comments were regularly repeated in early YFC publications. For example, when Charles Neville of the secular *Saturday Home Magazine* praised YFC for its work at discouraging "juvenile delinquency" on Saturday nights, the praise was repeated word for word by YFC leader Mel Larson in his *Youth for Christ: Twentieth Century Wonder.*[51] Similarly, when Cliff Barrows, Billy Graham, and other YFC leaders were invited to meet with President Harry Truman in 1950,

Truman agreed with Graham's request to join in a moment of prayer. Barrows crowed in the national publication, "I am thankful that I live in America, where the leader of the nation [is] . . . willing to stop and bow in prayer."[52] Through such reports of their growing influence, YFC Evangelicals moved "from alienation to engagement, from separatist sectarianism to panevangelical cooperation, and from the pose of a prophetic faithful remnant to that of the nation's evangelists and chaplains."[53] Favorable attention from the public meant "the movement was newsworthy . . . it *mattered* in American life."[54] By teaching purity and patriotism, Evangelicals gained access to power. When Jimmy Carter was elected to the presidency in 1976, one of their own had made it. When Carter disappointed them with "liberal" social programs, they helped replace him with Ronald Reagan. Reagan's victory was widely attributed to the New Religious Right in both the Evangelical press and the public imagination.[55] As a key part of this "evangelical resurgence," YFC had helped the public and Evangelicals themselves to see: they belonged.

PURITY, PROFESSIONALISM, AND PRACTICES

If it was, then, unclear in its early years whether YFC primarily taught young people to be witnesses for Christ or warriors for the American way, since the fifties YFC has developed a more nuanced relationship with American culture. The movement has maintained relatively consistent membership (with a slight ebb during the late sixties and recently). Youth for Christ also has developed or spun off countless new ministries to form and educate young Christians. These developments fall under five basic types: clubs; camps; new-style rallies or spectacle ministries; professional leadership training and education; and social-service ministries. Youth for Christ and its spin-offs are still focused primarily on individual conversion and person-to-person witnessing (now often described simply as "relating" to youth), and the movement is largely still culturally confirming. But a shift from purity to practices is also clear. Building upon the classical Evangelical concern for social justice and compassion, YFC and its spin-offs have deepened and nuanced their earlier rapprochement with "American civic faith" to offer youth a significant range of ways to practice modern Christianity.

First, YFC Bible clubs—now called Campus Life—since 1960 have become the basic, grassroots units of Youth For Christ. Housed in more than two hundred local offices across the United States (and many more around the globe), local YFC units are generally run by a full-time youth minister and staff and numerous volunteers. Campus Life sponsors club meetings once a week at the home of a youth, at a church, or at a local junior high or high school. After icebreaker games, Bible study, skits, songs, and conversation about "something that seems to be prominent in [youth's] lives," the one-hour meeting often adjourns to a youth hangout such as a fast-food restaurant, where members continue "to talk about the meeting, to see friends who are working . . . and to [have] some fun," reports one local college-aged leader. These meetings intend to form youth spiritually in the following way:

> Not all of the kids in our group have a faith in anything but themselves. What we try to do . . . is get them to open up their mind to the Bible. We try to teach them that there is a God and that this God does care about each and every one of them. . . . We teach them to have better relationships with their family and friends, . . . to take care of themselves and of our Earth, . . . that God cares about everything, not just "God stuff" (to use a phrase one of the kids used).[56]

Gradually over the course of a year the percentage of "God stuff" increases in the meetings, and the Bible studies become more "in-depth." But even official literature now describes the primary purpose of Campus Life therapeutically as "relational ministry" to "kids."[57] To teach youth that "God does care" matters as much as extracting a narrative of conversion.[58] Not surprisingly, by 1994 YFC claimed a number of "counseling ministries" to go along with its Campus Life programs across the United States.[59] This turn to psychology has also been accompanied by an emerging social commitment among select YFC clubs: they routinely provide leaders and supporters for programs such as Habitat for Humanity, World Vision, and other socially oriented Christian missions.

Second, under the leadership of international staffer Bob Cook, YFC has developed since the fifties a range of ministries called the Youth Guidance Program. Youth for Christ was reaching "comparatively few from the so-called 'seamy side of town,'" Cook explained. "One reason is that so much of our advertising and programs are slanted to happy Christian youngsters. Let's do something to reach the teens outside." Begun in urban areas and led first by Gordon McLean and later by Wendy Collins, "the Youth

Guidance Program was operating 110 summer camps for delin-
quent youngsters" by 1963.[60] Since then the program has expanded to provide manuals, lesson plans, and other materials for
leaders with youth who are "at-risk" or "beyond risk"—youth who
live in impoverished neighborhoods or who have been in the juvenile justice system, treatment centers, or group homes.[61] Summer
camps remain a central feature of YFC and the Youth Guidance
Program, however, although they serve middle- and upper-class
youth as often as they do "delinquents."

One Evangelical camp, Word of Life in upstate New York,
originated in 1946 under the leadership of YFC founder Jack
Wyrtzen. Word of Life has been described in delightful detail by
Evangelical historian Randall Balmer, who visited the camp as a
youth and returned as an adult to cast a professional historian's eye
on the camp's contribution to the Evangelical subculture. Balmer
recounts with vivid images the songs, games, preaching, and ro-
mance that take place over the course of a week at Word of Life.
Everything leads up to the Friday night campfire at the end of the
week, called the "say-so" or "testimony service." Here the young
campers speak one by one, confessing their shortcomings, asking
for help in realizing their hopes—in short, witnessing to their
faith. "There is a remarkable uniformity to these gatherings,"
Balmer concludes, "the rhythms, the emotions, [and] the ritualized
adolescent behavior that takes place around the fire."[62] Witnesses
are still being formed at Word of Life and countless other Evangelical camps around the country.

Balmer also offers an insider's critique of these experiences in
becoming a witness. "The 'gospel' presented" around YFC and
other campfires was

> really an adumbration of the New Testament "good news." Much
> of the news I heard was bad—that I deserved damnation for my
> sinfulness and that if I didn't do something about it quickly I
> would certainly receive my just deserts. The solution to the pre-
> dicament, as I understood it, was not to rely utterly on the grace
> of God, as Martin Luther recognized in the sixteenth century;
> rather, the way of salvation seemed to lay [sic] in subscribing to a
> set of doctrines and then hewing to strict standards of morality,
> usually expressed in negative terms: Don't dance, drink, smoke,
> swear, or attend movies.[63]

Not all camps preserve the fundamentalist purity program so
clearly as Word of Life, and Balmer's critique is itself evidence of
the new Evangelical shift away from moralistic conformity with

American conventions and into deeper dialogue with the historic Christian tradition.[64]

Third, in part as response to the change of generations, YFC and other Evangelical youth organizations have adapted the 1940s rally to accord with the current cultural tastes of adolescents. Evangelical sociologist and pastor Tony Campolo describes ministering to punk rockers at an Evangelical "Jesus festival" with thirty thousand youth in attendance:

> Taking the stage just before I spoke was a musical group called the Rez Band. Their music . . . [and] antics seemed to be "off the wall." . . . The punk-rock types in the crowd were gyrating to the band's drum beats. . . . When the members of the band gave their testimonies of what the Holy Spirit was doing for them, the crowd cheered them with wild enthusiasm. And when the leader of the band asked for people who wanted to be filled with the Holy Spirit to come forward, literally hundreds came.[65]

Campolo concludes, "Something *holy* was going on."

At the same time, Campolo is a sage Evangelical critic of the potential excesses of this accommodation to the popular taste for spectacle. Rock music is today as much a marketed medium as it is authentic adolescent mayhem. Campolo warns that when Christian educators and youth ministers uncritically embrace and promote "Christian contemporary music" and the spectacle ministries that grow up around it, they can wind up promoting not compassionate disciples of Christ but fans who do little more than consume a marketed subculture.[66] It is a familiar pattern in the history of revivalism: the old-time gospel is dressed up in the most modern forms. How much of the gospel survives is the question.[67]

Fourth, a separate industry, Youth Specialties, Inc., of El Cajon, California, has grown out of YFC to offer a wide range of publications and leadership training for Evangelical youth ministers. *The Catalog for Youth Ministry,* published biannually by Youth Specialties, offers to youth ministers "teaching tools and videos," "discussion starters," "programming tools," "student spirituality and leadership formation" materials, dozens of books and journals, dramas, "clip art," and more.[68] Youth Specialties also publishes two journals, *Youthworker* and *Youthworker Update. Youthworker Update* is a monthly newsletter culling facts and opinion about youth from a variety of popular and church sources.[69] *Youthworker* is a quarterly of practical tips and substantive analysis, often with a topical focus. The fall 1994 issue, for instance, discussed sexuality in ways the old YFC publications would never have tackled.

Articles included "How Youth Workers Are Teaching Sex Education," "Assessing True Love Waits [a national program teaching ab-
stinence]," "Youthworker Roundtable: The Sexual Youth Pastor,"
"Ministry to Bisexual Teenagers," and "The Big M."[70] *Youthworker*
also puts Evangelicals in touch with the most current intellectual
trends, as evident in the January/February 1999 issue, entitled
"Postmodern Ministry." Finally, Youth Specialties coordinates an
annual National Resource Seminar for Youth Workers, held at over
one hundred cities across the United States and Canada each
spring. In 1998 over twenty thousand youthworkers from around
the country attended the seminars. Throughout its materials, Youth
Specialties evidences an Evangelical concern with social problems,
along with traditional teachings of prayer, Bible study, and personal purity.[71] "I love *Youthworker's* professionalism," one reader
responded.[72]

More than one observer, however, both within and outside
Evangelical circles, has noted with unease the increasing "professionalism" of YFC and related organizations. Campolo writes,
"Does Christianity somehow betray its essential nature when a
ministry engages in the 'routinization of charisma' and the establishment of professional leadership? . . . Are professionals, including youth ministry professionals, to a greater or lesser degree con
artists?"[73] Given how professionalism and the "cult of the expert"
currently dominate American culture, Campolo wonders whether
professional youth ministers can educate and form anything other
than witnesses to professionalism itself. More historically, Mark
Senter observes that the "routinization of charisma" has destroyed
ministries in the past and that a "coming revolution" may be the
only way for YFC to endure. "The future direction of Youth for
Christ USA appears highly uncertain," he concludes.[74] Insofar as
much of American culture is in thrall to the cult of the professional, the future direction of YFC seems no less uncertain than
most American institutions. The substantive question of how professionalism affects the gospel message and practices of compassion, however, remains.

Finally, in part as a response to professionalization, YFC and
other Evangelical youth organizations have increasingly turned to
practical politics and social service as ways to deepen compassionate witness among youth. Evangelicals now exist on both the right
and the left of the American political spectrum. The popular press
has focused most visibly on the Evangelical and fundamentalist
New Right, but in the last three decades an "emerging left-wing fac-

tion in Evangelicalism" has developed rhetoric, actions, and institutions that endorse social ministry not as a means to conversion
but "as an end in itself" and as a logical life-path of Christian witness.[75] Evangelical journals such as *The Other Side, Sojourners,* and
Radix, all begun after the midsixties, emphasize social concerns
and Christian compassion far more than personal purity or conversion. In fact, these publications come close to describing practices of compassion as the expression of purity. A typical issue of
Sojourners, for instance, contains such articles as "The Difference
That Faith Makes" (an interview with Marian Wright Edelman of
the Children's Defense Fund), "A Community Tackles Racism,"
"Theology and Revolution in Mexico," and "Peace as a Women's
Issue."[76]

Showing the same vigor with which they built Bible clubs and
colleges, Evangelicals have also developed international missionary agencies to challenge and involve youth in practices of Christian compassion. Historically a by-product of Evangelical youth
movements, many of these missionary organizations have also
largely transformed themselves since the sixties from converting
and colonizing enterprises into relief and development agencies.
The most notable perhaps is World Vision, begun by former YFC
leaders.[77] World Vision defines itself as "an international partner-
ship of Christians whose mission is to follow our Lord and Savior
Jesus Christ in working with the poor and oppressed to promote human transformation, seek justice, and bear witness to the
good news of the Kingdom of God." More specifically, World Vision promotes "community-based and sustainable development"
around the globe, "focused especially on the needs of children."
The agency also provides emergency and disaster relief and works
to promote justice by seeking "to change unjust structures affecting
the poor among whom we work." Perhaps the most successful
World Vision venture, in which thousands of youth participate
each year, is an annual 30 Hour Famine. Members of local youth
groups fast for thirty hours, raising funds for World Vision through
pledges and learning together about the problems of hunger and
starvation in the world through educational materials provided by
the agency. In 1998, more than six hundred thousand youth participated, raising over six million dollars. World Vision is only one
of the many agencies that have increasingly challenged Evangelical
youth since the midsixties through practices that bring them to
identify their witness with those who are poor and suffering.

How might we interpret this shift from purity to practices in Evangelical youth formation? On the one hand, it might mean that a split between "left" and "right," widely recognized (and lamented) in mainstream Protestantism, has also begun to affect the formation and education of Evangelical youth.[78] Perhaps Evangelicals will, like the Walther League in an earlier period, fall victim to the polarizing tendencies of American political culture. A more accurate explanation may be that "there is a genuine and paradoxical tension in [Evangelicalism] between a sojourner's alienation from the present age and . . . a 'custodial ideal,' a proprietary responsibility for American national morality."[79] The care of souls and practices of compassion in society are hardly polar opposites; in fact, in classical Christianity the concerns for purity and compassion merge. It has been a characteristic dilemma of twentieth-century Christianity in the United States that these two concerns—and the groups who represent them—have come to be separated by a gulf of theological misunderstanding. Youth for Christ was clearly adept at converting young witnesses when conversion meant increased respect for Evangelicals as individuals and as a subculture and when conversion meant conformity to American civic faith and its violent victories. In recent years, YFC and other Evangelical youth ministries have moved into deeper and more nuanced relationships to American culture, more in keeping with the classical Evangelical combination of individualism and social responsibility. Whether "the cultural hegemony of American civic faith" within much of Evangelicalism can be re-created into a more grace-infused path of witness is a concern shared by many.[80] It will be of no small consequence for American culture and for the history of Christianity if YFC fails to form witnesses attuned to both salvation and social concern, both purity and practices of compassion.

chapter 4

Forging Freedom

AFRICAN-AMERICAN YOUTH MINISTRIES, 1930–PRESENT

One Friday night in 1940, Maya Angelou graduated from the eighth grade at the all-black Lafayette County Training School in Stamps, Arkansas. Her pride at having accomplished this signifi-cant milestone gradually sank into despair, however, as she lis-tened to the evening's keynote speaker, Mr. Edward Donleavy, a white politician from Texarkana. Angelou heard Donleavy praise the graduates for their accomplishments as athletes and encourage them toward their bright future as "maids and farmers, handymen and washerwomen." Underneath, Angelou heard the subtext: "Any-thing higher that we aspired to was farcical and presumptuous. . . . The man's dead words fell like bricks around the auditorium, and too many settled in my belly," Angelou remembered.

After Donleavy concluded, he immediately left the auditorium to catch a train, and the class valedictorian, Henry Reed, launched into his address, entitled "To Be or Not to Be." "I marveled that Henry could go through with the speech as if we had a choice," Angelou recalled. After concluding, Reed turned his back to the au-dience and, to Angelou's surprise, began to sing "the Negro na-tional anthem":

> Lift ev'ry voice and sing
> Till earth and heaven ring
> Ring with the harmonies of Liberty . . .

As the entire assembly joined in the song, Angelou's despair dissipated. "I was no longer simply a member of the proud graduating class of 1940," she remembers feeling. "I was a proud member of the beautiful Negro race."[1] The setting was a school auditorium, but the song held sacred significance. It rang the harmonies of liberty forged in the midst of oppression, of solidarity asserted in the midst of struggle, and of hope surviving in the midst of despair.

These harmonies have been consistent themes in the efforts of African Americans to educate and form youth in faith during the twentieth century. The harmonies of liberty are complex, for the boundaries between sacred and secular have been fluid within the African-American experience: school assemblies sang sacred songs, and churches acted in politics and society. In other words, freedom as taught to African-American youth has been both spiritual and political, both freedom from sin and freedom for justice. By connecting Christian young people to congregations where members related to each other as kin, African-American churches across America have empowered young men and women through congregational and direct social practices.[2]

FREEDOM BORN AT BETHEL A.M.E. CHURCH, BALTIMORE, 1930–1970

Freedom for African Americans has been born in congregations across the United States. One that has been active for over two hundred years is Bethel A.M.E. Church in Baltimore. In 1784, the official congregational history records, free black men and women who were attending Methodist meeting houses on Strawbridge Alley and Lovely Lane of Baltimore found themselves increasingly restricted during worship (as their numbers grew) to certain areas of the church. Several small groups of these Christians decided to form their own congregations. They met in homes and, so the story has it, in the cellar of a bootblack's shop. In 1785 they gave themselves the name Beth-el, "House of God" in Hebrew.[3] Bethel began as a place where freedom was born out of oppression.

This pattern has continued. In 1816 the church became a founding member of the African Methodist Episcopal denomination.[4] Bethel was a center of abolitionist activity before and during the Civil War, serving as a station on the Underground Railroad and its pulpit providing a platform for abolitionist speakers.[5] Bethel has also been a leader in support of higher education for African Americans. Daniel Payne, the church's tenth pastor, was instrumental in the founding of Wilberforce University and became its first president in 1856. Coppin State College, founded in 1908, is named for Fannie Coppin, the wife of Levi Coppin, pastor of Bethel from 1881 to 1883. Between 1975 and 1988, Bethel's pastor, John A. Bryant, sent more than seventy-five young men and women from Bethel to divinity schools and seminaries around the country.[6] Bethel has also been a fixture in the social and intellectual life of the Mid-Atlantic states. The current senior pastor, Dr. Frank M. Reid III, is a third-generation son of the congregation and has degrees from Yale and Harvard and a doctorate from the United Theological Seminary.[7] Over the years, Bethel has supplied the African Methodist Episcopal Church with seven presiding bishops. Through the influence of its leaders, its support for education, and its commitment to cultural and social concern, Bethel has nurtured generations of young people in a life-path of freedom that includes both purity and practices.

During the depression years, for instance, Bethel was the headquarters for the City-Wide Young People's Forum. This agency, led by Juanita Jackson, who eventually became youth director of the NAACP, sponsored programs to "develop the intellectual and moral talents" of young African Americans. The forum also took direct action. Along with members of the National Urban League, Bethel's youth "picketed and boycotted the city's chain stores, which refused to hire Negro clerks. They also protested segregation at the Enoch Pratt Public Library, and held mass meetings to demonstrate against" two Maryland lynchings in 1932 and 1933.[8] By 1937, the congregation mobilized to include black police officers in the city of Baltimore. Meetings in the church's sixteen-hundred-seat sanctuary were held to discuss the issue of representation on the police force, along with other political matters troubling the community.[9] Through such meetings, and through Sunday sermons and Scripture readings, young black Christians learned and practiced liberation theology at Bethel A.M.E. Church well before it was given a name as a movement within Christian theology.[10]

Of course, Bethel's young people from the thirties through the fifties were also involved in many traditional youth ministry activities, such as Bible study, prayer, and song. But in the context of segregation, when blacks were excluded by law from full participation in American society, even the most apparently innocuous events held social significance. In 1956, for instance, Mayme Tilghman, president of Bethel's Laymens' League, enlisted many of the young African-American women of Bethel as models in a fashion show. Over two hundred attended. Sociologist Lawrence Mamiya draws out the significance: "Long before the black consciousness movement of the 1960s, these social affairs underscored the insight that black was indeed beautiful."[11] For young people en route from childhood to adulthood, affirmation of their body as beautiful is a significant theological and cultural affirmation. Another event in 1962, also led by Tilghman, demonstrated the creative way Bethel's youth were taught patterns of economic empowerment. Tilghman organized a campaign to collect trading stamps, including a "licking committee" to paste loose stamps into books. The campaign raised enough money to buy a school bus for the Sunday school and youth programs. Through such social and economic activities, Bethel's youth learned that freedom meant both freedom from oppression and for social responsibility. Indeed, the "church [has been] the most economically independent institutional sector in the black community."[12]

During the civil rights movement of the 1960s the potential of the life-path of freedom to reshape history became apparent. Not surprisingly, Bethel was a fixture in the struggle to desegregate Baltimore. Pastor Harrison J. Bryant recruited youth into events such as the March for Baltimore on March 30, 1964, when four thousand demonstrators, led by a young Dick Gregory, paraded throughout the city to signal their demand for equal access to fair housing and other benefits of life in modern America. Bryant was an honorary chairman of the event. Leaders of the national civil rights movement visited Bethel, where young people could meet them and learn from them. Among these leaders was the Honorable Thurgood Marshall, a Baltimore native who was prosecutor in the pivotal 1954 Supreme Court decision *Brown vs. Board of Education,* which paved the way for desegregation across the United States. Bethel celebrated Marshall's appointment as solicitor general of the United States with a grand reception in 1965.[13] Through the welcome of such prominent guests, the youth of Bethel were connected to "kin" with significant success in public life. Such figures demonstrated for black youth that the life-path of freedom had practical as well as spiritual benefits.

Simply put, the history of Bethel A.M.E. Church to 1970 demonstrates what the civil rights movement as a whole made plain:

when young people are taught to value freedom and can apply it from a community to which they feel connected, they can change history. The civil rights movement dramatically reshaped American society, but it was continuous with long-standing patterns of practice in African-American churches such as Bethel.[14]

NEW CHALLENGES TO FREEDOM

Not all black churches have been as significantly connected to the civil rights cause as was Bethel. In fact, for years a critical stereotype of the African-American religious experience depicted it as "other-worldly," compensatory, or an "opiate" to pacify blacks in the face of oppression.[15] Black churches tended to be theologically conservative, these critics pointed out. African Americans were (and are) predominantly Baptists or Methodists, and these groups have often favored a traditional theology focused on salvation, not social concern. Furthermore, the critics continued, a significant number of black congregations, especially in the African Methodist Episcopal Church, sought to suppress traditionally African cultural expressions in worship, such as the "ring-shout" and spirituals, and replace them with more "decorous" forms of worship akin to white Protestant traditions.[16] Finally, many black churches patterned their youth ministry programs after those in Evangelical Protestantism, emphasizing individual conversion and personal purity as the primary Christian life-paths.[17]

Recently a more nuanced interpretation of the black church, consistent with the evidence of the civil rights movement, has appeared. Following the pioneering work of theologian James Cone and historians Eugene Genovese and Albert Raboteau, sociologists C. Eric Lincoln and Lawrence Mamiya have proposed a dialectical model for understanding the black church.[18] According to Lincoln and Mamiya, an authentic tension has been manifest in African-American religious history between a number of key polarities, such as priestly versus prophetic functions of churches, other-worldly versus this-worldly theologies, and an accommodating versus a resistant attitude toward white Christianity.[19] In other words, members of black churches have struggled to teach both purity and practices to youth. Some churches have stressed one side or the other, but most incorporated both.

Since the successes of the sixties, however, new factors have emerged in American society to challenge Christian ministry among black youth. Lincoln and Mamiya contend that "among certain sectors of the black community, fissures in the previous dominance of the Black Church have developed and important challenges and problems are emerging, especially among younger people."[20] Urban migration has been one factor in this development. In 1890 about 90 percent of African Americans lived in the South, especially in the rural "black belt." By 1990 more than 80 percent of African Americans lived in America's urban centers.[21] This remarkable migration has dislocated families and eroded the hold of traditional institutions such as the church in African-American life. Another factor in the declining hold of the church has been the development of secular organizations to serve the African-American community. The NAACP, founded in 1909, and the National Urban League, founded in 1911, have had close connections with churches but have also emphasized primarily legal and political, not theological or ecclesiastical, solutions to the problems plaguing blacks.

Two other factors in the diffusion of power from black churches have been the rise of the African-American middle class (estimates put the number between 30 and 60 percent) and the growth of separatist black nationalism.[22] Among relatively affluent or middle-class blacks, careers in professions such as law and medicine have been at least as attractive as careers in the ministry—out of which the great leaders of the civil rights movement emerged. Black nationalism—inspired in the sixties through such organizations as the Student Non-Violent Coordinating Committee and the Nation of Islam—led some black youth to grow alienated from the "Uncle Tom" religion of Christianity.[23] A nationalist or separatist attitude in the African-American community was not new by any means, but after the sixties it grew more widespread than at any time since the days of Marcus Garvey.[24]

The most significant challenge to the black church and its ministries to youth, however, developed when a new form of racism appeared in the wake of the civil rights movement. No longer legal, racism went underground, embedded in systemic and ideological exclusions or exploitations of African Americans. These exclusions, which impacted especially black youth, were justified on economic or political, but not racial, grounds.[25] They were subtle but effective at perpetuating white privilege. For example, during the Vietnam conflict the Pentagon set up Project 100,000, which "opened up opportunities" for military service to young men who would previously have been disqualified for educational reasons.

Many of them turned out to be black. Most of them wound up serving on the front lines. Too many never returned.[26] After Vietnam, as the nation sought to recover from cultural trauma and as the Reagan and Bush administrations implemented "trickle-down" or supply-side economics, white support for explicitly African-American initiatives (such as affirmative action) eroded.[27] At the same time, public demand for punishment of street crime rose, which again disproportionally affected young black males.[28] The result of such subtle forms of racism has been widespread economic and social devastation in the urban black community.

Unemployment has consistently been higher among African Americans than the rest of the American population, and it has been highest among black youth.[29] In the eighties, unemployment jumped to between 40 and 50 percent among seventeen- to thirty-five-year-old African Americans, and in some urban communities the number of unemployed youth has been as high as 80 percent.[30] Welfare reform has exacerbated this problem. In New York City, one 1998 study determined that close to 70 percent of the people removed from the welfare rolls since the 1996 cutbacks had not yet found jobs. Many of them are black youth.[31] Teenage pregnancy has been another social problem besetting the African-American community—as it has the entire American youth subculture since the "sexual revolution" of the sixties. The rates among black youth, however, have been more than double those among whites.[32] Many of these problems stem from educational inequities built into the U.S. localized school system. Schools in impoverished communities simply do not have the tax base to support the kind of intellectual, social, and sexual education programs suburban schools take for granted.[33] Finally, street crime has claimed many African-American youth. Homicide has been the leading cause of death among African-American youth for two decades.[34] Nationwide, blacks make up nearly half of the prison population—more in some heavily urban areas.[35] In short, the *first violence* of poverty and powerlessness that remains institutionalized in systems of mainstream America has led to the far more widely noticed *second violence* in the form of black street crime.[36] Racism has gone underground.

Nathan McCall, now a reporter for the *Washington Post*, has dramatically described the formative power of street violence for an alienated African-American youth. One night as a high schooler, remembers McCall, he and a group of his friends started a fight with another gang called the Cherry Boys at a bus stop in Norfolk, Virginia. McCall had a gun:

> I drew the piece. I shoved it to the temple of a guy named Jimmy. . . . For a minute, I got so caught up in the excitement of the moment that I started to pull the trigger. . . . It was nothing personal; actually, he was a likable guy. . . . I don't know why I didn't shoot . . . [but] I calmed down and pulled the gun away, satisfied that I'd publicly chumped him down. I can never forget that moment. . . . I know the feeling of standing there with all that power literally at one's fingertips. For someone who has felt powerless and ignored all his life, that's one hell of an adrenaline rush.[37]

To confront this dynamic of powerlessness and empowerment has been a recurrent dynamic in Christian formation into freedom among African-American youth.[38] African-American churches are hardly alone in this struggle to discern how Christian freedom is neither the anarchic "freedom" of street license nor the "freedom" to consume cultural goods, but in many urban communities the challenge has increased.

Not all African-American churches are meeting it. Lincoln and Mamiya discovered in a survey of over two thousand black churches that close to half of the ministers of these churches reported "difficulty in recruiting and maintaining teenagers and young adults in their churches." Nearly 15 percent said their church offered nothing for youth. Almost half felt that youth left their churches because they were "not given a chance by adults to participate in a meaningful way in church programs" or that they were "bored or the church does not have a relevant program for them." Only 4 percent hired a special youth minister. Many stressed traditional programs for youth, such as youth choir, Bible study, and special groups or services for teenagers.[39] Like most Christian communities in the United States, African-American churches have struggled to pass on the faith across generations. In some cases, they have failed. In many others—and it is to several of them that we will now turn—they have succeeded in remarkable ways.

FREEDOM THROUGH BELONGINGNESS, WORSHIP, AND CULTURAL CRITIQUE AT "GRACE CHURCH"

Seminary professor William Myers has described one church's successful strategy for steering youth on the life-path of freedom.

Myers's book, *Black and White Styles of Youth Ministry*, details youth ministry at "Grace Church," a middle-class and urban African-American congregation with about five thousand members in a midwestern city. The church takes as its motto "Unashamedly black, unapologetically Christian." The pastor described for Myers how the "kinship model" of youth ministry favored in his church contrasted with that of the "corporate model" favored in many denominations. "When a church hires a professional youth minister to 'do' youth ministry," he explained, "that youth minister has been hired to run a second church, a 'youth only church,' *alongside* the intergenerational church. . . . Such youth ministry tends to promote a kind of 'us' versus 'them' mentality, never the 'we' of the church; never the *belongingness*."[40]

In contrast, Grace developed a "kinship model for youth ministry" that "centers on intergenerational, communal worship, and the empowerment of adolescents who can critique mainstream culture from a theological, African-American stance."[41] This emphasis on kinship has deep roots in African veneration of ancestors.[42] At the center of the kinship model of youth ministry at Grace has been the intentional involving of young people in the worship life of the church. The pastor has read the report cards of young congregants from the pulpit, young people regularly read the lessons, and at least once a month, during Youth Sunday, youth have preached. One youth reflected, "I actually preached, and everybody supported me in doing that. . . . It seems like I have five thousand parents, all watching me, because it seems like I know everybody.[43] The youth of Grace Church have been welcomed as members of the community who belong, rather than as problems to be managed or children to be kept pure.

Youth Sunday at Grace Church has involved young people in the entire process of the liturgy—opening prayers, choir (the Young Warriors), solos, readings, sermon, and benediction. Throughout, young people gain formation in a many-layered reality of both spiritual and political power. For instance, a high school senior named "Roberta" preached one Youth Sunday on King Ahab's need for political advice (1 Kings 21):

> Here we have four hundred prophets, all worried about keeping their jobs, holding those influence-producing long lunches, staying on the King's good side, and getting promoted; they *had their own agenda*. . . . We should beware of people who have their own agendas. . . . Some of today's educators comprise a myopic minority, a group who have internalized a completely Euro-centric

world view and who look on anything African with suspicion and disgust . . . [and therefore] mutilate our mentality and pervert our personality. Either they don't care, don't want to make waves, or are so brainwashed that they believe the racist lies they perpetuate upon our youth. Whatever the reason, they steal our education from us and turn us out of schools ready to serve the needs of the military-industrial system. Beware, Grace Church, of folk like these teachers—a myopic minority—who *have their own agendas*.[44]

"Having their own agendas" is the way this high school senior critiqued and articulated the alternative life-path of Christian freedom. Preaching a sermon, furthermore, is a rite of passage into a practice of considerable spiritual (and political) power in the African-American context, where the sermon has been central to the act of worship.[45]

To be sure, Grace Church's ministry with youth has shared many of the traditional features of white youth ministry, including its professionalism. Two of the church's fourteen professional staff, for instance, are designated to specialize in youth.[46] But what one observer of the black church called "the trinity that had bored into resentment and departure so many . . . Youth Choir, Junior Usher Board, and . . . Young People's Union," has been superseded in this congregational setting by a more dynamic model that utilizes the gifts of youth.[47] As a youth of Grace Church remarked: "[This] Church gives us the future, now. If you're told you're the future, but you just sit in the pew, then . . . who cares?"[48] Since the sixties, Grace Church has deepened its intergenerational, kinship pattern of youth ministry in a way that taught youth both spiritual purity and political practices and reflected the intentions of its members to be both "unashamedly black" and "unapologetically Christian."[49]

MENTORED AND INITIATED INTO FREEDOM AT ST. PAUL COMMUNITY BAPTIST CHURCH, BROOKLYN

The strategy of Grace Church to connect youth to a Christian "kinship network" and thereby teach them Christian freedom has found practical expression in thousands of African-American congregations across the country. One of them, St. Paul Community Baptist Church in Brooklyn, New York, has been described in vivid detail by Samuel G. Freedman.[50] In Freedman's book, kinship takes on a human face in characters such as Kathleen Wilson—a member of St. Paul's. Wilson has befriended troubled youth by taking them into her home, where she fed them, directed them on their schoolwork and other life skills, and involved them in the life of St. Paul's congregation. Wilson taught freedom to youth by practicing hospitality. She had, as of 1991, fourteen grandchildren tied to her by blood and about two dozen other youth who called her Gram because of the love she has shown them in the past or present.[51]

Ali Nurse, a seventeen-year-old African-American male, was among Wilson's "grandchildren." One night, after a defiant confrontation with his father led to a fistfight, Ali Nurse was without a home. After a few months of sleeping in cars or bouncing from apartment to apartment, staying with friends of friends (where he was frequently evicted after accusations of theft), Ali learned that he could stay one night at Kathleen Wilson's apartment. On the way there, he collapsed with torn cartilage in his knee. Wilson took him to the hospital and afterwards brought him into her own home, where she cared for him, even feeding him pints of his favorite ice cream, "Monster Cookies."[52] Ali's one night with Wilson extended through the summer, and then on into his senior year in high school. Wilson required only that Ali pledge himself to graduate by the coming June: "No ifs, ands, or buts."

Over time, Ali became a member of St. Paul's, and shortly thereafter he pledged the Yoke Fellows in Discipline—St. Paul's fraternity-like youth group.

> The Yoke Fellows formed the linchpin of Saint Paul's vision of itself as an extended family, a tribal village. The title derived from a verse in Lamentations, "It is good for a man that he bear the yoke in his youth," and the structure borrowed from the fraternities and sororities so popular in black colleges. . . . As pledgees, called Acorns, the teenagers dedicated every free hour to meeting the requirements for initiation. They received academic tutoring and SAT preparation courses on Friday nights, and physical training on Saturday afternoon; they wrote summaries of both services each Sunday, memorized such church chestnuts as the poem "Invictus," and practiced the extravagantly syncopated form of group dance known as "stepping." Their parents, too, were required to participate, checking homework nightly and soliciting monthly progress reports from school. But the surrogate parenting the Acorns received, particularly from men, was crucially important. Fewer than one quarter of the pledgees lived with a father at home.[53]

Taking twelve courses to graduate on time, Ali adhered to a schedule that had him at school from eight in the morning until six at night, followed by a ninety-minute train ride to St. Paul's and pledging work.

Ali's work culminated with initiation into the Yoke Fellows, or Sigma Mu Epsilon, as the group was more formally called. The initiation took place over two days in March, beginning with a Friday night talent show (featuring "stepping") and concluding with "crossing over" on Saturday morning. Kathleen Wilson attended both the show and the induction breakfast the next morning. The pledges, Ali now among them, received "a baseball hat, a T-shirt, and a wind-breaker, each emblazoned with the letters Sigma Mu Upsilon." These signs of new status signaled a successful rite of passage.[54] Ali's successes continued beyond formal rituals. With the help of his newfound kin, by June he had graduated from high school, been accepted at Norfolk State University (historically a black school), and begun to reconcile with his father. "It takes a village," often preached the pastor of St. Paul's, quoting a now famous African proverb, "to raise a child." It also took a person such as Kathleen Wilson, and a group such as the Yoke Fellows, to mentor and initiate youth into Christian freedom.

SANCTUARIES FOR YOUTH: "BEST"—A CONGREGATIONALLY RELATED MINISTRY

Historically, the lines between sacred and secular have been fluid in African-American communities. In light of the challenge of recent history, congregations have, in some cases, taken the lifepath of freedom beyond the walls of the church to begin independent nonprofit agencies. These agencies have sought to provide a sanctuary for impoverished youth, without any spiritual strings attached. Milbrey McLaughlin and a team of sociologists have described the history and work of "BEST"—Building Educational Strategies for Teens—a composite of several actual organizations and agencies.[55] Their study documents the needs many black churches have met by turning from purity to practices, including the most basic and simple practices of survival.

BEST began in 1965 as special youth ministry program of a congregation situated in a heavily African-American section of a midwestern city. From a staff of one, a budget of $25,000, and a church basement site, BEST became in less than thirty years an agency with over three hundred and fifty active students [ages six through eighteen], twenty-four full-time staff, and fifty part-time teenaged employees. By the midnineties, over two hundred and fifty volunteers annually participated in BEST's programs, which had expanded to two sites. The operating budget grew to well over $1,000,000. BEST also developed a comprehensive daily program of educational, mentoring, and recreational activities. Educationally, students worked on traditional curricular subjects but also undertook novel programs such as local oral-history interviews. In 1994 BEST ran five different scholarship programs that promised college financial aid to students who graduated from high school. Over two hundred youth participated. Mentors worked with young adults from their earliest enrollment at BEST until they graduated or secured a career. BEST also offered many youth their first paying jobs, in addition to providing job training and career search assistance to others. Nuclear families were involved (within flexible guidelines).[56]

From its inception, BEST included youth, parents, and staff in the decision making about the agency, and consequently the program took on an inherently intergenerational cast. One observer wrote,

> Everyday life at BEST in many ways resembles the typical family as many Americans imagine it. Youngsters come in after school, get themselves a snack (from the machines in the entry hall), do their homework at tables with their "brothers and sisters," take breaks to play games or work on special projects, and occasionally settle down with staff or other members for serious talk about long-range plans for a Saturday visit to a museum, the zoo, a big game or even for college or travel. While focused as an educational program, BEST provides both personal and academic resources as well as broadening experiences for the children and youth who come to the after-school activities and to summer day camp.[57]

Financial support for BEST, initially provided completely by the congregation, gradually expanded to include a broad-based network of grassroots, corporate, governmental, foundation, and individual donors, many of whom monitored accountability requirements through service on BEST's board of directors.[58] The director of the program in 1994, Michael Carroll, summarized the basic vision of the agency: "There is chaos outside, but when [youth] come through BEST's heavy steel door they can hope to find calm and security."[59] Such a sanctuary has become, in America's cities today, a necessary precondition of religious education and spiritual formation.[60]

One youth who benefited from BEST is Teri.[61] Teri, raised near a public housing project notorious for filthy living conditions and gangs, began her work at BEST while she was in high school. She identified with the boys in her neighborhood, who, as she observed: "just have so many things up against 'em. . . . I can even remember my kindergarten teacher or my first-grade teacher [telling] the boys, 'You're nothin' but a gangbanger,' and stuff like that." In such a deformative educational situation, a program such as BEST offered an alternative to youth who seemed, in Teri's words, to have "no future. Most of 'em probably didn't graduate from high school. [A lot of them probably thought,] 'Why should I go to school when I can get what I need?' A lot of 'em don't have an expectancy of living that long anyway, so [they think], 'Why not live it up while I have a chance?' "[62]

Teri saw the social situation as no better for young women. For instance, many remained unaware that something like date rape existed. Teri commented, "[Most girls thought,] 'I was saying no and he just did it, anyway.' They wouldn't even say, 'He raped me.' It wouldn't be rape to them." At the same time, Teri observed that young women in the 1990s began to initiate violence. "They just want control over people," suggested Teri. "They want you to be afraid of them. [In the past], girl gangs were mostly fighting each other over guys, but now it's like they fight *any*body. They had been associated with a male gang, but now they want a *separate* gang. . . . They know guy gangbangers [who give them guns]. It's just bad." If anything, the extensive community services and media attention devoted to the projects exacerbated the problems. "Community services is all we have," Teri concluded.[63]

Teri worked about fifteen hours at BEST as a tutor to small groups of students. "It just started out as a job," she noted, but without BEST "[I] would have been a totally different person. . . . I probably wouldn't have graduated [let alone gotten] on the honor role." Teri felt that "the majority of the people that attend [BEST] feel like maybe there's help, and they're trying to grasp it. . . . You have sisters and brothers who are looking toward [youth and] saying, 'He's gonna be somebody and she's gonna be somebody.' "[64] At BEST, the traditional kinship network of African-American congregational life has been extended beyond the boundaries of traditionally religious education and formation. Providing sanctuary is a practice with deep roots in Christianity. It is documented in the Bible, from Abraham to Jesus, and it has been a characteristic practice of Christian monastic communities and churches down through the ages.[65] Today some African-American churches have revived the practice of providing sanctuary under the new conditions of urban America. A priority of practices over purity emerged at BEST, out of necessity.

BETHEL CHURCH TODAY: PURITY, PRACTICES, AND THE QUESTION OF STABILITY

We come full circle: how has Bethel Church, the birthplace of freedom for so many, negotiated the challenges facing African-American congregations in their teaching to youth today? Bethel is solidly middle class and, although located since 1910 in an inner-city neighborhood, now has more than 50 percent of its members residing in the suburbs. So, when I drove to the church from my temporary residence in Washington, D.C., one Sunday in December 1998, mine was one of many cars in line to park two blocks away from the sanctuary. As I pulled toward an attendant directing traffic, I rolled down my window, and he asked me, "Are you going to church?" The question did not surprise me, since I was the only non–African American in sight. I nodded, and the attendant smiled as he pointed me toward a school parking lot. "Pull right in there," he told me, and he shouted as I pulled away: "We brothers!" I couldn't help but smile at the kinship reference.

I had spent some time at Bethel over the previous week, talking with the youth minister, Rev. David DeVaux, about the wide range of ministries for youth in Bethel's recent history. He had encouraged me to attend the early worship service (held at 8 a.m.) to see the youth in action. After walking the two blocks to the church, I entered the sanctuary and took a seat halfway down, on the right. A deep balcony wrapped around the church above me. The church was full; about fifteen hundred in all. The service began traditionally enough, with a responsive reading, doxology, and a hymn, "Oh Come, All Ye Faithful." After a Scripture reading from Isaiah, the mass choir in the back of the balcony began to sing the music of Beethoven's "Ode to Joy," set to the lyrics of Henry van Dyke, "Joyful, Joyful, We Adore Thee." I noted the choir's precise, staccato pronunciation of the lyrics and thought, "That's rather traditional." After two such verses, the organ crescendoed, and then the piano, drum, bass, and guitars joined in a gentle gospel blues arrangement of Beethoven's beautiful melody. Two young women appeared at the front of the church, dancing classical ballet in blue jeans and red turtleneck sweatshirts. After a couple of verses of gospel blues, the band took off on a driving hip-hop beat. Up the aisle came an army of youth, dozens of them, of all ages, dressed in jeans and red turtlenecks, stepping, jumping, sprinting, and dancing with abandon. Several did cartwheels. The members of the congregation sprang to their feet, clapping hands and swaying to the music, joining in the exuberance. A young man took the microphone at the front of the church and began a theological rap as a choir of young people massed behind him, swaying and singing and shouting with adoration. The young man standing next to me turned my way as we shared in the beauty of the moment, and exclaimed, "Now that's what I'm talkin' about!" It was pure joy, and youth played a key part.

DeVaux had explained it to me in advance, but I still was not prepared. "There's no separation of the secular and the sacred here," he said. "We try to teach youth about all of life, everything from Zechariah [a biblical book] to Puff Daddy [a contemporary hip-hop artist]."[66] The musical reference was not accidental. Music has been a key bridge between the generations in African-American churches. The lineage is long, deep, and direct from the early spirituals, through the freedom songs of the civil rights movement, down to contemporary gospel music. As Lincoln and Mamiya suggest: "The music performed in black churches is a major way of attracting members and sustaining their spiritual growth. . . . Among black young people . . . gospel music programs constitute the major drawing card" determining their church membership.[67] Members of Bethel's intergenerational choir included young people who also constituted a separate youth choir, Joshua Generation. The dancers formed the core of the church's step team.

Bethel's ministry with young people goes considerably beyond music. For instance, on the Sunday I attended, Frank M. Reid III preached a sermon that included youth and their concerns in almost every sentence. The title, "God Delivers Us to Develop Us," was a virtual incantation of the life-path of freedom. Urged on by congregational responses of "Amen" and "Alleluia" and of intense spiritual experience (including speaking in tongues),[68] Reid preached, "The church is still filled with spiritual babies because we got stuck in the sixties and seventies with deliverance, and forgot the development. But God wants us to develop into mature men and women. God wants to birth greatness, strength, and security." The reference to God giving birth was subtle, but unmistakable, and was an effective way to broaden youth (and adult) images of God beyond the traditionally masculine images of Christian history. In case his congregation missed it, Reid repeated the theme: "God is always a God of birth and giving." Quoting Lutheran theologian Dietrich Bonhoeffer and Martin Luther King Jr., Reid rang the changes on Christian freedom: "Only those who believe, obey; and only those who obey, believe"; "With opportunity comes responsibility"; "God delivers us to develop us." It was a sermon in which the move from purity to practices was manifest.

Youth ministry at Bethel is not restricted to music and preaching on Sunday mornings. For several years, the church has sponsored a Rites of Passage program for youth between the ages of thirteen and eighteen. The program is structured like a college course, complete with syllabus, tuition ($400 per student), and course requirements of reading assignments and community service projects. It is open to males and females, the syllabus explains, "who are God's handiwork, fearfully and wonderfully made, lovable, kind, respectful, responsible, accountable, and intelligent young people." The topics covered convey both spiritual purity and basic practices. Youth learn "how to pray for yourself, your sisters and brothers in Christ and others; how to cope with today's problems; how to improve your appearance and . . . care for your home; how to cook, set a table, and improve your table etiquette; to have Fun." No line is drawn between secular and sacred learning: youth discuss from a Christian perspective "guns and violence, money management and entrepreneurship, African-American history, and selection of schools." Biweekly meetings culminate in an Afrocentric Rites of Passage ceremony at the church on a Friday in spring, followed by a cotillion dinner at a nearby restaurant on Saturday.[69] Mamiya summarizes the significance of these programs: "By creating its own rite[s] of passage based on African tradition, the congregation was again reasserting its resistance to mainstream American culture and returning to its African heritage."[70]

Along with its emphasis on worship and rites of passage, Bethel has established a scholarship program to assist its youth who wish to attend college. Administered by the Daniel Payne Scholarship Committee (Payne was pastor of the church from 1845 to 1849), this program began in 1975 with $50 scholarships to high school graduates. By 1989, twenty-eight awards were given, totaling $28,000.[71] By 1999, the total had jumped to over $60,000 in awards annually.[72] These scholarships indicate the long tradition of self-help within African American congregations—with *help* understood not only spiritually but politically and economically as well.

Scholarships assist upwardly mobile black youth, but among Bethel's numerous ministries are others that reach out to troubled teens. Teen PEP (Pregnancy Education Program) educates young women about motherhood and encourages fathers to take responsibility for their children. Ezekiel's Army is a juvenile-justice ministry seeking to prevent crime among male adolescents. Freedom Now is a "Word-based counseling ministry for substance abusers and their families and friends." The church also sponsors a prison ministry, through which church members evangelize, answer correspondence, and conduct praise and worship outreach in penal facilities.[73] These various programs aptly demonstrate Bethel's 1998 "Statement of Purpose": "We are *determined* to make a *difference* by bringing people to Jesus Christ, *delivering* them from all forces that would stop them from *developing* into *dynamic* and *disciplined* members of the church who are equipped to participate in *life-giving, life-changing,* and *liberating* ministry."[74]

In places such as Bethel, "Grace Church," St. Paul Baptist, and "BEST," African-American church members have assisted black youth as they have sought to find the life-path that will free them from oppression and for practices of the faith. From participation in worship to direct community involvement, congregations have provided to youth the necessary sanctuary of security, the traditional comfort of kin, rites of passage, and manifold other ministries to help them resist exploitation and develop into mature Christians. As the black middle class grows, a critical question is whether churches will continue to provide such a presence in the inner city. Bethel, as of 1999, was in the midst of a building campaign centered on 256 acres in the western Baltimore County suburbs.

chapter 5

Four Life-Paths and Four Common Problems

According to historian Joseph Kett, modern American youth ministry was moribund, intellectually and socially bankrupt. Kett documented in his groundbreaking *Rites of Passage* (1977) how Christians helped to "invent adolescence" in the nineteenth century. Kett argued that Christian youth organizations, along with colleges and high schools, created "a self-contained world in which prolonged immaturity could sustain itself." Christian youth ministries were essentially hostile to "precocious youth," and they limited youthful choices by substituting "adult-led training" in place of voluntary associations of young people. Furthermore, "Christian youth organizations of the late nineteenth-century downgraded not only voluntarism but intellectuality and spirituality as well." Youth ministries were "vapid" and "naive," by-products of the "intellectual decadence" of turn-of-the-century Protestantism. Surely they would soon fade away, for Christian youth ministry constituted "the final act of a melodrama which . . . had exhibited sundry attempts . . . to 'save' youth from cities, gambling dens, grog shops, and bawdy houses."[1]

In the twentieth century, Kett saw the "fortresses of morality" that Protestants had built for youth come crumbling down.[2]

"Between 1920 and 1950," thought Kett, "the reformers and clergy-men who comprised the original architects of adolescence passed the scene." A few vestigial pockets of Christians interested in "training" youth remained here and there, but they offered youth only "conformity," "hostility to intellectuality," and "passivity."[3] Quoting observers of small-town Christian youth in 1949, Kett found their diagnosis "devastating but accurate":

> By segregating young people into special institutions such as the school, Sunday school, and later into youth organizations . . . for a few hours each week, adults apparently hope that the adolescent will be spared the shock of learning the contradictions of the culture. At the same time, they believe that these institutions are building a mysterious something called "citizenship," "leadership," or "character," which will keep the boy or girl from being "tempted" by the "pleasures" of adult life. Thus the youth-training institutions provided by the culture are essentially negative in their intentions, for they segregate adolescents from the real world that adults know and function in. By trying to keep the maturing child ignorant of this world of conflict and contradictions, adults think they are keeping him pure.[4]

Youth subjected to such Christian ministries were, Kett thought, "hollow youth."

Kett's image of hollow youth was borrowed, ironically, from Christian poet and literary critic T. S. Eliot, who felt it was the modern experience of evil and the absence of God that produced "hollow men." In that light, and in light of the evidence itself, it is Kett's interpretation that appears to be increasingly hollow. Kett simply ignored the fact that Christian youth ministries drew upon intellectual traditions and social practices with ancient lineages and well-articulated rationalizations. Christian youth ministries were not, furthermore, all alike. American Christians were not one-sided ideologues who simply wished social control over adolescents. Kett's ridicule of Christian youth ministries for creating hollow youth failed to recognize the complex ways these organizations mediated interactions between generations. There were always options, and youth could choose from a plurality of life-paths that stressed in relative degrees control or experimentation, purity or practices. Tone-deaf to theology and ritual, Kett could not comprehend the lifeblood of Christian youth ministries, and so he produced caricatures. Of course, a caricature is hollow; a fuller portrait is not. Each of the four youth ministries presented here represent complex language systems and social practices within the broad stream of Christian tradition. These life-paths sought both to shield youth from danger *and* to involve them in intellectual challenge and the contradictory problems of American culture.

To be sure, the leaders of the Walther League, YCW, YFC, and African-American congregations all sought to convey to youth normative life-paths with definable boundaries. They did not want young people to frequent grog shops and bawdy houses. But that is only half the story. Christians are people of paradox. Over centuries they have developed a worldview that lives with tensions between apparently irreconcilable phenomena: God and humanity, nature and grace, self-interest and altruism, evil and goodness, life and death. Furthermore, Christians have hardly avoided engagement with the contradictions of American political life. Christians were present from the founding of the republic, and they have often felt a custodial responsibility to correct what they saw as America's flaws. In short, both the paradoxes intrinsic to Christian theology and attention to the contradictions of American culture have been present in Christian ministry to youth since 1930. As we revisit the four life-paths to contrast and compare them, we will discover their distinctiveness, their commonalities, and some of the depth that made them anything but hollow.

"SINNING BOLDLY": THE LIFE-PATH OF CHRISTIAN KNOWLEDGE, CHRISTIAN SERVICE

A paradox was at the heart of Lutheranism from its inception. In his early Reformation treatise *Christian Liberty* (1520), Martin Luther expressed the contradiction directly. "A Christian," wrote Luther, "is a perfectly free servant of none, subject to none." But in the very next sentence, Luther asserted, "A Christian is a perfectly dutiful servant of all, subject to all." Luther resolved this paradox by a distinction between the inward freedom of a Christian, on the one hand, and the external duties that a Christian would fulfill, on the other. Spiritually, Christians were free from any demands of the law. Everything that mattered in life, and especially one's eternal salvation, was a matter of God's doing, and God was a merciful God who became a human in the person of Jesus to save people by grace through faith. This was true even for sinners, which all humans were. To ensure salvation, God implanted faith directly into humans through the words of Scripture and the sacraments of the church. Inwardly and spiritually, Christians were completely and truly free. They could "sin boldly," as Luther once put it and as his life itself demonstrated.[5]

Luther's phrase, however, alerts us to the fact that he recognized humans were creatures prone to pride and illusions of self-sufficiency. In this world, the law always accused. All fell short of the glory of God. At our best, our motives were impure and tinged with self-interest. No one could be a perfect servant of all, subject to all. This did not, however, remove the duty; in fact, it intensified it. The individual was accountable to God, and in this light nothing a person could do was good enough. Individuals were invariably enslaved by the desire for self-preservation; their wills were in bondage either to God or to Satan. A will in bondage to Satan would fixate on one's own destiny and thereby contradict grace by acting in defensive or prideful ways. A will in bondage to God would be activated by God to spontaneous practices of love. Good works of service to all followed from faith, which freed a person from self-preoccupation to attend to the other. A Christian did not live alone in inward solitude, Luther pointed out, but lived externally as a body in the world, as a citizen, a worker, a family member. A Christian was duty bound to all, even though the best a Christian could do would invariably be tainted by sin. So, the Christian should "sin boldly," as a perfectly free subject of none and as a perfectly dutiful subject of all.

The Walther League's life-path of "Christian knowledge, Christian service" sought to express this paradox of sinning boldly in the context of mid-twentieth-century America. League leaders such as O. P. Kretzmann, O. H. Theiss, and Elmer Witt and thousands of local church leaders sought to inculcate in Lutheran youth the Christian liberty that created spiritually free but publicly active youth. "Christian knowledge" of God's grace was all but assumed in the league publications and programs; after all, most young Lutherans had been taught the faith by Sunday school teachers and pastors in Confirmation classes well before they joined the league. Still, the importance of an inward knowledge of God, based in trust, appeared throughout the league programs. At Arcadia, youth such as Bernice Baker[6] were "carried along paths [they] never dared venture before" by lecturers who were respected as Lutheran intellectuals and church leaders. In league Bible studies, Elizabeth Zoller[7] came to know that she was "at-one with God" and had no reason to fear, even as she offered a homily during Holy Week. And through the *Walther League Messenger* and the *Cresset*, Lutheran youth learned that faith was an inward reservoir that strengthened them to critique Nazi anti-Semitism, to tackle the Christian church's complicity with racism, and to challenge conventional sexual mores that saddled many youth with guilt.[8] A Christian was truly free to learn.

And a Christian was bound to love. Walther Leaguers were remarkably adaptable and active in projects of service over the years. When their hospices to welcome youth to America's cities failed during the Depression, Leaguers channeled their resources into Wheat Ridge Sanitarium. When penicillin made the sanitarium unnecessary, they sent "mission builders" overseas to build homes and schools. When parallel federal and ecumenical programs in the sixties made Lutheran mission builders seem less necessary than a decade before, Leaguers turned their attention to the problem of racism at home and sent Prince of Peace Volunteers out into the streets to march alongside African Americans and dodge the bottles and bricks hurled by bigots.[9] Throughout its history, the league offered Lutheran youth a life-path that combined a passion for knowledge with a passion for service. Knowing, the free and inward acquisition of faith, paradoxically merged with service, the public and external practice of faith for others. A pure faith produced practices. The transition from one aspect of the paradox to the other was not always smooth, and over the years league leaders and members noticeably—for reasons that we will explore in chapters 6 and 7—moved away from education into Lutheran knowledge and toward practices of the faith that might be shared by any Christians. But the young Lutherans of the Walther League were hardly kept ignorant of the world and its contradictions. They were, in fact, educated and formed to follow a life-path of sinning boldly. Many did so and thereby brought their private Christian knowledge to bear in public Christian service to America and the world.

NATURAL GRACE: THE LIFE-PATH OF A LAY APOSTLE

The Young Christian Workers were formed in a paradox quite different from that by which the Lutherans of the Walther League lived. Catholics thought Luther was a heretic, but their theology was no less complex than his. Indeed, the basic contours of modern Catholic thought and practice had been formed well before Luther by St. Thomas Aquinas, a thirteenth-century Dominican friar and philosopher. During his lifetime, Thomas had few disciples and many critics. Only after Protestantism did Thomism become the nearly universal theological and ethical foundation for Catholic thought and practice. So it is no surprise that Thomism was interwoven throughout the YCW movement as its intellectual foundation.

Thomism took as its touchstone Thomas's stunning work of intellect known as the *Summa Theologiae*. The *Summa* began (and would have ended, had Thomas completed it before his death in 1274) with God. All of life had its source in God, and all living things found their fulfillment in God. God meant for humans to be happy, and consequently God gave humans the beauty and awesome power of nature, the wonders of our bodies, the freedom to make choices, and above all the capacity to reason. Unlike Luther, Thomas thought that supernatural grace cooperated with natural human reason and ability. Thomas thought that grace, rather than obliterating and completely subsuming the will under God or leaving it unaided to the devil, assisted the will to become more or less in harmony with God's own will. Consequently, Thomas found plenty of good works for humans to do with the aid of grace, beginning with the virtues of faith, hope, and love and continuing to include the virtues of prudence (wisdom), justice, courage, and moderation.[10]

Like Luther, however, Thomas expressed the way humanity and the divine cooperated through a paradox: there was a "natural law" common to all humanity that could lead even unbelievers to do good works, but believers needed the "New Law" of Christ's grace added to the natural law to bring humanity to its eternal fulfillment: "The law we have in us by nature is inwardly implanted in us in the way human nature is: the New Law is inwardly implanted by way of a gracious gift added, so to speak, to that nature, not only telling us what to do but actually helping us to do it."[11] In other words, in between the natural law and the new law was human willing, understanding, and God's action. A Christian lived by natural grace, using the gifts of one's will, reason, and the tradition and practices of the church to find a way in the world on the way to eternal life.

This paradox of "natural grace" was woven into both the theology and the practice of the YCW movement. Aquinas began not with faith but with what we see in the world. He felt that "God's existence is not self-evident, but must be made evident from the world we see."[12] The YCW's inquiry method followed Thomas's lead by asking workers to observe their situation and report back on it. The YCW was grounded in the empirical senses. It asked workers simply to *see* the realities of their workplace and culture. But empirical evidence alone is useless: we must order what we see, relate it to a hypothesis or causal conjecture. For Aquinas, this hypothesis was God. We could understand God, Aquinas thought, only through analogy. The best we could hope for with our limited vision was a provisional judgment about God's being, filtered through language and based on our experience of God's creatures and on our reason. The YCW followed Thomas's analogical path by seeking to bring youth to judge the relative adequacy of their situations, in light of both the gospel and what they had observed. Young Christian Workers were asked to compare—the essence of analogy—their experience with Scripture and tradition. And finally, Aquinas's theology was grounded in action. God was the First Cause. Everything flowed from this in a continual process of change: "Some things in the world are certainly in the process of change. This we plainly see. Now anything in the process of change is being changed by something else."[13] The YCW sought to institutionalize this principle of action among its members. They would be causes of change within their church and culture by drawing on the power and energy of the First Cause, God.

By causing change in accord with God's natural and revealed law, YCW members would act as lay apostles, as full members of the Mystical Body of Christ, the church. The apostles, according to tradition, were connected to the life-giving Spirit of Christ at Pentecost, which had itself come from God—indeed, was one with God. From Peter down to the latest pope there was a direct line. In YCW and other Catholic Action movements, this connection was extended to the laity. On the one hand, becoming an apostle meant freedom of the will: one could act as an autonomous learner and doer of the faith, without direct control by the hierarchy. An apostle had access to power that linked nature and grace in a way that could transform work, study, and family life into part of the apostolic mission of the church. On the other hand, becoming an apostle meant responsibility: one had to sacrifice time to attend Mass or YCW meetings or take on the rigor of Christian action in an often hostile workplace and culture. A lay apostle such as Red[14] had to observe that, unlike the stereotypes held by his fellow workers at the garage, Puerto Ricans were not greasy. Then Red had to judge that Latino poverty had more to do with class than character, and he had to discern that his own prejudice needed to change. Finally, Red had the responsibility to act on what he observed and judged: he learned Spanish, started a tutoring program, and extended hospitality to new immigrants.

Of course, the life-path of a lay apostle that taught natural grace was likely to be more or less successfully applied. Not all individuals share the same natural aptitudes, and not all share the same charisms, or gifts of the Spirit. Some Catholic youth dabbled in "dilettante apostolicity," taking part in YCW for its natural reasons alone, such as finding a spouse or beer drinking and bar-hopping. And not all YCW chapters followed the "Observe, Judge, and Act" application of Thomas's analogical theology in either letter or spirit—some were stymied, understanding grace only as a church matter and unable to link it to the natural problems of society.[15] Other YCW cells, however, did exemplify their purpose as members of the Mystical Body of Christ. They educated and formed youth to be perceptive critics of American economic and social practices by studying the facts about America, by judging them on the basis of a deep tradition, and by acting in public life. Hardly shielded from the contradictions of American culture, YCW members were encouraged to confront those which had the most direct impact on them.

BECOMING BY BELONGING: THE LIFE-PATH OF A WITNESS

The intrinsic paradoxes of Christian thought and practice manifested themselves in yet a third distinctive fashion in YFC. The theological roots of YFC were in Calvinism, as transplanted to, and modified in, America. Calvin, like Aquinas, wanted a rational religion. "When God opens our eyes, if we close them are we not worthy of condemnation for having perverted the order of nature? . . . God has not put men in this world to deny them any intelligence, for he does not wish them to be like asses or horses, he has endowed them with reason and has wished them to understand."[16] Calvin systematized this rational religion in his best-known work, *The Institutes of the Christian Religion*, a Protestant *Summa* comparable in many ways to Aquinas's.[17]

Calvin's thought expresses the paradoxes of the Christian gospel, albeit with less enthusiasm and rhetorical extravagance than Luther and with less philosophical clarity than Aquinas. Calvin finally rejected those who always wanted "conclusions in the fashion of the philosophers," because "such people have never known what it is to be touched by God and to endure his judgments. And why? God treats us so fiercely that everything becomes obscure. And in fact there are also incongruous things in us: sometimes we desire to live and sometimes we desire to die."[18] The gospel, for Calvin, contained many things "that seem unreasonable to human judgment, even mad." When Christians confessed that "the Son of God, who is eternal life, put on our flesh," or that "by his death we have acquired life," or that "in his damnation we are justified and in his curse we are saved," Christians affirmed propositions that rightly seemed "contrary to our carnal sense."[19] Like Aquinas and Luther, Calvin recognized that the Christian faith embraced apparently incongruous phenomena.

More like Aquinas than like Luther, Calvin developed a theocentric vision of the relationship between God and humanity that extended to all spheres of life. Humans were depraved by sin but found order through God's grace, which predestined those chosen to be saved, and left untouched those who would be damned. God was not only the predestining power who determined eternal human destiny but the *législateur et roy*, lawmaker and king, of the universe. "God has consecrated the entire earth through the precious blood of his Son to the end that we may inhabit it *and live under his reign*."[20] Living in Geneva, where he negotiated a politically intimate connection between ecclesiastical and civil authority, Calvin imagined a closer connection between the inner and outer aspects of Christian life than Luther. "We remain unworthy," argued Calvin, "to look upon heaven until there is harmony and unanimity in religion, till God is purely worshiped by all, and *all the world is reformed*."[21]

Consequently, civil government did not exist simply to maintain order and hold back chaos but to promote public religion. Political leaders were to punish heresy, blasphemy, and moral offense. Calvin contended:

> The function [of civil government] . . . does not merely see to it . . . that men breathe, eat, drink, and are kept warm, even though it surely embraces all these activities. . . . But [civil government] also prevents idolatry, sacrilege against God's name, blasphemies against his truth, and other public offenses. . . . In short it provides that a public manifestation of religion may exist among Christians.[22]

Calvin's moralism, noted often by William G. Bouwsma, the reformer's leading biographer, finds its fullest expression in passages such as the one above. To note only the moralism, however, is to miss the fundamental point: a person became a Christian by belonging to an integrated Christian community active in public life.[23]

Calvin's theology promoted a rational zeal, but this paradoxical combination was not often matched by later Protestants in either zeal or reason. The Reformation quickly developed in dramatically divergent directions in the sixteenth and seventeenth centuries. Some so-called radical Reformers developed the Reformation's emphasis on the individual Christian by stressing a spiritualist communion between the individual and God in a fashion similar to medieval mysticism. Anabaptist (literally, "rebaptizer") groups took the opportunity the Reformation provided to reshape the sacraments, especially baptism, to make them more consonant with both rising individualism and rationalism. Yet other groups developed the Reformation in radical political directions. Some were revolutionary activists—most notably in Cromwell's Puritan Commonwealth, and others were pacifist separatists, most notably the followers of Menno Simons (now called Mennonites). The Calvinist paradox of "becoming by belonging" unleashed dramatic change in European history.[24]

Many of the varieties of Protestant thought and action inspired by Calvin and the other Reformers eventually found their way to America. Protestant colonizers established their version of the one true faith in a number of colonies (and states—the last endured until 1833) and bickered incessantly about who was allowed in and who should be kicked out. Calvin's Geneva proved difficult to replicate in the "howling wilderness." If churches could not claim entire territories, perhaps they could redeem individual souls and particular moments. Consequently, the practice of revivalism flourished in nineteenth-century America. The Great Awakenings and the rise of Baptists and Methodists constituted (numerically, at least) a domination of American public life that would last at least for a century. Becoming by belonging meant, primarily, being "born again," then, perhaps, belonging to a local congregation of Christians, and then, most tenuous of all, belonging to a national or regional denomination.

Accompanying the rise of these various Protestant revivalist traditions was a subtle but definite change in theology. Calvinism, with its emphasis on belonging via God's predestination and moral government, was gradually shed in favor of a revivalism that stressed less God's grace than the role of the human will in creating moral order.[25] Revivalists such as Charles Grandison Finney (1792–1875) sat potential converts at the front of a church on an "anxious bench," where they were confronted with the call of Christ to convert and amend their lives. Conversion was not a miracle worked by God's predestining grace; it was a choice on the part of a sinner or an effect created by the revivalist's skill at using "the right use of the constituted means," as Finney put it.[26] Surely a conversion could be accompanied by miraculous signs and wonders, but it was not, in itself, a miracle, Finney argued. Many revivalists, like Finney, stressed "perfectionism"; all of them were moralists. If America could not be like Geneva, where the systems of society were ordered by Christian zeal, perhaps at least an individual life could conform itself to God's law and thereby act as leaven in "the world." Revivalists and converts alike struggled with the problem of those who converted and then "back-slid" in the context of pluralist America. Their solution was to build alternative institutions where purity could be perfected, such as Oberlin College, which Finney served as president from 1851 to 1866. Oberlin and other Evangelical institutions, such as the American Bible Society and the Women's Christian Temperance Union, quickly became hotbeds of both revivalist training and moral-reforming activity. There are, of course, many years and subtle changes between Finney's Oberlin perfectionism and Billy Graham's life-path of witness in YFC, but the line is direct.[27]

In YFC, young people became witnesses through their conversion. Witnesses were those who decided to relate themselves to Christ and who could, in a narrative of conversion, testify to the power this relationship gave them. A witness was, first of all, weak without Christ. He was a sinner, caught up in or tempted by vices—like the young person named Jim described at the outset of chapter 3. Or she was afraid to speak of her salvation—like Melanie, the other youth introduced at the beginning of that chapter. Through the power of a relationship with the supernatural source of all power, mediated through a powerful evangelist such as Billy Graham, an individual could become a Christian. After conversion, the life-path of a witness was formed through beliefs like those of the NAE, through study of the Bible, and through prayer. Through this relationship, an individual could become a Christian and convert vice to virtue, or fear to action, and witness in a way that gained the speaker joy and perhaps even public power.

For many years, YFC, like many revivalist-based Christian movements, struggled to turn becoming into belonging. Youth for Christ members were expected to join a church after their conversion, but the links between YFC and congregations and denominations were tenuous. As a parachurch organization, YFC faced the complaint that it formed a youth-only "church alongside the church" that rivaled, rather than complemented, intergenerational Christian communities. This ambiguity went beyond simple statistics. By segregating youth and seeking to foster personal purity, YFC often appeared to shield Christian youth from cultural conflict. In its early years, YFC *was* culturally accommodating. Youth were trained to uncritically accept middle-class gender conventions, American populist anti-intellectualism, and the growing national power and systemic violence of the United States. When YFC featured military heroes and patriotic rhetoric at its rallies, it often appeared as if the organization formed youth to become warriors for the American way as much as witnesses for Christ. Identifying Christ with culture is hardly a new tendency in Christian thought and practice, as H. Richard Niebuhr long ago pointed out. Of late, however, YFC has also begun to develop theologies and practices for youth where "Christ transforms culture," where Christ stands *against* culture and its injustices, or where Christ and culture exist in paradoxical tension.[28] Youth for Christ members now become Christians not only by becoming converts who belong to a pure America but by becoming members of the multiplying Evangelical churches and organizations around the United States. And some of these churches and organizations, such as Compassion International, World Vision, and YFC, have moved well beyond training youth to be passive and ignorant in the face of American injustice and violence.

"CONJURING CHRISTIANITY": THE LIFE-PATH OF FREEDOM

If young Walther Leaguers could trace their distinctive formulation of Christianity's paradoxes to Luther, and Catholics could hearken back to Aquinas, and Evangelicals to Calvin or Finney, from whom did African Americans learn the life-path of freedom? Until recently most scholars would have found an obvious answer to this question: African Americans were Christian because they had been converted by white Evangelicals, primarily Methodists and Baptists. African-American religious history was part of the Evangelical story.

This answer is no longer sufficient. Out of the crucible of the civil rights movement, a number of black historians and theolo-

gians began to discern (or acquaint people with) the deep and
complex roots of the distinctive branches of African-American
Christianity. Albert J. Raboteau in 1978 published *Slave Religion*,
which argued for selected continuities between traditional West African religious patterns and Christian religious life among slaves.
Raboteau did not downplay how thoroughly slave masters sought
to eradicate all traces of African cultures among blacks and how
a vast array of "factors tended to inhibit the survival of African
culture and religion" in America. With a careful eye, however,
Raboteau also found traces of adaptation and survival. "Even as the
gods of Africa gave way to the God of Christianity," he wrote, "the
African heritage of singing, dancing, spirit possession and magic
continued to influence Afro-American spirituals, ring shouts, and
folk beliefs."[29]

While Raboteau and others were working to recover a usable
Afrocentric past, theologians such as James H. Cone were unearth-
ing the theological implications of African-American Christianity
in the present. Cone's many works of the late sixties and early seventies, notably *Black Theology and Black Power*, *A Black Theology of
Liberation*, and *God of the Oppressed*, developed a consistent thesis:

> Christian theology is a theology of liberation. . . . [Theology's]
> sole reason for existence is to put into ordered speech the mean-
> ing of God's activity in the world, so that the community of the
> oppressed will recognize that its inner thrust for liberation is not
> only *consistent with* the gospel, but *is* the gospel of Jesus Christ.
> . . . There can be no Christian theology that is not identified un-
> reservedly with those who are humiliated and abused. . . . Any
> message that is not related to the liberation of the poor in a soci-
> ety is not Christ's message. Any theology that is indifferent to the
> theme of liberation is not Christian theology.[30]

Writing in the wake of the civil rights movement, Cone asserted
that in the United States the people most oppressed and most involved in the "inward thrust for liberation" were American blacks.

Cone understood well that historically many black churches
had taught freedom in what appeared to be traditionally super-
naturalist terms—as freedom from sin and for heaven. Cone also
clarified for a white readership the paradoxical double meaning of
the symbol of freedom in black Christianity. Freedom was not only
spiritual, not only for purity, but also for politics. When African
Americans sang the spirituals or gospel blues, heard the book of
Exodus or the Beatitudes of Jesus read aloud, or felt the Spirit take
over their bodies in conversion, they were encountering not only

freedom as offered them by white Evangelicals but freedom as they remembered it from Africa and as they reconstructed it in America. The paradoxes of Evangelical Christianity appealed to blacks because they found ways to adapt them to the integrated worldview of Africa, in which there had been no separation of sacred and secular. They turned the slave master's oppressive tool into a life-path of liberty.

Practices surrounding the Bible in African-American churches can serve as a case in point. The use of the Bible in these churches has often been misunderstood as the black equivalent of white fundamentalist literalism. In fact, the roots may go much deeper. Biblical interpretation in black churches tends to be multivalent—to carry meanings on many levels at the same time. For instance, when Grace Church's "Roberta" preached on Youth Sunday and used an ancient prophetic text to indict "Euro-centric" teachers who distorted black identity, she was freely interpreting and applying the biblical story to the present in an obvious critique of education.[31] The transformation of the text from past to present, however, also opened up other levels of meaning. Roberta's critique of those who "have their own agendas" was a critique not only of white privilege but also of black churches that refused to address the issue of Afrocentricity. On yet another level, Roberta's sermon sought to motivate her listeners to support the Afrocentric programs at Grace Church. This is how African traditions endured in Christianity: by turning texts inside out to find contemporary meaning in ancient words. Such imaginative application of a biblical text may be closer to the African tradition of "conjure"—magical incantations and spells to heal and provide hope—than to Evangelical defenses of the Bible against modernity. Theophus Smith has argued generally that "a covert transmission of African spiritual principles . . . lies hidden under the conventional Euro-Christian forms found in black religious traditions."[32]

Smith, indeed, directly contends that the Bible has been used in black churches as a "conjure book." The Exodus story in particular and the prophetic tradition more generally, including the Gospels, have been sources used by African Americans to "conjure God for freedom." "Freedom," Smith goes on, has been understood in black churches "not only as simple prophecy: that is, as a visionary prediction of the coming emancipation." Rather, freedom has been "understood as prophetic incantation: as religious expression intending to induce, summon, or conjure the divine for the realization of some emancipatory future."[33] Not strictly a vestige of traditional African spirituality, the practice of conjure in Christianity is viewed by Smith as "interactive biculturality," where continuities with traditional African spirituality are infused into, and interpenetrate with, the conventional forms and stories of Evangelical Christianity. "Conjuring Christianity" motivated African Americans to action.

With this background, we are enabled to see more clearly the distinctiveness of the African-American life-path of freedom as taught to youth. Classical Christian paradoxes have surely been present: God's power is found in love, Jesus saves through his cross, and the Spirit is present with hope even in the midst of oppression. But African Americans have also given Christian freedom a distinct meaning, encompassing without contradiction the ideas of freedom from sin and oppression and freedom for political action and personal responsibility. The paradoxes of Christian liberty have been brought into sharp focus under African influence and in the midst of American oppression. The African wisdom that refused to separate sacred from secular, magic from religion, and religion from politics has been deeply imbedded in teachings to youth in thousands of African-American Christian congregations across the country. The movement is from purity to practices. God converts, or baptizes with the Spirit, not only to purify but to impel. Purity conjures practices. One without the other suggests disintegration—a disharmony that threatens survival and fulfillment.

This life-path of conjuring Christianity has taken on concrete form over the years. At Bethel A.M.E. Church, when young women and men marched in the 1930s to protest lynchings, they were taking the purity of their faith into practices on the streets to conjure freedom. When Kathleen Wilson of St. Paul Baptist Church took Ali Nurse into her home, brought him to church, saw him through high school, and helped him join the Yoke Fellows in Discipline, she conjured a future of freedom for him that might have been impossible for him on his own. When BEST provided a sanctuary for a youth like "Teri," although the program appeared completely secular, in fact it conjured for her freedom from street violence and freedom to reach her fulfillment as a person. Finally, back at Bethel Church today, when the youth of the church stepped and cartwheeled up the aisles of the church to a hip-hop version of Beethoven, they were conjuring both the intrinsic paradox of Christian joy in adoration of the divine and the interactive biculturality of conjuring Christianity contextually embedded in the African

American life-path of freedom. Over time, conjuring Christianity has—along with the other paradoxical life-paths taught by Christians to youth—re-created American culture in rather dramatic ways, as we shall see more fully in chapter 8. For now, let it suffice to say that black Christian youth have hardly been ignorant of America's contradictions or passive in relationship to them. For them, purity produced practices.

THE PROBLEM OF PRIVATE AND PUBLIC THEOLOGIES

These four life-paths demonstrate some of the diversity and depth of modern American youth ministry, contrary to an academic stereotype that viewed them as intellectually and socially bankrupt. All four instances emerged out of distinct Christian traditions and represented distinctive life-paths for young people to follow. The groups who developed these life-paths, however, also shared at least four common problems. A first problem was the power of "civic faith" to disrupt, if not destroy, authentic Christian faith among youth. The private faiths of Lutherans, Catholics, Evangelicals, and African Americans were susceptible to the corrosive power of modern marketed culture, on the one hand, and the hegemonic power of the state, on the other.[34] Martin Marty has described the process well: private and public modes of faith in the United States interact in ways that affect both. Marty observes, "In life the distinct elements of what is 'private' and what is 'public' intersect, interact, and interpenetrate each other . . . [especially] when they appear in *voluntary and associational* 'modes.' "[35] No Christian since 1930 has been able to avoid dealing with the blossoming technology that modernity has provided or the rapid growth of federal programs and cultural constructions. Most have not wanted to avoid them. If technology and national expansion did not exactly create an "American civil religion," as some have argued, they did help shape public assumptions about being an American that invariably interacted with the private faiths of Christians.[36] All four historical settings of youth ministry demonstrated leaders and youth alike struggling to identify the appropriate intersections and interpenetrations of the private faiths of Christians and the public possibilities of American culture.

The problem crystallized over the issue of violence. For much of their history, and surely through the fifties, Christian youth ministries were marked by a strategy of violence avoidance, at best, and complicity, at worst. During World War II, the Walther League, YCW, YFC, and African-American congregations sent their young men and women off to war or enlisted them to support the war effort at home. National youth programs supported denominational "war relief agencies," youth at Camp Arcadia were housed in barracks called "Army" and "Navy," and YFC members attended rallies where religion and patriotism blurred. None of the programs were pacifist, and all of them found the preaching of private salvation compatible with the "service" of killing enemies. The pure way of Christ, which suggested love of enemies, was considered impractical if it was considered at all.

In the sixties, Christian youth ministries began to question the easy connection between salvation and Christian participation in violence—whether at home in systems of racial exclusion or abroad in war-time service. All four groups struggled to find common language and practices to make *love* more than a word. The progress was uneven. Walther Leaguers were encouraged to identify with their neighbors who were not Lutheran, whether at home or abroad, and to find Christ in them inasmuch as they were suffering and oppressed. *Arena* and *Edge*, the successors to the *Walther League Messenger*, both made the public role of Christianity obvious in their titles. Lutheran youth were to take their faith into the public arena, where they would constitute the leading edge of nonviolent social change. Both publications consistently opposed U.S. participation in Vietnam and were ardent in support of the civil rights movement. In the process, however, salvation—a key Lutheran teaching since the sixteenth century—seemed to drop from view. Consequently, traditional Lutherans found the Walther League no longer Lutheran: "Stop blessing this God-awful mess with the Lutheran label. Fold up and die nice," one "Christian" critic of *Edge* suggested. It died as Lutherans, under the pressure of increasing levels of public violence, were unable persuasively to articulate the connection between salvation and social concern, between inner grace and external opposition to violence and injustice.

The YCW fell prey to the other side of the problem of private-versus-public religion in the sixties. Leaders of YCW studiously avoided comment on political affairs, aside from their impact on workers. The interconnections within Catholic teaching on peace-and-justice issues never seemed to make their way into the YCW publications, as they did in groups such as Dorothy Day's Catholic Worker Movement, among activists such as Daniel and Philip Berrigan, or among the Catholics who joined Clergy and Laity

Concerned about Vietnam—a group dedicated to protesting the Vietnam War as unjust. Part of this avoidance was strategic: the movement was, after all, a workers' movement. A too narrow focus on the "plight of the worker," however, and halting attempts to expand the focus led to failure. Catholic workers were faced with decisions such as whether to work in a munitions plant or whether to dodge the draft. The issues surrounding the problem of violence could not be avoided. When YCW gradually moved toward a "youth movement," and then into an "educational movement," the leaders were indicating their struggle to articulate the balance between the Catholic and the American elements in YCW, between grace and nature. By the time the focus of YCW had shifted to Catholic "education," the workers had joined the American middle classes, and there were plenty of other ways they could learn about Aquinas.

Youth for Christ continues to struggle with the issue of relating private salvation to public concern. In its inception, YFC's theology was privately and publicly triumphalist: converts to Christ made good warriors for the American way. Even during Vietnam, the question was not whether Christian youth would go to war but when. Private salvation prepared youth to "sacrifice" for their nation, even if the nation's cause had more to do with anticommunism and economic systems than with Christianity. The way of a witness was to "kill in order to save" the Vietnamese, as one participant in the conflict explained the logic.[37] This was, ironically, not unlike the logic used to crucify Christ. This irony did not, of course, occur to the leaders of YFC or to YFC youth, who were as often killed as they killed on the battlefields of Vietnam. Martyrs for capitalist America were not exactly what the original phrase *Christian witness* encompassed. Only recently have Evangelicals begun to chasten their triumphal theology into a more relational and socially critical ministry that seeks to attend to youth's needs and discern the interconnections and contradictions between conversion and political life.

The violence facing African Americans was immediate and closer to home than in the rice paddies of Southeast Asia, which makes it all the more remarkable that the civil rights movement was, for most of its history, dedicated to nonviolence. Many black youth also were enlisted or drafted to "defend" America in Vietnam. That these youth were being asked to die for freedoms abroad that they did not experience at home occurred to more than one African-American observer. So they took that fact to the streets with them to struggle nonviolently to turn their private faith into public law. That the struggle was as much a Christian as a civil responsibility had been taught to Christian youth in countless ways in African-American churches across the United States, where salvation merged with social concern, private faith with public action, Christianity with conjure. With the rise of the black middle class, the challenge has increased to differentiate salvation from success and to remember that "God delivers us to develop us" in ways that include all youth, including those from the large black underclass who are most susceptible to violence.

A tension, in short, between private faith and public action was found throughout Christian youth ministry during this period and resolved more or less effectively in the various movements. It should not be surprising that this tension appeared. It is found within the tradition itself, where the Scriptures speak in two voices. On the one hand, the Scriptures encourage followers of God on a particularist path: God is on the side of God's chosen and will save them both spiritually and materially, even if this leads God's chosen to wage war. On the other hand, Scriptures encourage followers of God on a universalist path: God sides with the oppressed who cry out for justice, and will save humanity both spiritually and materially insofar as humans extend God's grace to each other. This tension within modern American youth ministry was therefore not only a problem youth had to face. It was a problem with which adults struggled, as they have for millennia. One thing is sure, however. The issue of violence is a problem Christian youth ministries today can neither avoid nor shield youth from. Public violence invariably has an impact on private faith. Simply put, there will be no salvation to offer other generations if Christians do not heal the breach between salvation and social concern, between private and public theologies. In a nuclear age, the prospect of apocalypse looms if Christians do not attend to the complex interaction between grace and nature, God and politics, in their teaching across generations.[38]

THE PROBLEM OF VOLUNTARY PROGRAMS

A second problem faced by all four youth ministries was that encompassed in the fact that they were all "voluntary programs." Youth chose to join the Walther League, YCW, YFC, or BEST. The four modes of ministry depended, at some level, on a decision of will by youth to participate. At the same time, all four voluntary programs were closely guided (if not dictated) by parents, pastors, denominational or organizational adult leaders, supervisors, and mentors. They were programs. Thus, in all four cases, the wills of youth were not so much left alone to choose adulthood as they were offered normative paths that would guide them into grace-filled living. Whether this direction of the will destroys, makes possible, or intensifies the paradox of grace and action is a perennial question.[39]

Early on, youth ministries could depend on relatively stable and well-defined denominational and ethnic cohorts to ensure a consistent body of young believers to join their cause. Young Lutherans graduated from Sunday school and Confirmation classes into the Walther League. Young Catholic Workers, similarly, were recruited out of parishes and neighborhoods where ethnicity and faith were intimately interrelated in everyday commerce and activity. Youth for Christ, as a parachurch organization, had the most tenuous volunteer base. Consequently, the program was initially limited to spectacular rallies where emotional conversions recruited youth into what eventually became a movement of small-group meetings and high school clubs where individual purity became the mark of belonging. Among African Americans, either youth were members of a congregation of kin or they were on their own to negotiate their way in a hostile white world.

By the 1960s, however, all four movements felt the strain as the stable neighborhoods and ethnic identities of the middle years of the twentieth century gave way to the mobility and blurring boundaries of the latter years of the millennium. The Walther League, obviously, folded when the activist program no longer enlisted Lutheran youth, who were kept from it by their worried parents or who chose on their own not to participate. The YCW was, for all practical purposes, absorbed into the reforms instituted within Catholicism by Vatican II. The normative life-path of a lay apostle was opened to all God's people, not just young workers, who could choose from any number of educational and practical programs offered by local parishes or sponsored by Catholic agencies interested in issues of peace and justice. Youth for Christ gradually changed its focus from spectacular rallies to steadier "relational ministry," connecting on the local level to like-minded Evangelical congregations and nationally and internationally to the burgeoning Evangelical network of relief agencies. Youth for Christ expanded the normative dimensions of Christianity beyond personal-purity issues, and the choices of groups to which young Evangelicals could belong also multiplied. Finally, among African Americans the number of choices available to middle-class youth multiplied, while the need for choices among the urban underclass intensified. Churches creatively adapted, forming rite-of-passage programs with teaching in both Christian doctrine and normative life skills, while at the same time seeking to make the programs fun for youth.

The problem of voluntary programs, then, has been one that Christian youth ministries have also negotiated with varying degrees of skill. In the absence of national organizations like the Walther League, mainline Christian groups such as the Lutherans have largely gone local in their youth ministries, with occasional denomination-wide "gatherings" for youth. Such ministries give youth choices but erode the possibilities for sustained, distinctively Lutheran theological education and normative formation as found in the Walther League. Both purity and practices may be imperiled by this turn to locally initiated youth programs.[40] Catholic youth ministry, similarly, has gone local. Professional or volunteer youth ministers meet with youth for activities, while normative elements of the faith are often communicated to youth through other programs such as the Rite of Catholic Initiation for Adults or simply by attendance at Mass. This diffusion of youth ministry makes for a widely divergent balance between the normative and voluntary elements of the faith from parish to parish. Youth for Christ is also locally based. The national office coordinates occasional leadership seminars and provides some curricular assistance, but local YFC leaders are free to tailor their programs as they see fit, and youth are free to join or drop out as they desire. Voluntarism prevails.[41] Finally, African-American youth ministries have, to a large degree, always been locally based. Some denominations created imitations of white Baptist Young People's Unions or other denominationally run programs, but voluntarism from the grass roots has been a consistent theme in African-American youth ministry. The normative elements of the faith emerged out of the experience of enforced isolation: a life-path of responsible Christian freedom was presented by black churches as mandatory for youth because the alternative was oppression.

The problem of voluntary programs is as complex theoretically as it is practically. For instance, can compassion be programmed? One danger for youth ministry is plain old flight. Who wants to identify with the suffering? In an age of immediate gratification,

with ample opportunities for entertainment and diversion, practices of solidarity with "Christ in one's neighbor" are not an easy
sell to youth. The competition is fierce, and the normative elements of Christian faith and practice do not exactly receive confirmation from popular culture. Another danger lies in the opposite
direction. More than one youth minister has romantically imagined heroic legions of youth standing with him or her on the
"edge" of Christian ministry but then has been left standing alone
in the unemployment line. It is a fine line between, on the one
hand, acceding to the demands of youth (and popular culture's
image of youth, which they internalize and thereby desire) and, on
the other, enlisting them in a romantically envisioned and heroic
crusade. The problem of combining voluntary membership with
normative life-paths is fortunately an old problem for Christians
of all ages in America. Youth and youth ministers are hardly alone
in struggling to discern when and where to follow authoritative tradition and when to blaze a new trail. The only accurate historical
answer is: they have done both.

THE PROBLEM OF BECOMING AND BELONGING

According to historian John Modell, Americans have come to
understand growing up in the twentieth century as a process of becoming. Youth pass through a series of transitions and passages, a
life course that enables them to be on their own as an adult. "The
way one grows up," Modell suggests, "is closely related to what one
becomes." Between the years 1920 and 1975, argues Modell, the
life course became malleable. Timing of transitions shifted and
blurred. Studying primarily courtship and marriage, Modell points
out that youth "live and experience their own biographies as aware
actors, who do not merely receive [life] patterns as in the nature of
things, but *construct and evaluate them as they move along.*"[42] Personal choice, more than conformity to adult expectations, has
come to dominate youths' coming of age.

Belonging, conversely, has eroded. The church's "market share"
in the process of maturation has been challenged by a complex set
of developments, many of which we will explore in the next chapter. The result, according to William R. Myers, is that, increasingly
in the twentieth century, "American youth become adults through
a myriad of individualistic ways . . . they dropped out of school,
got a job, owned a car, bore children, joined the military, com-

pleted high school, got married, or graduated from college or trade school."[43] The church, as a community, has often appeared to youth as a peripheral appendage to the institutions to which they "must" belong to negotiate their way into adulthood. They have, for several generations now, routinely fled the church during adolescence.[44]

The rise of youth ministry is, on one level, a response to adolescent flight and a strategy to enlist belonging. The four groups, however, were rarely so up-front about their purpose, and in many ways they also contributed to the general cultural understanding of adolescence as a time of becoming. The Walther League stressed that young Lutherans should become Christians who "sinned boldly," but in the process it found that young Lutherans, their parents, and pastors no longer belonged because they saw in the league only either sin or boldness. The YCW functioned not only to form lay apostles for the Catholic Church; it also assisted Catholic workers to become members of the American middle class. Natural grace was divorced into either nature or grace, either the culture or the church. Members of YFC became Christians through conversion, but no one held them accountable to belong to a local congregation. They became, but may not have belonged. African Americans held the tension together best, conjuring Christianity by becoming Christians but belonging to a community of kin who also asserted that they belonged in a more just America. Even in the black church, however, youth have increasingly found other avenues of becoming and belonging more attractive than churches.

Still, all four groups also demonstrated flexibility in their efforts to enlist youth and created commitment on the part of those who did belong. Early Walther Leaguers not only learned they were Lutherans; at annual conventions they also learned skills, such as oratory and debating, necessary to belong as citizens in a democracy. Later Leaguers learned how belonging to America also meant belonging to a Christian community that could critique the nation's policies and practices and offer alternatives. Similarly, members of YCW learned not only how to attend mass but how to belong as Catholic workers or lay apostles in American culture. Youth for Christ taught its members to belong to YFC's small groups, Campus Life clubs, but also, especially in recent years, to get involved in any number of other Evangelical organizations that addressed central problems of American society, such as hunger and homelessness. Finally, African American churches enlisted youth not only to belong to local parishes but to claim a place in American public life they had previously been denied.[45] If America's youth were "hollow," it was because they were not listening to the call of their churches and youth ministries, which invited them not only to become adults but to belong to their churches as active citizens in public life.

FROM PURITY TO PRACTICES

This book covers a span of time—from 1930 to the present—during which youth ministry has moved from primarily serving a shielding function (intended to keep youth *pure*) to providing activities that infuse Christian faith into everyday life and bring young people into contact with the problems of their culture (intended to teach youth how to *practice* their faith). In addition to this historical shift in the ways churches have implemented youth ministry, there has also been a movement from purity to practices that is intrinsic to Christian faith and that has been enacted in varying degrees by each Christian individual and community. All four groups studied in this book in one way or another had as a goal to nurture purity in youth, in ways distinctive to the various traditions, and to prepare them for public action, in ways also shaped by diverse expressions of Christianity.

The Christian life demands such a movement from purity to practices; the gospel stories of Jesus' life are rendered moot without it. The move is not easy, and all four instances of modern American youth ministry struggled to make it. It is easy to fall into purity alone, what the Walther League's O. P. Kretzmann called "icebound verities," or into practices alone, what Kretzmann called "mindless doing." It is difficult to sin boldly, to live by natural grace, or to follow a life-path of becoming and belonging. And it is difficult to be free. The difficulties have not, however, kept youth from learning Christian life-paths across generations and from putting them into practice.

The key is theological. Modern progress in the material conditions of everyday life has not been matched by progress in life quality and meaning. Modernity produced not only technological wonder but also the "iron cage" of bureaucracy and the disenchantment of nature and society.[46] Theologians and church leaders, no longer among the most sought after and well rewarded of professionals, have struggled to comprehend the rapid changes.

Adult Christians in the United States from mainline, Catholic, Evangelical, and African-American backgrounds have encountered problems when they failed to offer youth *theologies* that both demonstrate authentic continuity with the depths of their traditions and apply to the changing circumstances of youth. The paradoxes of authentic Christian faith have often been watered down or been made stagnant when presented to youth. It is in the nature of human institutions to fix symbols and images, seeking to perpetuate themselves and their presence. But as youth move away from parental control and seek to create a future for themselves, they become critical thinkers.[47] All four movements failed, to some degree, to recognize the critical abilities of youth, their intellectual gifts, and their constructive potential.

They did so either by abandoning the depths of their own traditions, as in the case of the Walther League, or by failing to keep up with the changes in modern America, as in the case of YCW. Youth for Christ has gradually worked its way into a deeper understanding of classical Christianity while also tempering some of its early uncritical (and unconscious) adaptation to American mores. African Americans have kept pace best—both drawing upon the depths of conjuring Christianity and dressing the message in the idioms and styles of modernity. In any case, the movements came closest to each other when they were truest to their own visions while also attending mindfully to the realities of modern America. Context determined much, as we shall see in chapters 6 and 7.

It may not be the case, however, that the reader as yet discerns this task of finding both depth and malleability in youth ministry as a theological, rather than a social, problem. Modern America has seemed oddly vacant of God's presence in the absence of scientific certainty and yet filled with shrill or strident theologies. Simply put, adults have often failed to recognize before youth where they or their peers within (or without) America's churches have mislocated God's presence. God has been identified with American culture and institutions, with a particular brand of Christianity or ethnicity, with a charismatic preacher, youth minister, or youth, or even with particular images of God. To fail to recognize this mislocation of God into human fabrications is to fall into what the tradition has long called idolatry. And if Christians have in fact offered youth idols, rather than the living God, then they should hardly be shocked when youth absent themselves from worshiping them. If adults do not understand the movement, intrinsic to Christianity, from purity to practices, how can they teach it to youth?

Still, in all four movements were found adults who offered youth a way to identify God's presence with integrity and who led young people onto life-paths of authentic Christian living. Youth emerged from the Walther League, YCW, YFC, and African-American congregations able to understand and apply the paradoxes of Christian faith and to confront the contradictions of American culture. In the process, they changed the meaning of purity, the way the church interacts with culture, and the meaning and process of becoming a person in America. Fuller evidence for these points will have to wait until chapter 8.

For now, though, we have perhaps begun to see how, along with Jeremiah long ago, youth learned through modern American youth ministry that God was, in some sense, with them to deliver them and that, having been freed, they could develop themselves, their churches, their faiths, and their culture without fear. That many youth were also drawn to the powerful images of an increasingly violent culture was nothing new in history. The twentieth century is not the first to confuse God's presence with the power of violence. It was into such a culture that Jesus of Nazareth came, teaching a way of knowledge and service, making apostles, calling for witnesses, and offering freedom to the violated through his passion and compassion. The gospel has not changed between then and now. But in the last sixty years, American culture has changed dramatically.

chapter 6

Revolutions and Responses

Youth ministry is one of the remarkable social innovations in the past century of Christianity, for it has become a specialization across diverse denominations. Until very recently, however, the history of young people has been all but absent from accounts of U.S. history. Few books document the historical experiences and contributions of youth, and still fewer historical studies of youth ministry have been published, even within the field of American religious history.[1] The reasons for this neglect are many. Adolescents seem to live at the margins of American society. They do not generally work full-time, only began to vote in 1976 (at age eighteen), and are experiencing a brief segment of the life cycle. The ephmerality of youth in the flow of time makes writing their history difficult.

If young people themselves constitute a marginal, ephemeral, and difficult historical object of study, a further, deeper reason exists for the neglect of youth ministry as a historical topic. Social scientists are drawn, like most Americans, to novelty and progress. They therefore either overlook tradition-based social movements (unless they become reactionary) or tend to reduce conservative impulses to other causes—psychological fear, status anxiety, or buried economic interests on the part of traditionalists. That people might want to preserve something because they authentically deem it worth preserving seems a hypothesis hardly worth academic attention. Sociologist Edward Shils called this bias "the blindness of the social sciences to tradition."[2] Youth ministry was an innovation within Christian history, but in any given generation the point of youth ministry is to preserve the Christian tradition across generations. It appears to be inherently conservative in function. Historians have therefore been blind to it.

Still, youth ministries have been less conservative than one might think, and have been anything but static since 1930. Shils points out that traditions change in two broad ways: from causes without, which he calls "exogenous factors," and from causes within a tradition, which he calls "endogenous factors."[3] Two exogenous factors in the American context produced revolutionary transformations in American culture between 1930 and the present, and these revolutions in turn impelled changes in American youth ministries. First, as the United States became a world power, youth ministries also became more internationalist and had to contend with the fissures in American cultural consensus that U.S. international involvements produced. When, in the mid–twentieth century, America's providential story, whose plot emphasized anticommunism, became entangled in the quagmire that was Vietnam, youth ministries were caught up in the conflict. The shift was not linear or consistent, but from World War II through Vietnam and beyond, as Americans increasingly resorted to violence to solve their problems, youth ministries generally moved away from militancy and missionary zeal toward practices of culture critique and international relief.

A second set of exogenous factors emerged to change youth ministries when the rapidly expanding federal programs from the Roosevelt through the Reagan administrations were joined with burgeoning educational and market-inspired opportunities for youth. Federal programs, educational opportunities, and consumer goods and services provided competition to youth ministries in their efforts to gain the attention of youth. Women entered the workforce in unprecedented numbers, and families changed from hierarchical relations based on production needs to companionate relations based upon consumption preferences. Rites of passage for youth were provided from multiple sources in twentieth-century America, and if churches wanted to maintain any "market share," they had to focus and tailor ecclesiastical "products" to consumer demands in their particular "niche." These two revolutions in American culture—the dawn and debacles of the "American century" and the economic growth of the nation and its institutions from the New Deal to the "Reagan Revolution"—helped propel the shift from purity to practices within modern American youth ministry.

When American Protestants began specialized youth ministry in the mid-nineteenth century, the often explicit context for this work was militancy: the churches needed soldiers for Christ. Youth were "trained" (often with formal military exercises), and then many of them were sent overseas as missionaries. Such youth ministry accorded well with an American culture that was itself expanding both internally and in global influence. Along with militancy in youth ministry came the purity program that Joseph Kett accurately perceived as a part of (especially evangelical) American youth programs.[4] Christian leaders taught youth what they ought to avoid: vice, urban strangers, and precocious behaviors such as smoking and sex. Youth ministry had its origins in Protestant dominance, as a way to maintain Protestant hegemony across generations, to pass on the privileges and "burdens" of power.

By at least the late nineteen-sixties, it was clear that youth ministry had failed in its effort to perpetuate Protestant power. Consequently, this ministry has appeared to many within the churches to be in decline. When they did not eliminate agencies altogether, mainline Protestant leaders cut national youth ministry budgets and staff in what an observer called a "dramatic dismantling of youth bureaus and services [beginning] in the early 1960s."[5] Locally, pastors and congregations struggled to keep young people active in the church. Fully 80 percent of baby boomers recently reported leaving the church or lessening their participation in it during adolescence, and their children (and grandchildren) have fared no better.[6] Among the current generation, a precipitous drop in church participation is evident as children age: 60 percent of elementary school children participate in church education programs, but this drops to 52 percent by junior high and to 35 percent by high school.[7] Churches also struggle to keep youth ministers. The average employment period for a Protestant youth minister is eighteen months.[8] Facts such as these produce the sense of decline in youth ministry. At their most optimistic, church experts see a "fundamental paradigm shift" under way.[9] At their most pessimistic, they wonder whether youth in the church today are "youth without a future."[10]

A more complex and accurate view of the history sees less decline than diversification, on the one hand, and ideological and social focus, on the other. Early youth programs seem strong to the eye of nostalgia because they often had clear ethnic or denominational identities and because they were militant and separatist. Youth were segregated into separate institutions and trained to become soldiers for the church.[11] Since few statistics are available on the actual number of participants, people can imagine a glorious past when youth were integrally woven into the fabric of congregational, denominational, and American public life. Such nostalgia can also fuel alarmist accounts of the "decadence" of contemporary youth and thereby legitimize the flow of resources to organizations serving adolescents, whether juvenile detention centers or youth ministry programs. Although we await careful studies of selected youth ministry organizations in the late nineteenth and early twentieth centuries, it is likely that this nostalgic view of the past will not prove accurate.[12]

A more accurate perspective sees institutional diversification *and* ideological focus in modern youth ministry. Youth ministry occurs at multiple sites in modern America. There are countless sources from which youth can receive education about Christianity, both within and outside the churches, and there are numerous opportunities for youth to be formed in practices of the faith. Pluralism has promoted, not destroyed, youth ministry by diffusing sources beyond local congregations and denominations. Within youth ministry, furthermore, denominations and congregations have both broadened and grown more focused in their ministries to youth than in their earliest years. Youth ministries have abandoned, by and large, the attempt to create "soldiers" for the church, and have both imitated cultural trends to entertain youth and focused on teaching the faith and providing opportunities for practices of Christian compassion. The next two chapters will show how, in response to exogenous and endogenous factors, modern American youth ministry shifted from purity to practices, finding a variety of media available to form youth in faith and focusing increasingly on ministries in accord not only with modern American culture but also with the historic Christian message and tradition.

THE AMERICAN CENTURY IMPACTS YOUTH MINISTRY

When the United States dropped atomic bombs on Hiroshima and Nagasaki, Japan, in 1945, Americans responded with a mixture of pride and fear. The victory produced by dominant American technology also produced despair at the destructive forces unleashed. World War II had been a popular war, but the victory through atomic technology produced destructive cultural fallout. "The atomic bomb that leveled Hiroshima also blasted openings into a netherworld of consciousness where victory and defeat, enemy and self, threatened to merge. Shadowed by the bomb, victory became conceivable only under the most limited of conditions, and an enemy too diffuse to be comfortably located beyond national borders had to be confronted in an un-American spirit of doubt." "The American story," which featured the inevitable progress of democracy through technical mastery and which had "helped order [Americans'] sense of history for almost three hundred years," began to unravel.[13] Simple progress was complicated by America's new internationalist role and by the destructive forces unleashed with atomic power.

A sense of what Tom Engelhardt calls "triumphal despair" seeped down to the most local levels of American society. Historian Paul Boyer surfaced the reflections of a young mother in 1945:

> Since [the bombs dropped,] I have hardly been able to smile, the future seems so utterly grim for our two little boys. Most of the time I have been in tears or near-tears, and fleeting but torturing regrets that I have brought children into the world to face such a dreadful thing as this have shivered through me. It seems that it will be for them all their lives like living on a keg of dynamite which may go off at any moment, and which undoubtedly will go off before their lives have progressed very far.[14]

Such despair was the underside of American triumph throughout the latter years of the twentieth century.

Still, America's victories had been based upon military and industrial prowess, and the link between military might and industrial production was unbroken throughout the postwar period. On the eve of his retirement from office in 1960, former general and president Dwight D. Eisenhower warned Americans to be wary of what he called "the military-industrial complex." Noting that before World War II the United States "had no armaments industry," Eisenhower lamented that the United States had been "compelled" to create one, along with a large standing army, on which the government spent more annually "than the net income of all United States corporations." Eisenhower pointed out, "This conjunction of an immense military establishment and a large arms industry is new in the American experience." Its "total influence—economic, political, even spiritual—is felt in every city, every State house, every office of the Federal government. We recognize the imperative need for this development. Yet we must not fail to comprehend its grave implications. Our toil, resources and livelihood are all involved; so is the very structure of our society."[15] The very structure of a society, down to its youth and including its spirituality, was likely to be impacted "gravely" by the institutionalization of violence, even if it was the legitimated violence of "defense."

Housewives and presidents were not the only ones sensitive to the problems the American century posed. Diffuse anxieties promoted among otherwise "normal people" what historian Richard Hofstadter called "the paranoid style in American politics." Writing in the wake of the McCarthy era and the assassination of President John F. Kennedy, Hofstadter traced a tendency among Americans to resort to conspiracy theories in efforts to explain the causes of cultural dilemmas. Senator Joseph McCarthy represented the paranoid style in its most dramatic form. McCarthy, a Catholic from Wisconsin, found Soviet-affiliated communists everywhere, including at the highest levels of government: "How can we account for our present situation unless we believe that men high in this government are concerting to deliver us to disaster? This must be the product of a great conspiracy."[16] McCarthy was eventually exposed as a fraud, but while in power he used religious rhetoric that resonated with many Americans to justify his witch-hunt: "Today, we are engaged in a final, all-out battle between communistic atheism and Christianity. The modern champions of communism selected this as the time. And, ladies and gentlemen, the chips are down—they are truly down."[17] Anticommunism was America's consensus ideology during the Cold War, and while it exaggerated nuclear anxieties, it also provided Americans with enemies within and without to contend against.

In Vietnam the Cold War turned hot, and the anticommunist consensus began to unravel. American involvement in Vietnam was a spiritual as well as a political crusade, as documented by theologian Walter T. Davis. Davis traces the causes of U.S. intervention in Southeast Asia to "the American dream," closely akin to what Tom Engelhardt identified as the American story. For Davis, the American dream held "imperialistic pretensions that [were] masked by a theology of special calling wedded to an optimistic, progressive view of history." America's God-given destiny was to contain "atheistic" communism, and U.S. intervention in Vietnam was only one of its manifestations. Vietnam, however, was where this dream was shattered, according to Davis: "The American war in Vietnam destroyed the national consensus regarding who we are and what our mission is at home and abroad."[18] Engelhardt concurs: in Vietnam, the American dream met the "nightmare, the quagmire, and the bloodbath" in a "reversal" that "ended victory culture."[19]

The median age of combat soldiers in Vietnam was 19.6 years, compared with over 25 years in World War II.[20] The conflict invariably changed youth ministries. Most of the young men who fought in Vietnam were conscripted rather than enlisted—leading to widespread evasion of the draft, often as religiously inspired conscientious objectors. Young people themselves developed organizations to protest the fighting, of which the best known was the Students for a Democratic Society (SDS).[21] By the conflict's end in 1975, nearly all of the mainline Protestant denominations were opposed to the war, as were many Catholics, and African-American Christians felt betrayed by the promises of programs such as Project 100,000 and the realities of young black men coming home in body bags.[22] If Vietnam did not end victory culture and the American consensus of anticommunism, it surely gave them a severe jolt.[23] Since the 1980s and the demise of the Soviet Union, anticommunism has all but ended as a rallying cry for U.S. cultural consensus.

Churches responded to these challenges posed by America's new internationalist role. All four settings of youth ministry—the Walther League, YCW, YFC, and African-American congregations—both changed their programs and took advantage of the opportunities U.S. global prominence provided. On the one hand, U.S. global involvement was an opportunity. Youth had access to cultures beyond their own to learn from and interact with. On the other hand, the American century and its responsibilities produced a problem. If youth programs were not the church's equivalents of armies and navies, what were they? The struggle within American Christianity to answer this question—although no one put it in quite these terms—began during Vietnam, and it has not yet been resolved.[24]

The opportunities and fissures of the American century changed all four settings of youth ministry by promoting both international involvement for youth and the move from purity to practices. The Walther League sent Mission Builders around the globe and Prince of Peace Volunteers to America's cities, not to convert heathen or promote American anticommunism but to build houses and hospitals and provide support for causes of social justice. When league leaders invited the slightly "pink" Pete Seeger to sing at their national gathering in 1965, Lutheran anticommunists reacted and effectively ended the league's history. The YCW emerged out of an internationalist church and brought young workers together in Rome and elsewhere to study and worship, but it carefully avoided official involvement in either anticommunism or war protests. The implicit anticommunism of the movement surely helped it propel young Catholics into the middle class, but when YCW leaders avoided the political turmoil of the sixties, they doomed the movement to irrelevance. Historian Mary Zotti observes that while YCW was saying nothing about the war, young Catholic men were "either going to Vietnam or going to college to stay out of Vietnam, or becoming conscientious objectors."[25] Youth for Christ generally supported the anticommunist consensus, even through Vietnam. Since the end of that conflict, however, YFC has abandoned the efforts to establish overseas "beachheads" through conversion-centered crusades. Now YFC collaborates with World Vision and other international relief agencies and sets up Campus Life Counseling Centers around the globe. Finally, since the sixties African American churches and their youth ministries have, as in the cases of Grace Church, Bethel, and St. Paul Baptist, promoted "Afrocentricity," which depends upon the global interconnections American internationalism provides. African Americans also became critics of government policies that enlisted young black men to fight as "warriors" for freedoms they did not experience at home. In short, the American century produced responses from within modern youth ministries across the United States. The move from purity to practices was promoted by the revolutions in American politics. Youth were participants in these revolutions, often on the front lines. In such a context, purity preaching made little sense, except as a thinly veiled escape from atomic despair. Some youth ministries survived the end of victory culture, others did not, but none was unaffected.

COMPASSION, COMPETITION, AND A CULTURE OF CONSUMPTION

The turn from purity to practices in Protestant youth ministry initially received a significant boost from the New Deal programs of President Franklin Delano Roosevelt. Roosevelt's programs were tailored in response to the stock market crash of 1929, but they had deep affinities with, and were shaped by, experts and professors from within Protestant, Catholic, and Jewish ethical traditions. The wide range of New Deal programs also involved millions of youth, since they were often the last hired and the first fired in economic downturns. In the thirties the National Youth Administration, to take one example of a New Deal program tailored for youth, developed apprenticeship programs for over two million jobless young men and women and provided work-study grants for other youth to attend colleges.[26] The Civilian Conservation Corps (CCC), also a jobs program of the New Deal, enlisted young men in a series of camps around the country to build roads and trails, plant trees, and stock fish.[27] The *Walther League Messenger* took note of these New Deal programs for youth. "The C.C.C. experiment," observed Walther League leader Alvin Klatt of South Dakota, who also served as chaplain to one of the CCC camps, was a story "of salvaged human hopes and confidence."[28] It was also a step toward the demise of youth programs with a national scope such as the Walther League. According to historian William J. Leuchtenberg, the New Deal replaced generations of local and church-based charity with a "philosophy of governmental responsibility for people in need."[29] Programs of compassion could be efficiently administered, without sectarian bickering or theological baggage, by the government.

This philosophical revolution of the New Deal continued through the Eisenhower, Kennedy, and Johnson administrations. Johnson's vision of a Great Society depended upon a rhetoric that contrasted American wealth and power with the responsibility of compassion. "We have the opportunity," the president argued in a 1964 address, "to move not only toward the rich society and the powerful society, but upward to the Great Society." The Great Society would be marked by "an end to poverty and racial injustice . . . where every child can find knowledge to enrich his mind and to enlarge his talents." Indeed, the Great Society would be "a place where men are more concerned with the quality of their goals than the quantity of their goods." Governmental spending for social programs grew exponentially under Johnson, in projects such as Model Cities, Medicare, and Operation Head Start. The changes wrought by the early years of the civil rights movement made the Great Society seem like more than mere rhetoric. Well-being seemed within the reach of all.

Consequently, average Americans developed lifestyles that stressed economic and social consumption. This culture of consumption dramatically impacted the family and thereby intergenerational interactions. "The legendary fifties family," writes historian Elaine Tyler May, was not "the last gasp of 'traditional family life,' but rather the first wholehearted effort to create a home that would fulfill virtually all of its members' personal needs through an energized and expressive personal life." Home ownership jumped dramatically with the boom of G.I. Bill loans. By the late fifties, Americans, like then Vice President Richard M. Nixon, worshiped the "model home within the price range of the average U.S. worker" as the essence of American freedom. Adorned with suitable modern appliances such as clothes washers, refrigerators, and televisions, the home was no longer a site of hierarchical production but a site of "consumption" by family members who treated each other as "companions."[30] From the turbulent sixties through the economic booms of the eighties and nineties, a "silent majority" of America devoted itself to a private spirituality of home, where men, women, and children could express love to each other and find fulfillment with modernity's technological trappings, bolstered by a strong economy and mighty military.[31]

In the administration of Ronald Reagan (and, with less success, those of George Bush and Bill Clinton), this combination of military prowess, business expansion, and "family values" constituted what Reagan called a "second American revolution." Reagan's rhetoric was extravagant, as were his expansion of some federal programs and his contraction of others. Reagan hardly undid the New Deal. Despite his rhetoric of "small government," Reagan presided over massive economic programs that doubled the national debt in less than six years.[32] Reagan's emphasis on economic growth was consistent with every administration from FDR to the present. "There are no constraints on the human mind," argued the former actor in his 1985 State of the Union Address, "no barriers to our progress except those we ourselves erect. . . . Our economy is not getting older and weaker, it's getting younger and stronger; it doesn't need rest and supervision, it needs new challenge, greater freedom." Competition would trigger economic growth that would "trickle down" to all Americans. "This government will meet its responsibility to help those in need," argued the Republican leader, "but policies which increase dependency, break up families and destroy self-respect are not progressive, they are reactionary. . . . Minorities will not have full and equal power until they have full economic powers. . . . Let us resolve that we will stop spreading dependency and start spreading opportunity; that we will stop spreading bondage and start spreading freedom."[33]

Youth ministries were caught in a bind by this "second American revolution." On the one hand, federal welfare programs had duplicated or replaced many of their traditional functions, and, more important, had created a philosophy of entitlement that expected government intervention in social problems. On the other hand, when government leaders such as Reagan reduced the meaning of freedom to economic power, the culture of consumption that competed with (if it did not contradict) Christian ministries of compassion received new impetus. The quest for personal fulfillment, especially when linked with the eighties' and nineties' reduction of social controls on business greed, made youth ministry programs a hard sell. Youth, like their parents, were caught up in the ethos that defined happiness and freedom in terms of economic power. Consequently, when George Bush called for a "thousand points of light" to replace welfare and when Bill Clinton began dismantling "welfare as we know it," churches were being asked to assume responsibility for practices of compassion without the cultural or institutional resources necessary to motivate and enable members to do so.

Youth ministries were challenged by these dramatic developments in American macroeconomics, but they had been impacted even more by the educational opportunities and expectations that Americans created for adolescents. A dramatic increase in school attendance throughout the twentieth century rendered many youth programs redundant. Mandatory schooling through twelve grades became increasingly the norm after 1930. In 1900 only 11.4 percent of fourteen- to seventeen-year-olds attended high school. By 1939 the number was 73 percent. In 1980, fully 94 percent of eligible American teenagers were enrolled in high schools.[34] As schools grew, youth ministries struggled to redefine their focus. It no longer seemed essential for an organization such as the Walther League, for instance, to educate young Christians into basic skills to support democracy. Attempts to do so that endured were likely to be duplicated, with greater scope, on the public level.[35]

An example is available in the area of recreation. Every youth program sponsored recreational or sporting activities for youth, and most ran their own leagues. The Walther League had, throughout the forties, organized dozens of local basketball conferences, drawing into competition thousands of young men and women, eventuating in a national Lutheran World Series of Basketball held on a college campus.[36] By the sixties, when parochial and public high school basketball leagues drew off the best athletes and most spectators, only the benchwarmers participated in youth group leagues.

Young people of all faiths increasingly had their time occupied by publicly funded schools and programs. School bands, choirs, and talent festivals made the necessarily smaller and less well funded parish programs seem second-rate. School curricula began to incorporate teachings about religions and "the Bible as literature," and school clubs devoted to special studies or activities duplicated many efforts previously undertaken by churches. Finally, nationally organized social service programs such as the Peace Corps and Vista provided ample opportunity for young volunteers to spend time working for social change. It is no surprise, then, that by the late sixties a former YCW chaplain felt that "social evils were no longer recognized as giants to be toppled; [we believed] government would solve society's problems with new programs."[37] As this faith and hope proved illusory during the eighties and nineties, youth ministries, most notably those for African-American youth, again were forced to adapt to meet needs for sanctuary and development still very much unmet by the government.

The affluence of American culture also affected youth ministry by making college possible for many Christian teens. Lutherans, Catholics, Evangelicals, and African Americans all became increasingly able to attend college as an avenue to social advancement. Lutheran college attendance, for instance, increased by five times between 1940 and 1959.[38] As the older young people who had once led denominational youth programs were siphoned away from congregations and into colleges, they encountered currents of thought that often challenged the faith they brought with them.[39] Colleges provided another new site for youth ministry, and while American higher education produced notable innovations in church work with young people, such as the Newman Center movement in Catholicism and campus ministries among Protestants, it also diffused the sources of youth ministry and made integration difficult.[40] High schools and colleges, in short, dominated the efforts of youth ministries to serve as agencies for mediating cultural meaning and value across generations.

Youth ministries were also directly impacted by the increasing affluence of American youth. Youth entered the consumer culture with a vengeance. Young Americans returned to work (usually part-time) in the postwar period and consequently had discretionary income at their disposal. In the ten-year period between 1944 and 1954, the number of adolescents working outside the home jumped from 17 to 31 percent. Since then, the number has increased even more.[41] Any number of sources demand the income generated by young workers—saving for college, dating, clothing, and entertainment, such as attendance at movies and concerts. The churches have laid claims, in some ways, on youth's discretionary income, but they have not found methods for teaching youth to use their money compassionately with anywhere near the effectiveness with which television has persuaded youth to spend their money on commodities. Bible clubs are simply a hard sell. Little wonder they meet at McDonald's.

They get there, as often as not, in their own automobiles. Henry Ford's invention revolutionized transportation in America and reshaped both the physical and the cultural geography of the United States. With the exception of a slight lag during the Depression, new-car sales and vehicle registrations climbed continuously during the twentieth century.[42] Americans grew attached to their cars and to the ribbons of gravel, concrete, and asphalt that transformed the American landscape. Young males seemed especially susceptible to the dream of "autopia." By 1950 they could expect to acquire a driver's license upon turning sixteen and perhaps could purchase a jalopy of their own to customize with the help of *Hot Rod* magazine, which began publication in 1948.[43] The auto industry has been a leading U.S. business for decades, and cars have become more than simple consumer items. They function as status symbols, enable a mobility that the horse-and-buggy age could hardly have imagined, and create a semiprivate space through which courtship rituals have moved from the front porch or church basement to the back seat.[44] Youth with wheels could choose to go wherever, whenever they wanted, with or without parental or ecclesiastical approval.

Rituals of all kinds, especially in the areas of courtship and coming of age, competed with church efforts. The possibility that evangelical boys might invite their girls to a date at the YFC meeting, for instance, was dwarfed by the probability that they would attend together some form of public entertainment or a school-sponsored activity, such as a prom. Prom and high school graduation ceremonies became dominant rites of passage for American middle-class teenagers in the twentieth century, as any parent or youth of the period can attest. The prom offers historians of popular rituals an especially interesting set of practices to examine as a rite of passage whereby youth demonstrate their ability to meet tests of adult status. High school juniors and seniors who attend prom dress up in formal wear, rent limousines to take them to expensive dinners, and spend the evening dancing (and often drinking) in imitation of adult patterns of behavior. Graduation day provides youth a more somber but no less significant rite of passage to compete with Christian efforts to form and educate youth. Adolescents are offered multiple paths as they come of age, and many of them are far better marked than those offered by churches.

Christian youth ministry, then, often seems to have declined in response to these dramatic developments in twentieth-century America. In fact, the competition was a catalyst for change as youth ministries shifted youth's attention from purity to practices, from separatism to public engagement, from ethnic or denominational enclaves to central concerns of American society. Churches learned to share the nurture of "their" youth with other institutional sources and to act as leaven in the midst of an officially secular culture. Thus, Lutherans and Catholics may no longer run separate youth basketball leagues parallel to those of the public schools (although some do), but urban Lutheran or Catholic congregations may cooperate with secular "midnight leagues" in inner cities to provide alternatives to gang participation. Catholic or Evangelical churches may no longer be able to persuade their young people to abandon public school proms, graduation days, or even attendance at movies, but both have developed alternative high schools and colleges, and YFC Bible clubs across the country have taken to gathering in high schools for prayer meetings. Furthermore, mainline denominations provide "servant events" and camping ministries that challenge the commitment and compassion of Christian young people in ways comparable to the challenges extracurricular activities of public schools pose to youth as they come of age. African-American churches have adapted, too, and are beginning, with some success, to develop their own rites of passage programs, which integrate both secular learning and Christian education and formation. Youth ministries have, in short, responded to the revolutions in American economic and social life. Diversification and focus, rather than decline, accurately describe the way in which youth ministries shifted from purity-centered movements to movements focused on practices.

The adaptation did not come easily. Churches were especially stymied in response to the subtheme of violence and destruction that wove its way throughout the American century. As political power was increasingly concentrated in the federal government and as the military-industrial complex churned out its products, America often sent its youth off to war. In little more than fifty years, four major military conflicts (World War II, Korea, Vietnam, the Persian Gulf), countless smaller skirmishes, and a massive military buildup of nuclear and conventional weaponry made Americans adapt to living with awesome destructive power. Youth ministries became less militant in this context, but they did not, by and large, commit to nonviolence or pacifism.

The destructive consequences of American technological prowess were also felt close to home. The environment became a source of concern for many, and "green" programs for youth ministries began to develop.[45] At times, American society as a whole seemed unable to find a center beyond economic prosperity. Wealth became concentrated in fewer hands, and the expectations of affluence were beamed to every citizen through mushrooming mass media. When educational and other social systems were not adjusted quickly enough to include all in the benefits accruing to supply-side economic prosperity, crime escalated, especially among youth. Corruption by presidents, duplicity and white-collar crime by public elites, and scandalous breaking of vows by ecclesiastical leaders have been matched by escalating acts of domestic and street violence by adolescents. This violence is in turn met by further violence in the form of enlarged police forces and more jails. Little wonder that the youth of America, given such a "moral compass" by adults since 1930, have opted out into an indefinable Generation X.[46] Only in anonymity does there seem to be safety from the systemic and random violence of adult America.[47] Youth ministries have had to overcome a significant generation gap as youth view adult hypocrisies with suspicion. Since the sixties, this gap has gone underground, but it has hardly ended.

Churches have been confused by these changes and have often struggled to identify a distinctive voice in response. A sense of decline has paralyzed many. Youth ministries have proven to be adaptable and resilient, however, and resources are deep and enduring in the traditions of youth work found in every major American Christian community. Facing competition but potentially more focused than in the past, churches and their youth ministries have not only been reactive since 1930. They have also produced changes from within. Most of these changes, as the next chapter will show, have focused youth more intently on the distinctive teachings and practices of historic Christianity. The move from purity to practices within modern American youth ministry came from within churches, not just in response to American culture.

chapter 7

Convergences and Choices

"As the state goes, so goes the church." This cliche, like most, conveys only a half-truth. Youth ministries and American churches were not simply passive while American culture, or "the state," changed dramatically during the last half of the twentieth century. Christians also changed their traditions intentionally, from within; that is, they were changed through what sociologist Edward Shils has called "endogenous factors." "There is something in tradition," writes Shils, "which calls forth a desire to change it by making improvements in it. . . . In each generation a further step forward from the point previously reached is possible." Shils argues that "rationalization," "correction," and the "imagination" serve as the primary endogenous factors through which traditions change. "Rationalization is a process of being made more rational, that is, clearer, more consistent, and more comprehensive" than before. Correction occurs when people attached to a tradition see "defects" in it and move to correct them. Both rationalization and correction "proceed from a state of satisfaction with much of the tradition." Changes in the content of a tradition, or in patterns of adherence to it, occur as people rationalize or correct what has been passed down.[1]

Beyond rationalization and correction, Shils finds the imagination to be the primary endogenous factor causing traditions to change:

> Sometimes the imagination works in an unarticulated manner to add small increments to the received patterns of action and to make small subtractions and elisions. . . . At other times, the imagination . . . engenders large changes in a short time in the circumstances to which multitudes of persons must adapt themselves. . . . Imagination, directly or indirectly, is the great modifier of traditions.[2]

Charismatic figures, for instance, change a tradition by imagining and articulating better ways for it to serve as "the guiding pattern" in people's lives. As new adherents are drawn to the tradition, they in turn change it. Using the example of Jesus, Shils points out that "he had the gift of arousing in others an acknowledgment or attribution of charismatic qualities. . . . He had to have the tradition as his point of departure; he had to have an audience which had the same tradition as its point of departure." Like other rabbis before and since, Jesus imaginatively reconceived the Jewish tradition through story and practice, in ways that led it to find "a reception far beyond Palestine and the Jews."[3]

For the vast majority of people in the United States, Christianity in one of its many forms serves as a guiding pattern, or tradition, in their lives. Like their founder, Christians did not leave tradition unchanged as they experienced the revolutions in modern American politics, economics, and mores. Christians adapted during the American century not only in reaction to these changes but out of the resources of their own streams of the tradition. They imaginatively rationalized and corrected Christianity, changing youth ministries in the process. We will examine two broad areas of change. On the one hand, churches converged. On the other, they offered people choices. Mirroring the centralization of the federal government, but with reasons well grounded in the Christian faith, mainline Protestant, Catholic, Evangelical, and African-American churches cooperated publicly more than at any time in their history, correcting decades (if not centuries) of mutual hostility and competition. This ecumenical movement spawned organic unions of church bodies, interdenominational dialogues, and nondenominational parachurch agencies—including youth ministries—over the past seventy years. The corrections and rationalizations of Christianity in twentieth-century America also went beyond institutional reconfiguration. Christians converged in the ways they undertook missionary work, in commitment to the study of Holy Scripture, in forms of corporate worship, and in their engagement in various forms of social activism. These convergences all affected youth ministry in dramatic ways. Converging, activist churches produced converging, activist youth ministries, dedicated less to denominational or moral purity than to practices of Christian faith in a changing world.

Christians also gave people choices, mirroring the consumer boom of American culture, but again with reasons deeply embedded in the Christian tradition. Churches found resonance within their traditions for an "expressivist" and "therapeutic" ethos, which dominated the era. Often dismissed as cultural accommodation, in fact these changes in Christianity provided people with something Christianity has always sought to provide—personal meaning and significance. Christians also created internally pluralistic churches during the late years of the twentieth century. Many churches built into their institutional structures, for example, an increase in the public roles for women. Finally, Christians were imaginatively active in rethinking their traditions. Across denominations, an explosion of theological writing took place. The most basic symbols and doctrines of Christianity were subject to imaginative revision as Christians turned to diverse social contexts to ground theological reflection. In short, during the last half of the twentieth century, Christian churches increasingly became communities that valued, in varying degrees, personal spiritual expression, pluralistic tolerance, and socially grounded theological reflection.[4] Youth ministries followed suit, providing youth with choices in which practices took precedence over purity.

CHURCHES CONVERGING

The revolutions of the American century were matched by endogenous changes in Christian churches. Churches converged in ecclesiastical structure, world missions, biblical studies, worship, and social activism, not only in reaction to modernity but as a logical expression of their own traditions. As churches converged, boundaries blurred. Youth ministry diversified, not out of weakness or decline but because lines of loyalty were constantly being redrawn. As churches changed from ethnic or denominational enclaves to places for public practices, so did their youth ministries.

Of course, Christians did not agree on everything; as they converged, they often produced heated debate. Their debates helped rationalize and correct the tradition, and kept Christian perspectives and life-paths alive in American public discourse and society. Naturally, there were implications for youth ministry in both the debates and their outcomes. Churches debating the nature of missionary work were churches concerned about how best to send youth—who historically constituted a significant cohort in the missionary corps—into the world. Churches debating how to interpret the Bible were churches that cared about how the stories of the faith were passed on to a new generation. In all cases the Bible was a key part of youth ministry. Churches debating principles and forms of worship and forming new ones were churches that cared about the symbolic forms through which faith was expressed across generations. Finally, churches arguing over which forms of social activism were most intrinsically related to Christianity were churches likely to involve youth in practices, albeit with a number of differing agendas. The turn from purity to practices in modern youth ministry came from changes within churches as well as from without.

The ecumenical movement is the first and most obvious example of how churches converged in twentieth-century America.[5] Christians in America, present in record numbers, cooperated unlike at any time in their history. American Protestants joined the World Council of Churches (WCC) in 1948 and, along with members of Orthodox churches, formed the National Council of Churches (NCC) in 1950.[6] Twelve agencies and twenty-nine denominations were charter members of the NCC, which by 1999 represented about fifty million Christians across the United States.[7] Catholics, although not official members of the WCC or the NCC, were frequently present as observers at ecumenical gatherings and in dialogues throughout the century, especially after Vatican II. Official Protestant observers were invited to this revolutionary council. Such rapprochement between Catholics and Protestants was remarkable after centuries of competition, mistrust, and hostility, if not outright warfare. Evangelicals also did not join the WCC or the NCC, but they did converge in 1943 to form their own ecumenical association, the National Association of Evangelicals (NAE). The NAE was intentionally designed as an alternative to liberal ecumenism, but it provided its four million members with "a level of cooperation similar to that practiced by the 'mainline' churches in the 1920s," according to one observer.[8] The NAE also found many points of agreement with the NCC in the late nineties as Evangelicals became more active in American public life.[9]

Along with these agencies came national and local dialogues and, in some cases, church unions. For example, three groups of Lutherans—including many who had participated in the Walther League—converged in 1988 to form the Evangelical Lutheran Church in America. The church numbered at that time about five million members.[10] Lutherans were hardly alone in the urge to merge. Other mainline groups had preceded them, notably the Congregationalists and German Reformed in 1957 (United Church of Christ), the Methodists in 1968 (United Methodist Church), and Presbyterians in 1987 (Presbyterian Church [U.S.A.]). When joined with the ecumenically active Episcopal Church, these mainline groups represented over eighteen million Christians across the United States.[11] Even when churches chose not to join the NCC or to merge institutionally, they may have engaged in bilateral, trilateral, and even more complex dialogues.[12] In a most notable ecumenical dialogue in the nineties, Lutherans and Catholics discussed the central issue of justification, which had been a sticky theological issue (to put it mildly) for nearly half a millennium.[13] Locally, churches that had once competed for souls now cooperated on food pantries and CROP WALKS for hunger; they even signed "covenants" together and held joint worship services.[14] Churches have converged.

They have done so not only in response to the American century but for reasons intrinsic to Christianity. In *Church Unity and Church Mission,* among the first of his many publications, a former Walther Leaguer, Martin E. Marty, argued in 1964 that churches could and should unite, and indeed had already united in many ways for the sake of the church's mission. He did not mean by "mission" that the church was primarily to "save souls" but, rather, that the church was "to be at the side of the revolutionary and the sufferer, not merely reflecting but molding a new world." Marty found rationale for ecumenism in the prayer of Jesus as recorded in John 17: "I ask . . . on behalf of those who will believe in me . . . that they may all be one." The church needed unity so that it could carry out its mission of transforming the world.[15]

Church convergences often emerged from church missions. They also changed them. Competition in international missions had long seemed a scandal to many missionaries, who, while the twentieth century continued its violent course, grew further chastened as they listened to the voices of indigenous peoples.

Drawing upon historically based biblical scholarship that recognized that Jesus was not a modern American but a first-century Jew, missionaries began to distinguish between the gospel and its cultural manifestations.[16] No longer were missionaries to be covert agents of Americanism; instead they were to offer to indigenous cultures a "Christian presence . . . listening before we speak, . . . involved in the fierce fight against all that dehumanizes, ready to . . . identify with the outcast, merciless in ridiculing modern idols and new myths."[17] The most liberal missiologists—as students of missionary theory are called—encouraged pluralism. That is, they argued that Christian missionaries could and should work together with people of other faiths to address common problems the indigenous people themselves had identified. The goal of a missionary was not to convert individuals but to work with people of many faiths to create a more just and loving world. God's work was humanity's common work, no matter how (or if) the humans used the word *God*.

Evangelicals initially opposed these changes. Billy Graham and others insisted that proselytizing for Christianity abroad was as important as it was at home, and he was reluctant to recognize that Christian proselytizing had in the past been linked to European conquest. Gradually, however, and especially after 1970, Evangelicals also changed the balance between evangelism and social action within their rapidly multiplying missions. Harvard historian William Hutchison explains: "As the evangelical contingent, like its liberal opposite number, held its meetings increasingly in nonwestern locations . . . western evangelicals heard pleas for change more compelling than those they had been hearing, and in general resisting, from western or white-American colleagues. . . . An attitude of penitence . . . [gradually] replaced . . . triumphalism." Not numbers of "souls saved," but "dialogue" and "justice" became Evangelical catchwords.[18] "A self-styled Chosen People were coming to accept their real-world status as . . . a people among peoples," concluded Hutchison.[19] Youth ministries no longer needed to be the ecclesiastical equivalents of armies and navies. They could be occasions for international dialogue between young people across cultures.

Of course, there were exceptions. The most conservative Christian groups—Hutchison called them "oldstyle cultural and religious imperialists"—continued the tradition of "soul-winning." Even among them, however, things had changed. "Some of the most theologically conservative mission groups outdid all others in 'going native' and blending with the local culture," contended

Hutchison. In general, then, "American attitudes and American churches had . . . come a long way since the 1930s. Further maturing along the same lines, whether produced by an internal dynamic or by the pressures of history, would mean that the modern-day American missionary would at last be perceived less as a chaplain to the old imperialism, more as someone intent on maintaining Christian effectuality within the new religious and cultural pluralism."[20] Youth ministries, which had often supplied the churches with eager missionaries, faced a similar prospect. The center of Christian adherence was shifting away from America, in part because of American Christian intent to disentangle Christian faith from American power. What this lost for Christians in cultural influence, it gained for them in ideological and social focus. Youth could concentrate on practicing their faith as Christians, without also making converts to the American way.

If Christians expended energy debating about and changing missions during this period, they nearly exhausted themselves in Biblical studies. Historical-critical study of Scripture—a staple in Europe since the nineteenth century—immigrated to America in the twentieth and found a welcome home. The trend to read Scripture in its context, as reconstructed through archeology, history, and sociology, created both passionate devotees and passionate critics. To some, it seemed to make the Bible fallible. To others, it made the writings of the New Testament believable as the theological reflections of the earliest Christians. In any event, historical study of Christian Scriptures opened the door for the Bible to make its way ("back," some would have it) into American higher education. Following a series of Supreme Court rulings, state colleges and universities began to develop programs or departments of religious studies, and biblical scholarship began to move out of its denominational and parochial enclaves. The Society of Biblical Literature—the leading academic guild for professional exegetes—claimed seven thousand members in 1999, drawn from the many brands of faith and no-faith in American culture. If the Society of Biblical Literature was little known outside the academy, many of its members were not, as popular books informed by scholarship on the Bible became best-sellers.[21] Youth learned about the Bible not only in their churches but at college, or at their local bookstore, or, increasingly, in public schools.[22]

Christians debated about how to interpret their sacred text. Through their often heated arguments, however, churches demonstrated a common commitment to using Scripture in ways honed by Christians over the centuries—as a source of inspiration, as a moral guide, and as a revelation (however understood) of God's intent for humanity. Christians did not only battle over the Bible; they pored over it (often in the original languages of Hebrew, Greek, and Aramaic) to create numerous translations and commentaries. These new versions of the Bible were intended not only to update the archaic English of the King James Version but to correct it. The Revised Standard Version (1952; New Revised Standard Version, 1989) and *The Interpreter's Bible* (1951-1957) became, as intended, standard among mainline Protestant groups and in biblical scholarship.[23] Among Catholics, a flood of critical study of Holy Scripture followed Vatican II, leading to the New American Bible in 1970 and *The Jerome Biblical Commentary*, begun in 1962.[24] Evangelicals came to favor the New International Version (1978) and any number of available commentaries, including some informed by a return of Evangelicals to the academic guilds.[25] In 1930, American Protestant youth were memorizing "thees" and "thous" in church basements from the King James Version. In 1999, they might very well have compared ancient Near Eastern flood myths (including the one with Noah), now translated into modern English and available online, in a high-school class entitled "The Bible as Literature."[26] Churches converged on the importance of serious Scripture study while expanding dramatically the media through which it was available. If youth ministries had multiple and sometimes competing media available to teach about the Bible across generations, they generally agreed that it was important to use them.

Churches—and their youth—also converged on a number of issues related to public worship. A liturgical-renewal movement transformed worship among Catholics and mainline Protestants. Altars, once placed up against walls in the east of the chancel away from the people, so that a priest or presider officiated with his back to the congregation, were moved to the center of churches. Now the priest or presider faced the congregation, thus indicating a renewed understanding of liturgy as "the work of the people," including its youth.[27] Young people served as acolytes, readers, and, in selected cases, preachers. Led by the turn to vernacular worship in the post–Vatican II Catholic Church, Lutherans, Episcopalians, Presbyterians, and Methodists all issued new hymnals and service books that offered worship in vernacular English. All of the books stressed options. "Flexibility and adaptability became favored goals in modern liturgical revision," wrote one historian of worship.[28] Following a series of experiments with "folk worship" in the sixties and seventies, "Christian contemporary music" spread across denominations, especially among Evangelicals. "Professionally trained church musicians felt shouldered aside by guitar-plucking teenagers," noted one not-too-sympathetic observer.[29] Among African Americans, traditional worship forms were often infused by a neo-Pentecostal movement that opened up the service to enthusiastic participation by the laity. Across the board, in short, Americans returned worship to the people, including youth, in the late twentieth century.[30]

Finally, churches converged in turning to activism—on a number of fronts—in the American century.[31] "Church . . . became a place to get things done. A modern church was judged by the activities it kept." Mainline Protestants helped to promote a "'new awakening' to peace issues in the early 1980s," led a "heroic mobilization against hunger at home and abroad during the mid-1970s," and gave a "magnificent showing . . . on desegregation and racial justice" in the sixties, according to one historian.[32] Youth often provided both leaders and followers for these Protestant causes. Catholics, with energy unleashed by the election of John F. Kennedy to the presidency in 1960 and by Vatican II, also entered American public life in unprecedented ways. The National Council of Catholic Bishops released numerous statements articulating Catholic views on pressing public issues, and Catholic laity—including youth—could join any number of activist agencies to address issues from abortion to nuclear disarmament.[33] Evangelicals also joined in the public fray. Ralph Reed, leader of the Christian Coalition, put the impulse well in the title of his recent book *Active Faith*.[34] Reed spoke for only a segment of the Evangelical community, but the impulse he articulated was widely shared. For instance, Evangelicals Millard and Linda Fuller founded the remarkably successful housing ministry Habitat for Humanity and involved thousands of youth in the Campus Chapters and Youth Programs division of the international organization.[35] One of Habitat's bumper sticker friendly mottos expressed the principle around which Christians of many stripes were converging: "Faith must be active in love."[36] For African Americans, activist Christianity was nothing new: their churches had long been places not only of pastoral presence but also of prophetic and political practices.[37] The point should be clear: activist churches produced activist youth ministries. The move from purity to practices within American youth ministry came from endogenous changes in churches, not only from changes "forced" by American culture.

It is impossible to determine the relative weight one should ascribe to the various causes of change within youth ministry. Historically causes intertwine and intermingle. Exogenous and endogenous factors cause changes together, not separately. It is, furthermore, possible to overstate the convergences: we have painted with a broad brush. The case for convergence must be balanced by another part of the story. While converging, churches have also changed by offering their members choices. What one historian called "the lively experiment" of Christianity in the United States continues.[38] Christians found resources within their traditions to embrace the value placed on personal expression, a therapeutic spirituality, and cultural pluralism in late modern America. Christians imaginatively reconceived their streams of the tradition to shape, as well as react to, the American century.

SPIRITUAL CHOICES IN THE MARKET ECONOMY

Along with formal convergences on missions, the Bible, worship, and activism, Christian churches changed to emphasize "spiritual empowerment" of individuals in accord with the expressivist and therapeutic ethos of the market economy. They did so not only to accommodate the culture but because they participated in creating that culture. The links between Christianity and a capitalist market economy are many and complex, as Max Weber recognized some time ago, and the influence has not been one-way. Finding resources within their traditions to do so, Christians encouraged a turn to spirituality during the past half century. While this turn to private meaning eroded denominational identities, it also engaged diverse people in practices of the faith. Women, in particular, experienced new opportunities in the churches, as some denominations corrected years of patriarchy and sexism. Theologies—the products of Christian imagination—multiplied, but they shared a grounding in specific social contexts, and they shared a desire to activate Christians for participation in public life. Youth ministries were, naturally, caught up in these dramatic changes in Christian faith and practice.

Christianity has always intended to empower people, but intent has not always matched reality in eras when ecclesiastical hierarchies were entrenched or orthodoxies rigidly enforced. Neither situation has been present in the past forty years of Christianity in America. An "age of the laity" has dawned, where believers young and old have been given, or have taken, responsibility for the life of their communities. The consequences have been dramatic. Churches have found a welcome place within what religious historian R. Laurence Moore has called America's "commercial culture."[39] Churches have accepted that they must market their meanings and symbols, tailoring them to the needs and desires of religious "consumers." The entire phenomenon of youth ministry is one example of church "niche" marketing. In an effort to meet adolescents where they are, churches have developed specific programs for them.

The marketing of religion has had its detractors. Several decades ago psychologists Philip Rieff and Christopher Lasch penned widely read denunciations of a "triumph of the therapeutic" and a "culture of narcissism" they saw sweeping American religions and culture. Both contended that the self-directed language of psychology had eroded traditional motives for religious commitment and created generations of self-absorbed consumers.[40] More recently, theologian William Placher decried "the domestication of transcendence" as the way "modern thinking about God went wrong."[41] Throughout, sociologists such as Robert Bellah and associates have contended that religion under the sway of market influence has impelled individuals into "a competitive race to acquire . . . [which] minimizes, if it does not neglect . . . altogether . . . any larger moral meaning, any contribution to the common good, that might help it to make sense."[42] They have stressed repeatedly the conflict between the "individualism" of the market and "commitment" to the common good, most notably in *Habits of the Heart*, where they wrote, "We are concerned that individualism may have grown cancerous . . . and may be threatening the survival of freedom itself."[43]

Most recently, however, sociologists such as R. Stephen Warner have unearthed a different view of market-tailored Christianity. "Organized religion thrives in the United States in an open-market system," contends Robert Ellwood.[44] Warner puts it more sharply: "Individualistic tendencies in American religion are consistent with its history" and do not prevent religions from serving as "vehicles of empowerment" for individuals and groups. "U.S. religious institutions are constitutively pluralistic, structurally adaptable, and empowering." But according to Warner, "the empowerment functions of religion are [largely] latent." People may use specifically

religious language and therapeutic theology not so much to retreat
from commitment as to take a necessary step in the transformation
of individuals and traditions where "political empowerment appears [as] a by-product of religion."[45] This process is complex, but
its operation has become apparent in different aspects of American
life. For instance, in a careful study of American holiday celebra-
tions, Leigh Eric Schmidt discerned how twentieth-century Christian "consumers embraced, 'bought', and helped create the market
versions of [American] holidays, imbuing these rites with their
own hopes and desires, recognizing in them resonant and fluid
symbols of love, family, faith, prosperity, and well-being."[46] Despite high-brow disdain of the process, American Christianity has
flourished in the past fifty years by using the market to meet the
spiritual needs and desires of ordinary people. People have continued to find Christianity a source of strength for personal and public life, and Christianity has changed in order to meet people's
needs in terms they will understand. Old boundaries blurred, and
Christianity diffused in the late years of the twentieth century to
provide people plural paths to spiritual meaning.[47] Personal autonomy, including both an enlarged arena of voluntary choice and
an enhanced freedom from structural restraint, became a hallmark
of American Christianity.[48] Youth ministries followed suit, diffusing their earlier emphasis on purity into diverse, if not contradictory, practices.

To see these changes in Christianity as simple accommodation
to the market is to miss again the impulse for change within the
faith itself. Nowhere have these changes been more dramatic, and
better grounded, than in the roles of women within America's
churches. After centuries of being relegated to the home or church
periphery, women began to move toward full participation in
many denominations in the late twentieth century. Although a few
churches ordained women in the nineteenth century, it was not
until after World War II that many began to do so. Congregationalists led the way, but the African Methodist Episcopal Church voted
to ordain women in 1948, and Presbyterians and Methodists followed a decade later. The first Lutheran woman was ordained in
1970, Episcopalians joined the trend (after a long debate) in 1976,
and "the number of ordained women in the mainline denominations grew rapidly in the late 1970s and early 1980s."[49]

These changes were not simply accommodation to market
needs or to a broader secular impulse for women's liberation. They
were grounded in the Christian tradition itself as scholars and

church leaders rationalized and corrected it. A 1964 report from the WCC identified two key theological developments that promoted ordaining women. First, Christians came to recognize that "it is a basic tenet of the New Testament that the whole body [of Christ] is called to witness to the name of Christ; all members—men and women. . . . This basic Christian truth was for many centuries overlaid. It has been rediscovered in our own day by all parts of Christendom." Second, "it is an essential element of the Christian message that men and women are created in the image of God and are therefore of equal dignity and worth."[50] To ground these assertions, biblical scholars examined the Gospels, especially the practices of Jesus, and found a remarkable openness to women on the part of Christianity's founder, while historians unearthed centuries of women in leadership roles as teachers, writers, mystics, and activists.[51] Some Christian groups—most notably the Roman Catholic Church—balked at these rationalizations and corrections of the tradition, but youth ministries were generally sympathetic. Even within Catholicism, youth ministry was an area in which women learned to lead, quite apart from the church's official refusal to ordain them.[52]

All of these changes were grounded in a remarkable efflorescence of American theologies in the late twentieth century. The Christian imagination was highly active during the American century. Beginning with the neo-orthodox movement during World War II, Christian theologies began to take seriously their context. Neo-orthodoxy, represented in the United States by Reinhold Niebuhr, responded to the unprecedented suffering of World War II and the Cold War by urging Christians to take refuge in the sovereign God who "sets limits to our personal and collective megalomania."[53] Other Protestants, many of them informed by Paul Tillich's turn to anthropology and existentialist philosophy, were less resigned to "immoral society" than Niebuhr and the neo-orthodox and advocated a theology that celebrated cities and Christian agency in history and that urged Christians to commit to the struggles of "'being' (war), 'having' (poverty), and 'belonging' (race)."[54]

Within Catholicism, countless voices emerged after Vatican II to "open the window" and spread fresh air throughout the church. Europeans such as Karl Rahner, Teilhard de Chardin, and Hans Küng tackled long forbidden topics, and Americans such as Daniel and Philip Berrigan, Thomas Merton, Rosemary Ruether, and Richard McBrien responded to the injustices and suffering of modernity from a Catholic point of view.[55] Most notable of all, Catholics in Latin America such as Gustavo Guttierez began to develop the liberation theology that mirrored and encouraged African-American theologies, all of which stressed emphatically the mandate of theology to take seriously its social context.[56]

Evangelicals were also active theologically during this period, not only defending traditional Christianity but articulating anew the import of Christianity for the public sphere. Thinkers including Carl Henry, Mark Noll, Gabriel Fackre, and those in the New Right urged Evangelicals to assume a prominent place in public life as an increasingly "minority" voice. Women similarly asserted their distinctive theological perspectives. Feminist, womanist (black female), and "metaphorical" theologies were developed by Catholic, mainline Protestant, and Evangelical Protestant women writers.[57] Any and every topic was open for discussion. God, creation, Jesus, the resurrection, and prayer all came in for serious debate and questioning. The pluralism was bewildering, but the multiple perspectives, in fact, shared a common commitment to context: theology emerged from the life and language of people, and theology mattered for life. This turn to context has linked theory and practice—or praxis, as liberation theologians describe it—in a way unprecedented in Christian history. As theologies turned to praxis, so did youth ministries.

The roots of this turn to context lie in Christian efforts to respond with imagination and compassion to the modern experiences of suffering, using all available tools of modern social sciences joined with the deep spiritual resources of their traditions. Christians have always sought to respond to suffering. That their theologies would do so should hardly be surprising, since these theologies are the closest Christians get to "social-scientific" rationales for their faith. Evangelical theologian Gabriel Fackre writes,

> With new capacities for radical evil or good in human hands, the theological problematic moved from the vertical to the horizontal: from alienation of the sinner from the righteous God to the estrangement of rich and poor, black and white, male and female, young and old, East and West. While other quandaries persist . . . the riveting question of our epoch is human *suffering,* personal and social. . . . The variety of theological views throughout this era testifies to American initiative and creativity.[58]

The Christian imagination has been active in the late years of the twentieth century, rationalizing and correcting the faith on the cusp of a new millennium.

All this dramatic change within America's churches produced, in turn, dramatic changes in American culture. In America, as the churches go, so goes the state. The initiative and creativity of American Christians in the twentieth century helped to end what Yale historian Sidney Ahlstrom called "the great Puritan epoch" in American religious history.[59] Ahlstrom felt that American history from 1558 to 1960 could be conceived of as a whole—as an era when Puritan thought and practices dominated in American religion and culture. From the death in 1558 of Mary Tudor, the last Catholic queen of England, down to the election of Catholic president John F. Kennedy in 1960, Protestants influenced by a Puritan ethos ruled America, not only as presidents and public leaders but by dominating and shaping the everyday institutions and structures of society.

Ahlstrom documented how the Puritan epoch ended slowly, in a glacial rather than a revolutionary movement. A new Catholicism, immigrants from Eastern religions, the activism of African-American churches, and changes within the mainline all contributed to the rise of "post-Puritan America." Changes escalated especially in the sixties, as a "radical turn in religion and morals" dramatically transformed the religious landscape of the United States. Among the causes were the convergences and choices noted in this chapter. Even more significant, however, in ending the great Puritan epoch were the changes in youth ministry and youth cultures. The shift from purity to practices in youth ministry was a key factor in the demise of Puritan America. Youth and youth ministries, as places where generations met to negotiate the future and as marginal spaces where cultural change could occur almost without notice, assisted in ending the great Puritan epoch. Put even more provocatively: Christian youth and youth ministries actively re-created American culture and its churches over the past fifty years. As they turned from purity to practices, Christian youth and youth ministries proved to be catalysts in the creation of a new, post-Puritan America.

chapter 8

Re-Creating America

The great Puritan epoch in American religious history ended in the 1960s, and Christian young people and the youth ministries that served them helped to end it. Throughout that decade and since, young people have resisted traditional purity programs and created activist alternatives. Youth ministries were, since the sixties, a site of negotiation where both resistance and cultural re-creation occurred. The two processes happened simultaneously. As historians Joe Austin and Michael Nevin Willard—among the few to begin forays into the history of young people—point out: "Youth cultures are often at odds with the interlocking network of social forces, representations, and institutions that attempt to control and guide them. . . . Youth have challenged, *innovated*, and redirected social and cultural practices."[1] In the sixties, youth challenged and redirected traditional youth ministries through an innovative trinity of practices that together have come to be summarized as "sex, drugs, and rock 'n' roll." As young people increasingly engaged in sexual relations, experimented with drugs and alcohol, and created new forms of music, they used these practices as rites of passage to mark their "maturity" and to resist incorporation into traditional patterns based on a Puritan ethos. Youth min-

istries were not, as one might expect, unilaterally opposed to
these changes but in fact promoted them, at least indirectly. The
practices of young people—including many Christians who were
involved in youth ministry—signaled the dawn of post-Puritan
America.

Of course, not all American teenagers since the sixties have engaged in promiscuous sex, smoked dope, and listened to the
Stones. The numbers who did are, by and large, impressive—even
among Christians—but they are matched by the number of youth
who engaged in other practices that re-created American culture in
equally dramatic ways. Youth did not only end the great Puritan
epoch by resisting traditional purity preaching through rites of passage of their own creation; they redirected the churches and culture
through other practices as well. Youth ministry has provided a
forum for youth to assert their hopes, dreams, and visions for
America's churches and for American culture. We will examine
four. First, Christian young people had historically been active
as overseas missionaries. Over the past seventy years, Christian
youth helped the church to rethink an old competitive pattern of
missionary work and helped create a church in which internationalist and ecumenically cooperative service took precedence over
conversion-centered, "imperialist" missions. Second, at home,
Christian youth demanded knowledge, and they flocked to colleges and universities that offered them not only material advancement but also information and opportunities to reshape the world
by service. Third, Christian young people also clamored for (and
created through their youth ministries) more "relevant" theologies
and forms of worship, which generally meant theologies and worship forms that addressed human sexuality and "embodiment"
honestly. Gradually, the music and teachings of many churches
changed to accommodate their tastes. Finally, young people joined
the front lines of many activist causes—most notably during the
civil rights movement, in ways that significantly reshaped the
American cultural landscape. Through participation in youth ministries that shifted their focus from purity to practices, American
Christian adolescents re-created America in the latter years of the
twentieth century and helped end the great Puritan epoch.[2]

This chapter is hardly the last word on this topic; I hope
to write another book exploring this hypothesis in greater detail
and using a wider range of evidence, such as biography, autobiog-
raphy, diary, and correspondence. The purpose of this brief chapter is not to prove that religious youth played a key role in

twentieth-century American history but to provoke further study
into the roles Christian young people have played in American cultural history. Youth have, over the past decades, dominated American popular culture in countless ways. Most youth are Christian, at
least nominally and in many cases significantly.[3] Millions have
participated in youth ministry and America's churches. A case,
then, can be made that Christian young people and the youth ministries that served them played a key role in ending the great Puritan epoch in American religious history. We will begin with the
way youth have shaped for themselves rites of passage involving
sex, drugs, and rock 'n' roll, and then will turn to four other ways
Christian young people and youth ministries re-created America
over the past seventy years. The story is not a romantic one of
youth succeeding in leading America to new glory. In fact, adolescents have been among the victims of the quiet revolution they
have wrought.

THE "SACRIFICE" OF YOUTH IN MODERN AMERICA: RITES
OF PASSAGE IN AMERICAN POPULAR CULTURE

Youth have resisted the purity programs designed for them by
churches and other cultural institutions by acting in ways that directly contradict these programs. They have often been motivated
to do so as they observed adult hypocrisy. One young woman, noticing the sexual double standard for women in the early twentieth
century, exclaimed, "The hypocrisy, and phoniness, and pretense—
women must have been enraged!"[4] A young man complained to
Harvard psychologist Robert Coles about American violence and
corruption: "Did *we* invent war and crookedness and corruption?
All this sleaze today—look where it's coming from. . . . There are a
lot of hypocrites around."[5] A third member of Generation X ech-
oed the refrain in slightly different terms: "The buzz in the background, every minute of our lives, is that detached, ironic voice
telling us: 'At least, you're not faking it, as they did, at least you're
not pretending, as they did.' "[6]

Youth have contradicted adult preaching of purity not only
with their voices but with their behavior. By being sexually active,
by experimenting with drugs and alcohol, and by creating and consuming alternatives to classic Euro-American culture, youth test
their abilities to participate in what they perceive unvarnished
adult culture to be like. This testing fits the classic pattern for rites

of passage as developed initially by Arnold van Gennep and refined by Victor Turner and others, according to which there are three stages: separation from the community of origin, a period of testing or trial (called "liminality"; literally, "being-on-the-threshold"), and, finally, reincorporation with recognition of new status.[7] Sexual activity, drug experimentation, and rock 'n' roll subcultures all involve youth in liminal tests that challenge their ability to engage in "adult" behaviors.

Over the past seventy years, adolescents in America have become increasingly sexually active. The numbers are obvious. Data for earlier years are hard to come by, but as late as 1960, only 27 percent of eighteen-year-olds reported having had sexual intercourse. By 1987 that number had nearly doubled to 52 percent. In 1995 the number was 66 percent. Numbers were slightly lower when eighteen-year-old students were asked in 1995 if they had experienced intercourse in the past three months: only half responded in the affirmative.[8] Nevertheless, the number of virgins in America's high schools dropped dramatically during the past half century.

The broad context for this change is important. The sexual revolution of the sixties took place in the midst of the other revolutions of the American century. Historian Beth Bailey explains:

> It is easy to forget how rigidly controlled sex was in the postwar era, and how closely a woman's value was linked to her sexual morality. The sexual revolution was not just about the right to have sex with a stranger met at a singles' bar and to depart the next morning uncommitted and guilt free. It was also about the right of unmarried people to express love sexually, and centered around a rejection of the understanding that equated a woman's value with her "virtue."[9]

In this light, the way youth ministries created leadership roles for women becomes significant, as does the way youth ministries routinely brought together members of the opposite sex. Youth ministries—like high schools—became places where adolescents could meet and court with relatively minimal adult supervision and where women could gain experience as leaders. All of the youth organizations intended to promote meeting of the sexes and involved women as speakers and leaders. The Walther League universally held "mixed meetings," as did YFC groups and African-American churches. The YCW movement initially segregated sexes but changed to mixed-gender meetings in the late fifties to "capitalize on the natural tendencies" of youth. No one has yet explored how these opportunities for peer interaction, provided by churches, contributed to the sexual revolution or how youth ministries helped to propel women into leadership positions in the church and culture. My hypothesis is that they did.

The sexual revolution was not, however, only or even primarily about the "right" to have intercourse. Teens wanted power, and sexuality was one way to find it.

> The sexual revolution was not only about sex. It was about the struggle for power and for freedom, equality, and autonomy—a struggle in which sex played a key role. The struggles between the sexes . . . took place in so many spheres . . . the boundaries blur. . . . Freedom made courtship less certain. It undermined the rules. . . . Conventions are no longer so coherent, their meaning no longer so clear. . . . Living together has become a conventional step in the path to marriage and an acceptable arrangement on its own terms. Sexual intercourse is a conventionally assumed part of long-term relationships (even among teenagers, for better or worse), and a clear possibility on first dates.[10]

Many of these changes are loudly protested, especially by conservative churches, but churches have, through youth ministry, also provided teens with some power. They have not, by and large, been successful in promoting sexual abstinence.[11]

Adolescent sexuality is often about power. Young people, of course, express desire and intimacy through sexual behavior, but they also use sexuality to demonstrate their "adult" status. A recent survey of adolescent males and females between the ages of thirteen and fifteen discovered that nearly two-thirds of those who engaged in sexual intercourse did so primarily because they wished to gain popularity and impress their friends.[12] One high schooler reported, "The guys say how many girls they did it with. With the girls, it's *who* they did it with."[13] For evidence of this pattern of status seeking through sex among older teens, we can recall the Spur Posse, a sex–for–points "club" uncovered in 1993 in Lakewood, California. Boys in the Posse, named for their favorite basketball team, the San Antonio Spurs, competed to collect points, with one point being scored for each orgasm with a different girl. The winner had accumulated sixty-six points.[14]

Adults were not unaware of this competition. One father of a Posse member compared his son to Wilt Chamberlain, who claimed to have had sex with twenty thousand different women. Another claimed that "there wouldn't be enough jails in America if boys were jailed for doing what he has done." A third boasted that his son was now "all man."[15] Sex was a rite of passage through which this teenager earned the title "man." His rite of passage had been completed. This incident is not isolated if one listens to the voices of youth and reflects on the statistics. Sex for adolescents is as often a quest for status as it is an expression of intimacy. Psychologist Mary Pipher concludes, "Losing virginity is considered a rite of passage into maturity."[16]

A wildly popular 1994 song by Trent Reznor of Nine Inch Nails vividly described the religious, or ritual, character of much adolescent sexuality. Youth sang the lyrics out loud on the dance floors or in their cars, shouting out the vulgarities when the radio or DJ censored them. The song is entitled "Closer," and its lyrics are graphic:

> you let me violate you, you let me desecrate you
> you let me penetrate you, you let me complicate you
> help me I broke apart my insides, help me i've got no soul to sell
> help me the only thing that works for me, help me get away from myself
> I want to fuck you like an animal
> I want to feel you from the inside
> I want to fuck you like an animal
> my whole existence is flawed
> you get me closer to god

Youth have discovered what adults know: sex and spirituality are closely connected. America's churches and youth ministries may not have taught this fact explicitly to youth, but some church leaders did, over the past few decades, relax considerably an earlier moralism and encourage the integration of sexuality and spirituality.[17] Churches also brought young men and women together, and gave them power within their own small groups. Almost any youth group meeting is sexually charged, as practitioners from the field routinely report.[18] Youth ministries, then, at the least provided occasions for youth to learn the power of sexual expression. Even when they were taught purity, the statistics demonstrate that youth often resisted and turned to practices.[19] Some young people discovered the hard way that "adult" behaviors have often violent consequences. America's youth have suffered through rapes and abortions, and they have had to grow up quickly as teenaged parents.

If sexual activity is one rite of passage modern American youth have turned to as a way to resist traditional purity programs, so too is drinking and experimentation with illicit drugs. The numbers again tell the story, although this time they do not indicate dramatic increase but steady experimentation. The first reliable national data stem from 1975, when 45 percent of high-school seniors reported having used an illicit drug over the past year. Marijuana predominated; 40 percent of the whole sample reported using it. Between 1975 and 1995, numbers of users dropped slightly. Thirty-six percent reported using an illicit drug in 1995, with marijuana again the leading choice, at 30 percent.[20] These numbers hardly indicate an epidemic worthy of the multibillion-dollar "war on drugs" of the past two decades; they do indicate a significant drug-using subculture among youth.[21]

Alcohol is another story. In 1975, 68 percent of high-school seniors reported alcohol consumption in that year. In 1995, the number was 76 percent.[22] Binge drinking—having five or more drinks in a row—reached a high of 41 percent in 1980 but remained at 30 percent in 1996.[23] Experts suggest three reasons for these numbers. First, youth use drugs to seek community. As they break away from parents, adolescents begin to establish their first adult relationships, based upon choice. Youth look to peers as much as to parents for life-paths. Thus, "drug use by adolescents is frequently associated with drug-using peers."[24] Teens imitate each other's practice of drug and alcohol consumption in an effort to fit in among the "adultlike" friends they have chosen. Second, youth use drugs to tranquilize the turbulence of adolescence: drugs help them cope with the conflicts and crises they experience growing up. They choose drugs to cope because they have ample evidence of this practice from their parents, who have turned to taking drugs to deal with everything from baldness to real (or imagined) aches and pains. Finally and most significant, youth use drugs to seek sensations. Psychologist Marvin Zuckerman writes, "the term 'sensation-seeking' was defined as the need for varied, novel, and complex sensations and experiences and the willingness to take physical and social *risks* for the sake of such experience."[25] Youth use drugs and alcohol, rather obviously, to get high.

So do adults. Teenagers imitate what they see in adult culture when they take drugs and consume alcohol. There are, then, not surprisingly, ritualistic behaviors associated with both practices. Teenagers usually consume alcohol before dances, parties, or dates, which are courting rituals in their own right. Games might be played—bar dice, quarter toss, or others—that deflect attention from the actual practice (and the amount consumed) and help build community. All rituals, especially rites of passage, seek to create community. Anthropologist Victor Turner identifies *communitas*—

defined as a feeling of "oneness" with fellow initiates—as a key part of a rite of passage.[26] Youth seek *communitas* through alcohol in imitation of what they see happening regularly among adults, who consume gallons of fermented spirits at social occasions.

Use of harder drugs is even more ritualized than use of alcohol. Anthropologist Terry Williams spent a year observing behavior in New York City's crackhouses: "The way the drug is prepared, the language that is used, the bartering of sex for drugs, and the business of smoking are very much the same throughout the city's crackhouses. This is not ritual perpetuated for the obvious purpose of getting high; it serves some intrinsic . . . purpose. The ritual is used to focus attention, to help create a situation that allows total absorption."[27] This is religious language, parallel in many ways to the ideals of faith. Believers are to have their attention focused during worship and to be totally absorbed in their experience of God and in the life of faith. The parallels are drawn explicitly, if negatively, by drug users. One crack addict called her pipe "the devil's dick, because the more you smoke the more you want."[28] More generally, the symbolic language for the sensation produced by drug use, "getting high," has obvious resonance with the Christian tradition's tendency to identify God as a sky god and to locate heaven "up there." In short, drug use for many adolescents is a rite of passage. They know it is dangerous. The risk is part of the lure as they seek to experience intense sensation; indeed, the risk constitutes a key element in the test of their survival ability as adults. Binge drinking makes sense in this context. Youth binge because they want to prove their capacity to consume; they want to demonstrate their ability to be an adult.

Youth are on the cusp of the adult awareness of mortality. They may routinely act as if they are immortal, blithely ignoring the negative consequences of their actions, but most also perceive the impending end of childhood and seek ways to cope with it. One young woman reports, "I specifically pursued substances, because I wanted to separate myself from my past." Such separation is the first phase in any rite of passage. A young man claims, "When I was in the altered states . . . intoxicants provided, I felt like I could do or be anything I wanted." Such is the experience of *communitas* or being on the threshold. And a third young person explained, "I was not willing to face my past and myself quite yet. I sought to escape through drugs and alcohol."[29] By using drugs and alcohol, young people simultaneously defy death and separate themselves from adult control of their childhood past, but they do so through ritualized means well legitimized (at least since 1930 and the end of Prohibition) within adult culture.

It would be perverse to suggest that youth ministries are responsible for drug and alcohol experimentation among America's youth, and of course, it must be pointed out that some youth fall from experimentation with drugs into abuse. Some do not survive the test. Furthermore, no Christian youth minister in America would keep her job if it became known that she shared a joint with her youth group as they sang "Pass It On" around a campfire. Still, most drug users are middle-class, and many are at least nominally Christian: they have the money to support experimentation. It may not be far from true, then, to suggest that youth (including Christians) seek, through drug use, to experience what adults hope Christianity would provide them: experiences of community that help them cope with anxiety and that give them a sensation of transcendence in the midst of mundane reality. Drug and alcohol use offers teens a more intense and physical test than most youth ministries but not one that is radically different in symbolic function. Drugs serve as a rite of passage for many American teens.

Finally, then, that rock 'n' roll can function for teens as a rite of passage should be apparent to anyone who has attended a rock concert. Rock concerts are *communitas* fests. At them, young people (and some not so young) dance, sing, and touch indiscriminately, lifting each other aloft (and dropping each other) as they "mosh" to the music. These ritualized behaviors at concerts make sense when it is remembered that the roots of theater and drama are in religion.[30] It should therefore be no surprise that the entertainment cultures created by and for young people can provide them with both a sense of community and a test of their adult status. Music has power, and by creating and consuming their own music, youth assert their claims to power. Initially, rock 'n' roll was perceived by adult authorities as dangerous. It emerged out of the spirituals, gospel blues, and jazz from the margins of American culture, as a language of humane, even soulful, resistance to mainstream culture. It was created for and by young people. To "rock around the clock" was a ritualized way to assert youthful independence from adult control and to practice pleasure (or at least dancing) independent of adult prohibitions.

Rock has become part of mainstream American culture. The music is ubiquitous—on the radio and television, in films and videos, at sporting events, and in churches. What once was the music of resistance has become the music of America. The mediated rites of passage of American culture have also become increasingly complex. Today, for instance, rock music and video images combine to constitute the cutting edge of how entertainment cultures serve as rites of passage for teens. That these media have been used by adults to exploit adolescent fears and hopes almost goes without saying.[31] The phenomenon of the "cinema of adolescence" will illustrate the point.

Since 1950, teenagers have become the biggest consumers of film in the United States.[32] For a Hollywood production to succeed, it must market itself to this audience, especially to adolescent males. One way Hollywood has done so is by producing a genre known as "splatter" or "gore" films, or, more broadly, "horror and adventure" films, which combine graphic violence with rock music soundtracks. Teens flock to these films to terrify themselves. The best-studied example of this genre is *Halloween* (1978, with eight sequels, the last in 1998), but there have been countless imitators, including *Friday the 13th* (1980, with nine sequels), *Prom Night* (1980, with four sequels), *Graduation Day* (1981), and, most recently, *Scream* (1997; two sequels so far).

All of these films focus on youth in crisis, usually in some ritual context (Halloween, prom night, graduation day). The plots are highly stylized. At least three bloody murders, usually many more, occupy the ninety minutes or so of screen time. Most of the murders are graphically depicted, often with a first-person camera angle, where the viewer sees the murder through the eyes of the killer. Youth are depicted as isolated from adults, as driven by sexual desire, and as hapless and unwitting victims of brutal violence—often inflicted by teens themselves. As Roger Ebert put it in his review of *Friday the 13th, Part II*, the "primary function of teenagers" in these films "is to be hacked to death."[33]

Alternatively, however, a primary function of teenagers in these films is to hack each other to death. Realizing this variant reading of the film—that teens are hackers as well as hacked—is the key to seeing how attendance at them can function as a rite of passage. *Halloween* and other films in the horror-adventure genre crystallize teen fears that they will in fact be "sacrificed" in modern America as their elders keep hold on their secure economic places and sexual privileges.[34] The films routinely depict teens getting killed for having sex, for choosing adult pleasure over adult responsibility. The viewers, however, all survive. Every person who bought a ticket to the film walks out alive. Thus teens who attend these films invariably identify not primarily with the victims but with the killers. The first-person camera angle makes this explicit, as does teen behavior at the films, where the murderers are often applauded. Youth participate (voyeuristically) in the ritual sacrifice of some of their peers. That the killing is a ritual is obvious: no one really dies. The actors are all symbols, playing a role. The young actors who "die" in these films represent rivals of the viewers at the altar of adulthood. Adults themselves are generally absent from the films, which thus represent to youth the fact that they are largely on their own to negotiate their transition into adulthood. *Halloween* and other films in the horror-adventure genre test youthful willingness to imitate the hidden (but looming) adult prerogative to use violence to solve problems in the modern world.[35]

Youth, of course, pay for this rite. These films—and rock 'n' roll generally—are now huge businesses in America. My point is not to scapegoat them—they are hardly the root cause of teen violence. My point is a simpler one: American popular culture provides youth with rites of passage that allow them to demonstrate their willingness and ability to endure whatever sacrifice is necessary to enter adult status. Adults in America practice violence in all kinds of institutionalized and legitimized ways. It would be odd, indeed, if we as a culture did not create some way to mark for youth the violence they have to be prepared to endure as adults. Hollywood producers and rock 'n' roll stars have met youth's demand for rites of passage into American violence. They have become like the shamans of old. They tell stories of horror to teens isolated around images flickering from a fire, or sing songs to them of violence and abuse through the loneliness of Sony Walkmans.[36] The cinema of adolescence, and rock 'n' roll more generally, have become ways to exploit the desires of young initiates as they are embroiled in the long liminality between child and adult in the United States. These cultural products test teen worthiness to be incorporated into the tribe of consumers, a tribe whose practices include war making, crime and punishment, racism, sexism, and more. American Christians have not created this tribe alone. They are among its members.

Youth ministries have, again, not been responsible for the turn to sex, drugs, and rock 'n' roll as rites of passage among American teenagers, but they have contributed. The turn from purity to practices in American youth ministry matches well the expressed desires of youth for autonomy and power, articulated through sexual and substance experimentation. Similarly, the way churches have tailored their message to the market economy and the way Christians have given at least tacit support for all kinds of legitimized violence mesh well with the tests offered to youth by rock 'n' roll. The demands of youth, the accommodation to those demands by youth ministries, and developments in American pop culture together ended the great Puritan epoch in American religious history. Still, this is only half of the story. No Christian youth ministry has explicitly encouraged youth to have promiscuous sex, to smoke crack, or to hack each other to pieces. The ministries have, in fact, cultivated other ways for youth to be tested that meet the desires of young people for community, for transcendent sensations, and for danger. In the process, they have involved youth in practices that have transformed America's churches and cultures in ways that do not exploit youth or invite their participation in destruction and violence but that engage them in a community seeking nothing less than the re-creation of America through the power of love.

RE-CREATING AMERICA

Christian youth and youth ministries remade their churches and American culture in at least four ways that go well beyond the stereotype of youthful sexuality, drug use, and rock 'n' roll. First, youth have been active in ecumenical endeavors and in national and international service. Second, they demanded knowledge and supported institutions that offered to them not only facts but meaningful passages into the future. Third, youth in a variety of ways reshaped ecclesiastical practice and theology. They expressed their sexual fears and hopes, experimented with worship styles, participated in sports, and enjoyed nature in ways that helped lead the church toward an incarnational theology in which the body became a key focus of theological reflection. Finally, youth led churches in a number of activist causes, most notably the civil rights movement. Participation in these tests—of service, knowledge, praise, and action—helped youth re-create America's churches and culture while emphatically ending the great Puritan epoch in American religious history.

Youth have been notable experimenters with religious dialogue across denominations and cultures. High schools and colleges are hotbeds of religious pluralism, after all—and youth do not generally have long experience or vested interest in maintaining institutional structures. Youth have often pushed churches to reject old boundaries and create new communities. For instance, adolescents have participated in the international ecumenical movement. Youth began meeting ecumenically well before the founding of the WCC in 1948, notably at an international youth gathering in 1939 at Amsterdam. There, reports one observer, young Christians "broke down dividing walls of denomination, culture, history and race and strengthened the hidden bonds of a world-wide fellowship."[37] At the founding of the WCC in 1948, youth were present to help create a Youth Department as part of the council. This agency eventually sponsored a wide range of programs, such as camps, leadership-training events, intercultural meetings, interdenominational dialogues, and youth service opportunities. The latter resulted "from numerous requests received from young people who desired to give a short period of voluntary, unskilled service wherever there was need." Youth became increasingly active in the WCC during the sixties. One observer recalled that "the political enthusiasm, the ecumenical iconoclasm and the quest for radical Christian ethics of youth reached their climax at the Uppsala Assembly [of the whole WCC in 1968]." Youth sat in, walked out, and otherwise vocally made their presence known. "Youth wanted action in the world," and they were convinced that "disunity among Christians is caused by basic human conflicts." Youth argued that "the churches should render a common service to the poor, the suffering, and the exploited of the world and so demonstrate that they maintain the same apostolic faith, proclaim the same gospel, break the same bread, and unite in common prayer."[38] Since that explosive meeting, the WCC has, not surprisingly, sought to integrate youth into its various agencies and bureaus. The understanding of ecumenism articulated by those youth in 1968 has also come to be widely shared across ecumenical Christendom, as we saw in chapter 7. In short, young people "were deeply involved in . . . the renewal of the church," as Philip Potter, one of the early directors of the WCC Youth Department, points out.[39]

Were it an isolated incident, this ecumenical leadership by youth in the WCC could be dismissed as an aberration, but similar patterns crop up in the national and local records, including those of the selected groups we have already studied. In chapter 1 we met Linda Gerling Schroeder, who attended an international ecumenical assembly in 1960 and who reported back to the *Walther League Messenger* on "the pain of disunity." We also noted that the Walther League leaders pioneered in Lutheran ecumenism by retiring the

venerable *Walther League Messenger* in the early sixties and by re-
placing it with publications jointly produced by three Lutheran
church bodies, which more than two decades later would merge
many of their members. In chapter 2, we learned that YCW members were well prepared for the ecumenical openness created by
Vatican II. One participant recalled, "Vatican II was never a big surprise for me, because it was what we had been talking about for
years in YCW."[40] In chapter 3, we saw how YFC, though solidly
Evangelical, was intentionally a nondenominational movement.
Youth for Christ groups welcomed any comers, and young Catholics and mainline Protestants have joined the Evangelicals in their
high school Bible clubs and at summer camps. African American
youth were similarly bold in boundary crossing: many were members of mainline, Evangelical, or Catholic churches, and many predominantly black churches welcomed young white visitors or
members.[41] In short, Christian youth were often boundary crossers
in the past few decades, and youth ministries were often sites of
ecumenical convergence on both the national and the international levels.

Youth were not alone on the ecumenical vanguard. There is no
need to romanticize their contribution to recognize its significance. A WCC document put it well. On the one hand, "youth can
experiment courageously and dangerously with traditions and reject inherited value systems." On the other hand, "the search for
security can make [adolescents] ruthlessly egocentric and conservative."[42] In ecumenical circles, the experimenters prevailed. Writing in 1985, ecumenical activist Ans Joachim van der Bent opined,

> Young people are deeply aware of and oppose the increasing
> intransigence, irrationality and inhumanness of concentrated
> political, economic, technological, and military power which
> undergirds the doctrine of national security. They also expose
> and resist the mysterious powers of ecclesiastical institutions, so
> far only partly demythologized. Christian youth searches and
> yearns for a power which absorbs "powerful power" rather than
> counters power with power.[43]

Youth who sought "powerful power" may have chosen to be
active in one of the many ventures of national and international
service sponsored in the late twentieth century by both secular
agencies and churches. They may also have joined in nonviolent
protests against "the establishment." Youth manned the work
camps of the Civilian Conservation Corps in the thirties, they
joined the Peace Corps and Vista in the sixties, and today they

serve as Americorps volunteers.[44] Churches have, as we have noted, enlisted youth in various volunteer ventures that have proven to be very popular. The Lutheran Volunteer Corps, the Jesuit Volunteer Corps, World Vision, Habitat for Humanity, and many others explicitly challenge young people to national and international service.[45] Millions have accepted the call and spent a year or two or more actively working for justice, living in intentional faith-based communities, and otherwise reshaping local communities around the globe. They have done so to christianize the world not into any nineteenth-century "muscular Christianity" where numbers mattered more than substance but into a Christianity based in practice that was comfortable with pluralism. Where youth have been active as volunteers, democratic dialogue and social service has often prevailed over conversion or colonialism.[46] Young people, including many Christians, led the protests against American involvement in Vietnam and have insistently called for a more loving America.[47] They have thus been catalysts to christianize America in the late twentieth century, in populist and pluralist, if not Puritan, ways.[48]

Youth also demanded knowledge, and churches (and the culture) met their demands. The Walther Leaguers flocked to Lutheran universities such as Valparaiso, Catholics attended Notre Dame or one of the many Loyolas, Evangelicals populated Wheaton or Calvin, African Americans went to Spelman or Morehouse, and young people of all religious stripes went to the relatively affordable state schools, whose populations boomed.[49] Numbers alone hardly tell the story of how these young people transformed their campuses. Colleges gave up, some slowly, others dramatically, on the ideal of *in loco parentis*, according to which college administrators and faculties had parental responsibilities to keep youth pure. Teaching—long a hierarchical transmission of knowledge from an expert to a pupil, gave way to dialogical teaching, where students were engaged with faculty as active learners. Finally, a wide range of internships and service-learning opportunities further expanded the walls of the classroom, at the demand of students for "relevant" teaching that would prepare them for places in public life.[50]

Not all of these changes were inspired by student demand, and historian Beth Bailey has authored an important caution against romanticizing "youth" as the key agent in social change. Young people acted to create changes in colleges, Bailey points out, but "they did not frame their actions primarily through the construct of youth. Instead . . . students were participating in a larger struggle over the shape of American society, one that pitted concepts of individual growth against traditional moral strictures in the search for a citizenry capable of sustaining democracy in an increasingly complex world."[51] Youth—including Christians—have hardly been in agreement on the issues they have faced; they have, however, acted in ways that have transformed higher education and American culture over the past decades, often in radical ways.[52]

Indeed, college itself serves as a rite of passage now undertaken by the majority of American youth. Psychologists Miriam Dror and Flynn Johnson write,

> While we might like to believe that young people arrive at college having completed the "turmoil" of their adolescent years, what we know, of course, is that though they've been through turmoil, this has not delivered them into adulthood. In fact, in our culture the years of adolescence and youth span over an enormous period of time with few if any points of conclusion, let alone celebration of entry into a recognizable and welcoming community of adults. The college years . . . can serve as a means to create a passage.[53]

There is, again, no need to romanticize or homogenize youth—Christian or otherwise—to recognize how they have, by their numbers, voices, and actions, re-created American higher education over the past seven decades.

Youth have also re-created churches by forcing them to be open to issues regarding sexuality and the body in ways unthinkable in the recent past. We have already noted how youth ministries were "marriage bureaus," but as the age of marriage has been increasingly postponed in America, more direct issues of sexual responsibility have found their way into many church youth programs. The Walther League, YCW, and African-American churches all sought to teach young people sexual responsibility as they faced contemporary sexual activity and problems such as teenage pregnancy and sexually transmitted diseases. And as already suggested, leadership in youth groups paved the way for many women to seek ordination or other leadership roles in the church, although any conclusion to such a suggestion would have to await the careful study of biographies and autobiographies.

Even Evangelicals, long committed to traditional sexual purity, have begun to emphasize rules less and responsibility more. Tony Campolo, a leading Evangelical speaker at youth gatherings, contends that "instead of looking at biblical texts that either condemn or affirm sexual activities, it may be more useful to explore how the Bible instructs young people to view those persons with whom they become romantically involved." Utilizing Jewish theologian Martin Buber's "I-Thou" understanding of personal relations, Campolo concludes, "If the 'other person' in a romantic relationship is viewed as a mystical incarnation of God, then the two people will respect what they say and do to each other. Exploitation . . . will be out of the question. . . . Sexual interaction suddenly possesses a sacred dimension."[54] Today mainline, Catholic, Evangelical and African-American churches have all been confronted with the increasing sexual precocity of their youth, and according to *Youthworker Update*, "virtually all groups agree that some sort of sexual education needs to be taught to youth."[55] This virtual agreement stems from a vital fact: youth not only re-create, they procreate America.

More substantively, youth programs during this period have almost universally favored (even if they have not articulated it as such) an incarnational theology focused on personal experience and human needs, especially those of the body.[56] Given the changes puberty brings about and the heightened self-awareness that comes with bodily maturation, this should be no surprise. Yet it is, perhaps, surprising to observe the degree of uniformity, in both theoretical and practical emphases on the body, in Christian work with youth across the United States during this period. Walther Leaguers encountered Christ inasmuch as they offered food to, built houses for, or visited others to meet their physical needs. Members of YCW expressly articulated a theology of the Mystical Body of Christ, which, although a metaphor, was nevertheless carnal. Campers at Word of Life sang "Kum Ba Ya" ("Come by here"), recognizing the presence of God among them as they sat together around a crackling fire. And Kathleen Wilson extended the gospel to Ali Nurse through the medium of a pint of Monster Cookies ice cream. Theologies can be practiced as well as preached, and preaching is invariably shaped by practices. Christian youth have, at the least, had ample occasion to experience an incarnational "theology of the body" over the past seven decades, and they have, in many ways, put it into practice.[57]

For instance, they have played sports and games. A theology of the body at risk—call it a theology of the cross—was practiced by young Lutherans each time they jumped off the ground to reach for a rebound in a Walther League basketball game. Catholics had similar opportunities. A young Catholic linebacker at Notre Dame may have "observed, judged, and acted" in ways not intended by

Cardinal Cardijn, but that he re-created both Christians and the culture was obvious to those who saw, and cheered or booed, his actions. That there is a danger in this path of theological formation goes without saying; sports can easily be exploited, and youth in sports can turn their theology of the body at risk into a theology of glory.[58] But countless Christian (and other) athletes have, over the past few decades, re-created American culture almost daily to the tune of packed stadiums and huge television audiences, where an incarnational theology oscillates (as most theologies do) between other-directed love and self-interested pursuit.

Perhaps the most obvious way that youth have re-created American culture and churches through an incarnational theology is music. Rock was widely condemned by Christians in its earliest years for the "sensuality" it supposedly endorsed. Now it is becoming a regular feature in worship across Christian traditions. Walther Leaguers invited Pete Seeger to their national gathering in 1965, and the children of YCW members can listen to the Holy Father, of all people, on a "world music" CD.[59] The YFC members attend concerts by Christian bands such as Jars of Clay and DC Talk, and African-American youth can listen to CDs by church-based hip-hop artists such as Kirk Franklin and Philip Hammond. The examples could be multiplied endlessly, in youth programs and local churches across the country. In many venues, youth themselves create or contribute to contemporary music for worship, through choirs and ensembles that let them test their skills and lead a congregation in praise. The music of resistance is being christianized by youth, who seek to "use it for good," as an author in *Youthworker* put it.[60] That rock has re-created American popular culture is obvious; that it can be a practice of incarnational theology should be apparent to anyone who listens to it with ears or plays it with fingers or lips.

The incarnational theology favored by (and for) youth has, in some venues, been extended beyond bodies to include the stuff of bodies—matter or nature itself. Although she did not do so, Catherine Albanese could very easily have studied Christian youth camping as a potent venue for the "nature religion" she found widespread in American religious history.[61] Obviously, hiking, camping, and swimming are not only physical activities; they take youth directly into contact (and sometimes into a contest) with the elements. While hiking through a breathtaking Colorado meadow, an Evangelical youth once exclaimed to her counselors, "We don't have the teensiest chance against God out here! You guys have got it rigged."[62] Camping not only brought youth out of cities; it brought them into contact, many came to feel, with God.

If the ways youth re-created American churches and culture through an incarnational theology appear somewhat diffuse and indirect, there is no mistaking what happened during the civil rights movement. Historian and sociologist Vincent Harding puts it eloquently in words that deserve to be quoted at length:

> [Young people] were in Little Rock, Arkansas, entering the school under the protection of the National Guard—but with no protection at all in the classrooms, locker rooms, and lavatories. . . . They sat in at lunch counters, knelt-in at churches, waded-in at beaches, slept-in at motels, and courageously took the punishment such a struggle required in hundreds of cities and smaller towns. . . . Young people were the heart of the movement. . . . They rode buses, and their vulnerable lives demanded that the federal government enforce its own laws. . . . Strengthened by faith and by one another . . . they continued to move forward, convinced they were working for the truth of a people, nation, and their own individual integrity. . . . Eventually, their courage and determination—and blood—forced their government to defend democracy, made it possible for everyone in America to have the freedom to ride, to sit, to eat, to go to the restroom, just about wherever they wanted. . . . Suddenly it strikes us: It was a phalanx of children, teenagers, and young adults who did so much to break the back of the deadly, generations-old system of legal segregation.[63]

Put far less poetically, the civil rights movement depended upon young Freedom Riders, the Student Nonviolent Coordinating Committee, youthful leaders of the Southern Christian Leadership Conference such as Jesse Jackson, and thousands of other adolescents from Baptist, Presbyterian, Methodist, and all sorts of churches. Walther Leaguers marched alongside African Americans in Chicago and had rocks and bottles thrown at them, Young Christian Workers were kicked out of segregated restaurants, YFC readers of *Sojourners* carry on the battle against racism today, and the parents of African-American youth currently in the Yoke Fellows in Discipline have literal and figurative scars to show for the dangers they faced in the struggle to re-create an America that lived up to its promises.

Harding has documented how the activism of youth and others during the civil rights movement transformed not only the structure but the meaning of the U.S. Constitution. "They nurtured the nation toward democracy," he writes of the Student Nonviolent Coordinating Committee, which more than any other single

group organized voter registration drives for "black southern bed-
rock communities." While imprisoned for their efforts, these students sang the Christian songs they learned as children:

> This little light of mine
> I'm gonna let it shine
> I've got the light of freedom
> I'm gonna let it shine
> Right in this jailhouse
> I'm gonna let it shine, let it shine, let it shine, let it shine.

Insistently, Harding points out, young people "demanded that the
focus of the Fourteenth Amendment be taken off fictitious persons
called corporations and turned toward real persons, faithful citizens, who needed justice, defense, and liberty."[64] This attention to
the person was nowhere more evident than in the nonviolence of
the movement. Christian nonviolent resistance, led by young
people, re-created America.

To recognize that youth and youth ministries contributed to
re-creating American culture is not, again, to romanticize them but
simply to acknowledge something that has, by and large, been
missing from the historical record to date. Like all of us, youth have
had their problems. Historically, they have often been marginalized and silenced, if not sacrificed. They have also been belliger-
ent and demanding. Youth can be saints and sinners, and usually
are a little of both. Historians need neither to glamorize nor to
treat condescendingly the contributions of young people to America's churches and cultures. But before they can do either, they have
to recognize that young people and the institutions that serve them
have made a contribution to history. This chapter has been a modest beginning. To study Christian youth and youth ministry is to
investigate a new area of grassroots history, and perhaps it can shed
new light on the many complex ways Christians (and youth from
other religions) interacted with American culture. It is a story that
is hardly over. Youth and youth ministries helped to end the great
Puritan epoch in American religious history. It is not clear what the
new era will bring. But youth and youth ministries will play a role
in shaping whatever will come.

Epilogue

THE LONG LIMINALITY: IMPLICATIONS FOR YOUTH
MINISTRY IN THE NEW MILLENNIUM

Over the past seventy years, American adolescents have come to experience a long period of liminality, of being betwixt and between, as they come of age. This long liminality has developed, in part, to meet the need for specialized workers in a market economy. It takes time to teach the job and personal skills people need to contribute to a complex culture.[1] What ought to be the church's role in this process? This simple question leads to a variety of others: How does the end of the great Puritan epoch in American religious history change the task of youth ministry? What directions can churches take to nurture young Christians in the new millennium? What difference does knowing the history of youth ministry over the past seventy years make for the practice of youth ministry today? Those large and long-range questions pale in the face of a more immediate one. As I was completing the final chapters of this book, teenagers in Littleton, Colorado, killed twelve of their peers and one of their teachers at Columbine High School, and then killed themselves. The event shocked the nation, in part because it was not an isolated incident. The questions it raised drove to the heart of both youth ministry and how Americans as a whole relate to young people. These were suburban kids, catered to with comfortable homes and commodities, and attended to with programs galore. Now *they* had turned violent. What could be done?

With the help of historical perspective, the tragedy of Littleton becomes part of a larger pattern in American history. We have provided young people with programs, including those of many youth ministries, and we have sold young people countless commodities, but we have not offered to them (and demonstrated for them) compelling, nonviolent life-paths with depth of intimacy, compassion, and community. America's youth have been left vulnerable to violence, and they have chosen violence themselves. One last look at this ironic outcome of the turn from purity to practices in modern American youth ministry, along with help from three influential theorists of religion, will enable us to answer both the broad question of the future of youth ministry and the immediate question of how we respond to youth violence. First, with help from anthropologist Mary Douglas, we can see how the move from purity to practices can, indeed should, continue and deepen in American youth ministries. Youth ministers cannot bury their heads in the sand. Leaders need to face the dangers of an American culture where an incident such as the one at Littleton can occur, while also assuring young people that they will not be left alone to face the challenges of coming of age. Second, with help from anthropologist Victor Turner, we can recognize the need for churches to re-create meaningful rites of passage for young people. Youth are telling us what we need to know as they participate in self-generated rites of sex, drugs, rock 'n' roll, and violence. Churches, in the rites they offer young people, can offer youth authentic intimacy, transcendence, community, and grace that rival, if not replace, the marketed rites of popular culture. Finally, with help from anthropologist René Girard, we can see how youth ministries can, indeed must, embrace practices and teaching of nonviolence as the logical application of the Christian message for youth today.

YOUTH MINISTRY AS A DANGEROUS CALLING

Youth ministry is a dangerous calling, but it is hardly as dangerous as an American culture without any spiritual attention to youth. Both dangers are illuminated well by Douglas's classic, *Purity and Danger*. Douglas's thesis is that humans create purification rituals and practices—and the categories of pure and

impure more generally—to order the very dangerous contagion, rivalry, and looming chaos unmediated experience suggests. "Ideas
about separating, purifying, demarcating," Douglas writes, "have
as their main function to impose system on . . . inherently untidy
experience."[2]

Understood in this light, Americans in the nineteenth century
created the category of "adolescence," and along with it youth ministries, in an understandable attempt to keep youth pure during the
long liminality that complex modern cultures require. Youth ma-
tured biologically, but Christians tried to keep them pure because
the many other tests that young people faced in modernity were
complicated and obscured by intimacy and attachment, not to
mention children. Nevertheless,

> whenever a strict pattern of purity is imposed on our lives it is ei-
> ther highly uncomfortable or it leads into contradiction, or it
> leads to hypocrisy. That which is negated is not thereby removed.
> The rest of life, which does not tidily fit the accepted categories,
> is still there and demands attention. The body, as we have tried
> to show, provides a basic scheme for all symbolism. There is
> hardly any pollution which does not have some primary physio-
> logical reference. As life is in the body it cannot be rejected
> outright. And as life must be affirmed, the most complete phi-
> losophies, as William James put it, must find some ultimate way
> of affirming that which has been rejected.[3]

Christian youth have been struggling, at least since 1960, to move
the church to affirm their existence as embodied beings. Preaching
purity alone fails. Youth recognize its hypocrisy and have found increasingly dangerous ways to point it out to us. That the church
has begun to recognize this and incorporate youth through an
incarnational theology expressed by diverse practices is a hopeful
sign.

It is also a dangerous one, for with the body come death and
vulnerability. Near the end of *Purity and Danger,* Douglas describes
the "central rite of Dinka [African] religion." Nineteenth-century
Euro-American observers recorded the rite as ritual murder, "the
brutal suffocation of a helpless old man." But Douglas argues,

> An intimate study of Dinka religious ideals reveals the central
> theme to be the old man's voluntary choosing of the time, man-
> ner and place of his death. The old man himself asks for the
> death to be prepared for him, he asks for it from his people and
> on their behalf. He is reverently carried to his grave, and lying in
> it says his last words to his grieving sons. . . . By his free, deliber-
> ate decision he robs death of the uncertainty of its time and

place of coming. His own willing death, ritually framed by the grave itself, is a communal victory for all his people. . . . By confronting death and grasping it firmly he has said something to his people about the nature of life.[4]

The nature of life, in short, requires recognizing that it has limits.[5]

Christian youth ministers can demonstrate the realities of limits to young people by symbolically being like this old man. Giving up on illusions of "totalistic" solutions and frantic forms of the denial of death, youth ministers can embrace the fragmentary and limited character of their ministries to young people in transition. They can symbolically confront and grasp death and its manifestations in institutional and cultural violence, as did the founder of their faith, in order to demonstrate for youth how to live. There is, in other words, a simple answer to the question much asked in youth ministries these days: What Would Jesus Do? That answer is: "He died."

This is why youth ministry is a dangerous calling. It calls for rare vulnerability and courage, and it calls for refusing to get too attached to conventions of church or culture. The core of Christian teaching, according to the Gospels, is that "those who want to save their life will lose it, and those who lose their life for the sake of the gospel will save it" (Luke 8:35). This spiritual truth—that true life is found not by grasping but by loving—calls youth ministers to the dangerous task of incarnating, each in his or her own partial way, the presence of God for youth. This is the only meaning of purity that will make sense to youth today, who know only too well the dangers that face them in everyday life. Youth ministers represent to young people the presence of the God who will go the distance with them, even through hell, and surely in the face of violence.[6]

Of course, no one individual can *be* Christ to any youth; ministers with a Christ complex invariably do more harm than good. The challenge for a youth minister is to join *the church* in embodying Christ's presence here and now, to make Christ known to youth through one's work. The ways to do this are many, and there are, fortunately, precedents to follow. Christians in America over the past seventy years have learned to work for knowledge and service, as apostles, as witnesses, and for freedom, as they followed life-paths blazed by youth ministries.

The life-path of knowledge, in particular, needs to be cultivated more rigorously in youth ministry than has been the case in the last few decades. The Walther League, YCW, YFC, and

African-American youth ministries all shared a contact with the depths of the Christian tradition, albeit in varying degrees and distinctive forms. They had, within their own stream of the tradition, intellectual integrity. Today a challenge for Christian youth ministry is to embrace the dangerous questions that contemporary culture poses to Christian thought and practice. Anti-intellectualism in Christian youth ministry must come to an end. Christians strengthen each other when they struggle together to identify the tough questions modernity poses to the Christian tradition and when they are prepared to answer them not with pat answers compatible with cultural or ecclesiastical conventions but in ways that convey truth as fully as we can conceive of it. Across the academy, theologians have been doing just that over the past seventy years. It would be good for youth ministers to take note and join them. There has been, for instance, nothing comparable to a liberation theology for young people. Surely a strong argument could be made, after Littleton, that youth in America need such a new vision of God at least as much as women needed a feminist theology, African Americans needed a black theology, and any other group who has been marginalized and violated has needed to rethink the Christian tradition.

It is time, in short, to open up the windows even further and let youth in not only on the practices of the faith but on the questions of the faith. They are already addressing these on their own. The truly dangerous course today is to refuse to let young people in on the debate and to imagine that we can keep them "safe." The move from purity to practices in American youth ministry must continue, indeed must be deepened in the direction of both social radicality and intellectual rigor. The Puritan epoch has truly ended. It is not inconceivable that a broader, more tolerant, more gracious era of American cultural history could dawn. Such an era would be marked not by imperialist expansion or Puritan negation but by the presence of a power that seeks not domination but democracy, not violence but love, not conquest but compassion. For anything like this vision to occur in the next millennium, youth ministry will have to play a role.

RE-CREATING RITES OF PASSAGE

When we listen to young people, which also means observing their behavior, they tell us what they need. That they have chosen, over the past few decades, rites of passage featuring sex, drugs, rock 'n' roll, and violence indicates something to which youth ministers would do well to give heed. Youth ministers will not answer youth's needs by offering them moralistic pronouncements of "Just say no." They will meet young people's needs when they provide them rites of passage that say yes to practices offering young people the intimacy, challenges, community, and grace they seek through the currently popular practices. At present, the rites of passage offered to teenagers in America lack coherence. Young people in America come of age in diffuse, if not contradictory, ways.[7] Indeed, today no one trial or test can prepare young men or women in the United States for the decisions they will have to face simply to survive. In this context, the church is relegated to the role of adjunct to, or critic of, the economic and political processes at the core of coming of age in the United States. This adjunct or critical role of Christian churches can, however, be liberating for youth ministries and can lead them to develop rites of passage that affirm young people in ways that separate them from childish things, challenge them to become authentic Christians, and incorporate them as part of a living community with deep roots and an enduring future.

Specifically Christian rites of passage might, then, follow the three classic stages of separation, threshold challenges, and incorporation as identified by Victor Turner and others, but they will infuse each stage with a particular meaning.[8] Separation for Christians means not only separation from parents but also refusal to attach oneself blindly to violent conventions of American culture. There are countless ways churches can mark these separations; indeed, having a youth ministry at all is one of them. The church needs more intergenerational activities; it also needs age-specific ones. Age-specific activities remain a necessity in the long liminality, for adolescents seek a community of peers to join them as they come of age and among whom they will discover intimate friends and partners.[9]

Youth ministers cannot, of course, steal children from their homes and take them out into the woods to test them through a rite of passage, as primal cultures did (although a carefully planned "kidnapping" might be a great youth group activity). Youth ministers can, however, expect attendance and attention in ways that clearly separate young people from childhood and that challenge youth to develop patterns of adult responsibility. Coaches of high school athletic teams, drama troupes, and musical ensembles, for instance, demand adult responsibility of their young members. Why should youth ministers expect less? Many youth, furthermore, will gladly leave home of their own volition to join a youth group work trip or other "adventure."[10] The first goal of Christian rites of passage, then, is to involve young people in practices that both separate them from their childhood patterns of behavior and invite them to engage as thoughtful Christian young people in practices that do not simply conform to a shallow intimacy, challenge, or community. The depth of the tradition—the presence of a gracious God who invites them all into a life of love—will draw them out of adolescent self-absorption and into intimacy, challenge, and community when it is presented and lived out.

For instance, at Christian camps and "servant events" around the country, young people leave home and live together for a period of time in a community where issues of intimacy, compassion, and community coalesce in dramatic ways. The community I know best in this regard is Camp Arcadia, in northern Michigan, where I have served as staff chaplain with twenty-six high school and college students for nearly three summers (see ch. 1 for its history). In this setting, all of the challenges of adult living eventually find their way into the lives of staff members as they work long days (and nights) to extend Christian hospitality to over one hundred and fifty guests per week. Staffers teach classes to children, lead singing and prayers, gather together each week for devotions and Eucharist, form friendships (and make enemies), prepare and serve meals, lead hikes and canoe trips, organize and star in talent shows, and much more, all in the interest of extending Christian hospitality to guests. Countless similar places exist around the country, functioning as testing grounds for Christian living, where Christian virtues and life-paths are honed. Young people who work there (or who attend, to a lesser degree) are experiencing a Christian rite of passage, marked by separation from childish things, engaging them in serious challenges, and incorporating them, after it is over, as people who faced the opportunity to become better Christians through the practice of hospitality. Such practices can occur anywhere and can take any number of different forms. Hospitality is only one of many Christian practices with salience for youth as they come of age.[11] Young people *can* be separated from their childhood and directed on Christian life-paths without falling into the violent conventions of American culture.

The second aspect of rites of passage—liminal challenges—can also be accomplished by churches in many ways. Most youth ministries already have this as their goal, but many programs are based on an intuitive grasp of "what youth need" rather than on an informed awareness of the challenges youth actually face. This problem is best addressed, among contemporary youth ministry materials, by those produced at Search Institute in Minneapolis. Search Institute has developed, on the basis of extensive scientific surveying of adolescents, youth ministers, and congregational members, a comprehensive vision of adolescent development. Search Institute uses, perhaps unfortunately, the language of the market to identify forty "assets" youth need to avoid violence and find fulfilling passage into adulthood. Not all, or even most, of the Search Institute assets are explicitly religious, but they are thoroughly grounded in Christian belief and practice.[12] They also emerge out of careful study of youth cultures and are correlated with the many diffuse institutions that already assist youth as they come of age, notably families, schools, and churches. Search Institute's forty assets also have as their goal to separate youth from thoughtless attachment to American consumption and violence and to create citizens and Christians (as well as people of other faiths) who care about their communities and who can contribute to the common good.

To ground its materials for youth ministry, Search Institute has developed an index of "faith maturity" that can be helpful to identify how to challenge young people in America's churches. "A person of mature faith experiences" faith in two dimensions, the authors of the recent report argue. First, people of faith experience "a life-transforming relationship with a loving God—[a] vertical dimension [of faith]." Second, people of mature faith experience "a consistent devotion to serving others—[a] horizontal dimension to faith."[13] Specific practices to nurture both dimensions already exist in most youth ministries, but rites of passage focused on any (or all) of the assets could be developed more intentionally and consciously. A key part of a liminal experience is for youth to experience a "reversal of hierarchy" in *communitas*, where they are invited to exercise "adult" power while still children. While the sacraments of the church historically intended to create this *communitas*, as currently practiced, they often do not.[14]

Youth can be challenged on the vertical dimension of faith by being asked to articulate their faith in both word and practice, through participation in study, prayer, meditation, worship, communion, and other means of spiritual formation. Conversion, speaking in tongues, and less dramatic practices such as participation in

Youth Sunday, common in some congregations, can be powerful rites of passage. I vividly recall the terror and elation of my first sermon. It was delivered at age thirteen, prior to my Confirmation, at the Easter sunrise service at Faith Lutheran Church in Appleton, Wisconsin. The last line of the homily I borrowed from a hymn: "Christ the Lord Is Risen Today! Alleluia!" It's difficult to get much more vertical than that. Teaching a life-path of attention and response to a loving God—the goal of any vertical aspect of faith— requires adults who themselves know how (and are not ashamed) to attend to God with mind, body, and soul and who are also willing to grant youth the chance to articulate the faith for themselves.

The same is true on the horizontal dimension. Christian youth cannot be expected to re-create America without adults motivated and willing to do the same. Intergenerational participation in such events as a CROP WALK or the 30 Hour Famine can serve as liminal challenges for youth, as can work with such agencies as Habitat for Humanity, denominational social services, or local soup kitchens. Youth also often bring to the church a love for music, both as listeners and performers. They also embody other gifts—as dancers, athletes, artists, and more. Camping, "adventure" ministry, sports, dance, even safely monitored forms of therapeutic massage (or at least back rubs) can engage young people in practices that involve them in adult problems and can move them to integrate devotion to God with work on behalf of human beings. Of course, adults need to honestly face the horizontal problems of American culture before they can engage youth with them.

That a need exists for greater integration of vertical and horizontal dimensions of faith among young people is obvious. In a recent survey of over twenty-five hundred youth, Search Institute discovered that only 6 percent of Protestant young people expressed predominantly vertical faith, 19 percent articulated predominantly horizontal faith, and only 11 percent integrated the two dimensions. Sixty-four percent had what the researchers called "undeveloped" faith, reflecting beliefs and practices high in neither horizontal nor vertical marks of mature Christianity.[15] If we expect youth to re-create America, we have to be willing to join them in the challenge.

Linking the vertical and the horizontal aspects of faith is the reality of language—to which youth ministries have, to date, paid little attention. Serious study of the Bible—using the resources of the best scholars in the field—is lacking in many youth ministries. This sells young people short intellectually and fails to meet them with the challenging questions they already are entertaining when they are allowed to be honest. Language is not only the medium of thought; it is the glue of most ritual, and attention to images used for God in worship—drawing on the diversity of images in the Bible and across the tradition—can be a powerful challenge for young people. In short, Search Institute materials identify a thoughtful and coherent range of challenges for youth ministries to offer young people as they come of age.

Finally, the third phase of rites of passage, incorporation, can occur in both informal and formal ways in youth ministries. Informally, youth can be incorporated after a successful rite of passage event with something as simple as a party or picnic, where generations mingle freely and where youth are welcomed into conversations and community. Simple presence, where young and old meet together as equals, provides *communitas* and reversal of conventional hierarchies. Churches can start with something as simple as getting elders and youth to learn each others' names. More formal ways to incorporate youth after meeting a test or challenge include inviting young people to participate in (and perhaps lead) boards or decision-making bodies of the church. Young people can, happily, be incorporated into the life of a community through committee meetings or other small groups. There young people can be delightful and constructive contributors to the common work of churches.[16] Elders can also serve as mentors for youth, not as hierarchical supervisors but as older peers who befriend youth and engage with them in solving problems together. Mentoring relationships such as this can be a powerful way for churches to provide recognition to adolescents. Mentors must be willing to assume such a role, but what they often discover in the process is that they change as fully as the young people. When mentors step down off their pedestals and walk with youth into more mature faith, the faith of the mentor is also invariably enriched. Authentic adulthood, after all, is a process as much as a state of being.

Most important, when young people practice their faith in public through successful rites of passage—whether in worship, at camp, with their minds, or through social activism—churches can acknowledge their accomplishments not with condescending praise but with adult recognition and thanks. There are symbolic ways that this occurs already: T-shirts are especially popular. But the symbol of all symbols in America is money, which means that youth ministries need the financial and other resources necessary to support rites of passage, mentoring programs, and education of youth leaders into the depths of the Christian tradition and into the problems of American culture. For better or worse, Americans associate value with money. Young people are, furthermore, sage observers of cash flow. They will know whether they are in fact being recognized by their congregations or whether their recognition is a token sign of condescension. We can expect them, in the latter case, to incorporate themselves elsewhere.

In the new millennium, then, churches can offer young people considerable clarity as they come of age. They will not do so by teaching them moral absolutes that negate their nascent adult desires. They will do so by engaging young people in rites of passage that intentionally demonstrate that the Christian faith is about solving complex problems in a community of people committed to using nonviolent, indeed gracious, means. One key to matching intention with practices is theological integrity: when elders and youth together understand and experience God as Creator, Redeemer, and Sustainer (these images for God are not absolute or the only ones viable), then the vertical dimension of faith, which we have called purity, will be present. Purity, in turn, when understood and experienced as God's gift rather than as a moralistic attainment out of fear, leads not to passive resignation or resentment but to practices of faith that are infinitely challenging. Here the classical Christian virtues of courage, patience, wisdom, and all the rest come into play. Christian rites of passage do not need, or even have to imagine, an America where everyone is a Christian, and they surely do not need a Christianity supported by government legislation. Christian rites of passage for the new millennium can have as the more modest (and yet challenging) goal to empower young people to live like Christians themselves and enjoy the company of all others, even their enemies. Christian rites of passage would seek to engage youth who become, in short, Christian pluralists.[17]

A CALL FOR NONVIOLENCE IN CHRISTIAN YOUTH MINISTRIES

We need ritual to mark life's passages, and constructive Christian rites of passage for youth will provide them with patterns to imitate that do not replicate America's tendency to solve problems with violence. After Littleton, however, more than ritual is necessary. The challenge to Christian youth ministry today is to speak

with one voice against violence and for nonviolence and to practice nonviolence intentionally and without reservation as a logical
development of Christianity in today's world. This is no small challenge, given the complicity many churches have had with the military, with prisons, with other manifestations of institutional and
cultural violence over the ages, and with the deep-seated rationalizations that have been used to justify such complicity. To understand why this radical step is necessary for youth ministry today,
we must first understand how young people have come to be
among the primary victims of violence and how teen violence,
such as the massacre at Littleton, indicates the front edge of a social
problem that demands Christian witness if Christian faith is to
gain authenticity in the next millennium. Our guide in reaching
such understanding will be Stanford anthropologist and literary
critic René Girard.

According to Girard, violence is learned behavior that follows
predictable patterns. People perceive a problem, usually rivalry for
resources stemming from mutual desire. This rivalry threatens to
disrupt, if not destroy, social order. People respond, then, by unit-
ing through cultural norms and institutions to create "scapegoats"
who are suitable for sacrifice. The scapegoat or scapegoats are then
expelled from the community; they are either actually or symbolically "killed." This expulsion temporarily creates unanimity in the
community; the rivalry of all against all has been transferred onto
one. Dissension is replaced with consensus, and people can then
go on with the pursuit of their desires, content that, for now, the
social order will remain intact.

According to Girard, this process of scapegoating repeats itself
endlessly in civilizations and is learned by people especially through
religion. Religious rites and teachings unconsciously reinforce the
scapegoating process and impel people to create scapegoats in
their midst who are sacrificeable for one reason or another. The
sacrifice "works," and the potential violence of all against all is
quelled by the limited violence of all against one. The solution,
however, is temporary. The problem of violence remains, for violence has been quelled with violence. The search for scapegoats
continues, and violence escalates as generation after generation
learns—through the dominant myths and rites—the cost of joining civilization.[18]

In America, the marginal status of young people, along with
the adoring (and punishing) attention paid to them through institutions, marks them as paradigmatic scapegoats. Sociologist

Mike R. Males, in *The Scapegoat Generation: America's War on Adolescents,* has recently argued this thesis. Males, who is apparently unaware of Girard's work, shows how national policies and cultural habits have led us to systematically (if unconsciously) blame young people for our cultural problems. We wage "war" on their underground trade in drugs, we build juvenile detention centers and prisons to house them when they rebel against their marginal status, and we refuse to fund education anywhere close to what we spend on defense and security. Violence is among the leading causes of death for all American teenagers. Among African-American youth, homicide has been the leading cause of death for over a decade.[19] We were, then, so traumatized by Littleton because it indicated to us that the scapegoats were beginning to fight back.

Youth violence is imitative behavior, drawing on patterns they have learned through observing a scandal-fascinated media, through living with their gun-owning and violence-accommodated parents, through noticing how their government solves problems, and through the tacit (and sometimes not so tacit) teachings of their churches. If violence is learned behavior, then young people have had plenty of sources to learn from in America. In Littleton and in youth violence more generally, we see young people expressing their inarticulate fears that there might not be a place for them in an American culture increasingly devoted to rivalry over resources. Teens are now resolving to kill, rather than to be killed; to scapegoat, rather than to be scapegoated.

So, what can churches and youth ministries do? What does the escalation of youth violence over the past seventy years teach us? First, churches and youth ministries have a particular responsibility to become aware of the dynamic of scapegoating and how religions often reinforce it. Second, churches and youth ministries have a particular responsibility to commit to being part of the solution of youth violence.[20] To do so, churches must replace thoughtless imitation, based on rivalry for resources, with imitation based in love. This sounds simple but is extraordinarily difficult. To unlearn violence, young people must have examples of people who refuse to join in systems that violate, and who speak out for and live a different way. Churches, especially youth ministries, can be a primary source of such examples, for, according to Girard, this is precisely the point of the Gospels. Jesus' passion points to a way of life beyond systems of death. Consistent with the compassion he taught and demonstrated with his life, the church's proclamation at Easter signals the victory of nonviolent love over any and all systems of domination and oppression. The challenge for churches today is to make nonviolence normative.

Violence in all of its forms is the manifestation of evil in our time. We are all capable of it and are all implicated in it. We can all also have a hand in clarifying for young people that violence solves nothing.[21] Until we do so, young people will continue to believe that it does.

Churches and youth ministries, then, are well situated to offer youth real presence: the intimacy, challenge, community, and grace that are like the presence Jeremiah found as he discovered his prophetic calling and faced his fears. The ways we can demonstrate this nonviolent presence are many. We can tell the stories of the prophets and Jesus in ways that make apparent their challenges to systems that violate. We can practice the sacraments not as token reinforcements of a church isolated from the world and its problems but as a source of solidarity for strength to engage "the powers." And we can mobilize communities to practice compassion—by feeding the hungry, housing the homeless, and befriending the outcasts. These practices are tried and proven ways to replace exploitation and violence, to which youth have often fallen prey, with life-paths of compassion like those taught through the Walther League, YCW, YFC, and African-American congregations. After all, the final petition of the Lord's Prayer, "Deliver us from evil," was also Jeremiah's prayer. The answer today is the same:

"Do not say, 'I am only a youth.' . . . Do not be afraid of them, for I am with you to deliver you."

Endnotes

NOTES TO INTRODUCTION

1. While writing this book I was Associate Professor of theology at Valparaiso University in Indiana, a private Lutheran school, worked as a part-time youth minister at First Christian Church (Disciples of Christ) in Valparaiso, sat in with the Valparaiso University Gospel Choir as an alto sax soloist playing gospel blues, and spent my summers as the spiritual advisor for twenty-six high-school- and college-age staff members at Camp Arcadia, a Lutheran family resort on the northeastern shores of Lake Michigan. In other words, I spent more time with youth and young adults than I did with anyone other than my own family members.

2. See George Gallup, *Scared: Growing Up in America* (Princeton, N.J.: Gallup Organization, 1995).

3. The choice of Jeremiah as a type for American youth is appropriate for a number of reasons, not least of which is the long tradition of jeremiads peppering American cultural history. See, for the origins of this pattern of language, Sacvan Bercovitch, *The American Jeremiad* (Madison: University of Wisconsin Press, 1978).

4. Less than a century after the founding of the first youth-serving organizations, the Young Men's Christian Association (YMCA) and the Young Women's Christian Association (YWCA), in the 1850s, M. M. Chambers counted over five hundred national clubs, groups, leagues,

societies, and fellowships dedicated solely to form and educate youth in the United States. Most were church related. See M. M. Chambers, *Youth-Serving Organizations: National Nongovernmental Associations* (3rd ed.; Washington: American Council on Education, 1948). For more recent catalogs, see Judith B. Erickson, *Directory of American Youth Organizations* (Boys Town, Neb.: Boys' Home, 1983); and Annie M. Brewer, ed., *Youth-Serving Organizations Directory* (Detroit: Gale, 1980). See U.S. Department of Health and Human Services. "Related Projects: Youth Serving and Youth Advocacy Organizations: Department of Health and Human Services Homepage," n.p., online: www.acf.dhhs.gov/programs/fysb/ ysyalink .htm; "The Adolescence Directory On-Line: Indiana University Center for Adolescence Studies," n.p., online: education.indiana.edu/cas/adol/adol .html; and "Search Institute Homepage," n.p., online: www.search-institute.org.

5. See R. Stephen Warner, "Work in Progress toward a New Paradigm for the Sociological Study of Religion in the United States," *American Journal of Sociology* 98 (March 1993): 1044–93.

6. See "Youth Homicides," HC 1.2b, in U.S. Department of Health and Human Services, *Trends in the Well-Being of America's Children and Youth* (Washington, D.C.: Office of the Assistant Secretary for Planning and Evaluation, Department of Health and Human Services, 1997); online: aspe.os.dhhs.gov/hsp/97trends/intro-web.htm.

7. National Council for Research on Women, *The Girls Report: What We Know and Need to Know about Growing Up Female* (Washington, D.C.: National Council for Research on Women, 1998). See also Mary Pipher, *Reviving Ophelia: Saving the Selves of Adolescent Girls* (New York: Ballantine, 1994).

8. See Peter L. Benson, *The Troubled Journey: A Portrait of 6th–12th Grade Youth* (Minneapolis: Search Institute, 1993).

9. Janet M. Simons, Belva Finlay, and Alice Yang, *The Adolescent and Young Adult Fact Book* (Washington, D.C.: Children's Defense Fund, 1991), 2, 3, 63.

10. William R. Myers, "Youth between Culture and Church," *ThTo* 47 (January 1991): 400–409.

11. Simons, Finlay, and Yang, *Fact Book,* 76. See also Mike R. Males, *The Scapegoat Generation: America's War on Adolescents* (Monroe, Me.: Common Courage, 1996).

12. The recent exceptions to this omission include Giovanni Levi and Jean-Claude Schmitt, eds. *A History of Young People in the West;* vol. 1, Ancient and Medieval Rites of Passage (trans. Camille Naish); vol. 2, *Stormy Evolution to Modern Times* (trans. Carol Volk; Cambridge: Harvard University Press, 1997); Harvey J. Graff, *Conflicting Paths: Growing Up in America* (Cambridge: Harvard University Press, 1995); and Joe Austin and Michael Nevin Willard, eds., *Generations of Youth: Youth Cultures and History in Twentieth-Century America* (New York: New York University Press, 1998).

13. I have begun research on another book which will expand the narrative beyond Christian youth to include Jewish, Muslim, Buddhist, Hindu, and other religious young people and their roles in American history.

14. Although, admittedly, these four groups were assigned to me as part of collaborative research sponsored by the Valparaiso Project on the Education and Formation of People in Faith, I found the assignment intellectually justifiable.

15. I will follow on this point, especially in chs. 6 and 7, the illuminating work of Edward Shils, *Tradition* (Chicago: University of Chicago Press, 1981).

16. This scenario is replicated in other mainline groups, such as the Luther League and the Methodist Youth Fellowship. See Dean Borgman, "A History of American Youth Ministry," in *The Complete Book of Youth Ministry* (ed. Warren S. Benson and Mark H. Senter III; Chicago: Moody, 1987), 61–74.

17. This does not imply that churches ought to reemphasize purity (negatively understood as the avoidance of adult behaviors and responsibility) in their programs to young people. The resolution of this dichotomy appears to be theological: when we teach youth to trust God, they will both understand and practice purity not so much as the negative avoidance of particular behaviors as a confidence in God's presence and grace that will empower them to take responsible and reasonable risks out of compassion. In short, between purity and practice is understanding— which should be the central task of theological education.

18. Sidney E. Ahlstrom, *A Religious History of the American People* (New Haven, Conn.: Yale University Press, 1974).

19. Victor Turner, *The Ritual Process: Structure and Anti-structure* (Ithaca, N.Y.: Cornell University Press, 1969).

20. Mary Douglas, *Purity and Danger: An Analysis of Concepts of Pollution and Taboo* (New York: Penguin, 1966).

21. René Girard, *Violence and the Sacred* (trans. Patrick Gregory; Baltimore: Johns Hopkins University Press, 1977).

22. Implicit here is a critique of the current tendency of churches to tailor services to the comfort level of their "consumers." A church that doesn't challenge its members to practices of compassion is not, so far as I can tell from the Scriptures and history of Christianity, worthy of the name.

23. Van A. Harvey, *The Historian and the Believer: The Morality of Historical Knowledge and Christian Belief* (New York: Macmillan, 1966), is a classic critique of "hard perspectivism" on the part of believers writing history. The tendency of most historians to locate the center of Christian thought in the supernatural does indeed create a problem for historical knowledge; a relocation of the center of Christian thought in the incarnation avoids many of these problems. My approach has been shaped by that of my mentor, Martin E. Marty, especially in *The Irony of It All*,

1893–1919 (vol. 1 of *Modern American Religion;* Chicago: University of Chicago Press, 1986).

24. See Robert McAfee Brown, *Religion and Violence* (Philadelphia: Westminster, 1987).

25. See Males, *Scapegoat Generation.*

26. See David R. Loy, "The Religion of the Market," *JAAR* 65 (Winter 1996): 275–90.

27. This is the viewpoint of Joseph Kett, *Rites of Passage: Adolescence in America, 1790 to the Present* (New York: Basic Books, 1977), which we will 'explore in more detail in ch. 5. According to Kett, the "youth problem" is an inevitable by-product of the mental category "youth" and an even more direct by-product of the institutions that "serve" them, and (once institutionalized) must justify their existence. Americans, and especially their churches, created a "separate sphere for youth in the same way that Victorian moralism sanctioned a separate sphere for women," with the same oppressive results. "By segregating young people into special institutions . . . [and] by trying to keep the maturing child ignorant of this world of conflict and contradictions, adults think they are keeping them pure" (p. 253, quoting from August de B. Hollingshead, *Elmtown's Youth: The Impact of Social Class on Adolescents* [New York: Wiley, 1949], 272, 298). It is undeniable that Christian youth programs began, and many continue, as middle-class, Victorian purity programs that sought to shield maturing adolescents from the knowledge—largely carnal—that would lead them to be critical of (and thus in conflict with) the conventions of church, state, or culture. Kett's critique is invaluable, but it will become apparent that his work, published over twenty years ago, has been badly dated by the development of youth cultures since then and by developments in historiography.

28. See Marcus Borg, *Meeting Jesus Again for the First Time* (San Francisco: HarperSanFrancisco, 1994), for a substantive theological critique of Christian and other "purity systems."

29. See Dorothy C. Bass, ed., *Practicing Our Faith: A Way of Life for a Searching People* (San Francisco: Jossey-Bass, 1997), for an explanation of the turn to practices within Christian theology.

30. This is the approach of Kenda Creasy Dean and Ron Foster, *The Godbearing Life: The Art of Soul Tending for Youth Ministry* (Nashville: Upper Room, 1998).

31. See Turner, *The Ritual Process.*

32. This is the implicit structure informing the dense research of Graff, *Conflicting Paths.* Graff's book is a wonder of archival research linked together with only the loosest narrative structure.

NOTES TO CHAPTER 1

1. I tell the history of the league in fuller detail in Jon Pahl, *Hopes and Dreams of All: The International Walther League and Lutheran Youth in*

American Culture, 1893–1993 (Chicago: Wheat Ridge Ministries, 1993). Based upon archival sources and interviews, it is available from Wheat Ridge Ministries, 1 Pierce Place, Suite 250E, Itasca, IL 60143; 1-800-762-6748; www.wheatridge.org. All proceeds benefit Wheatridge.

2. O. P. Kretzmann, "1856 Candles," *WLM* 42 (April 1934): 467.

3. The standard history (in need of revision) is E. Clifford Nelson et al., eds., *The Lutherans in North America* (Philadelphia: Fortress, 1980).

4. Fred W. Meuser, "Facing the Twentieth Century," ibid., 359–452.

5. I portray the Walther League as a mainline youth movement, but there are some distinctive features to Lutheran—and especially Missouri Synod—history not shared by other mainline groups. Although officially an independent Lutheran youth organization throughout its history, the Walther League was officially recognized as an "auxiliary" of the Lutheran Church–Missouri Synod in 1923 and drew increasing financial support from the Synodical Board for Youth Ministry. This pattern of denominational centralization matches the growth of many mainline youth ministries, and the story of the demise of the league closely parallels that of the other mainline youth ministries as well. Among the few recent historical studies of these groups of Christian youth, see Franklin B. Gillespie, "Youth Programs of the United Presbyterian Church: an Historical Overview," *Journal of Presbyterian History* 59 (Fall 1981): 309–82; "Luther League: 90 Years Young, 25 Years Strong," *Lutheran Standard* 15 (November 1985): 33–40; and J. Warren Smith, "Youth Ministry in American Methodism's Mission," *Methodist History* 19 (June 1981): 224–30.

6. See Jon Pahl, "Walther League Messenger," in *Popular Religious Magazines of the United States* (ed. P. Mark Fackler and Charles H. Lippy; Westport, Conn.: Greenwood, 1995), 494–500.

7. In 1939, Professor Ernest Chare of the University of Chicago observed, "The Lutheran Church of the Synodical Conference . . . has one of the most progressive youth programs in the country . . . the Walther League." Elfred L. Roshke, "Convention High Lights," *WLM* 48 (August/September 1939): 29–30.

8. O. P. Kretzmann, "The New Deal and the Society," *WLM* 42 (June 1934): 611.

9. "Bible Study: Jonah," *WQ* 29 (April 1958): 10.

10. See, on this school of thought within Protestantism, Ahlstrom, *A Religious History;* and idem., ed., *Theology in America: The Major Protestant Voices from Puritanism to Neo-orthodoxy* (Indianapolis: Bobbs-Merrill, 1963).

11. Elizabeth Zoller, letter to Jon Pahl, November 1991, including typescript copy of homily. Between 1991 and 1993 I solicited letters from and surveyed hundreds of former Walther Leaguers. These materials, currently in the possession of their author, will eventually be forwarded to the Concordia Historical Institute, St. Louis.

12. Ibid., 7.

13. Marilyn (Rook) Bernthal, letter to Jon Pahl, September 23, 1991.

14. "Should Girls Go to College: Yes! No!" *WLM* 59 (January 1951): 10; "Messenger Letters," 59 (February 1951): 22–24.

15. "The 'Why' of the Walther League," *WQ* 26 (April 1955): 2.

16. P. E. Kretzmann, "That Vexing Question of Dancing and Related Subjects," mimeographed, ca. 1939, in Walther League Collection, Concordia Historical Institute, St. Louis.

17. John Fischer, "Iowa West Highspots," *WLM* 59 (December 1956): 19.

18. Walter M. Wangerin, "We Like Singing Games," *WQ* 24 (April 1953): 23.

19. "League Mirror," *WLM* 61 (July 1953): 31.

20. "Church Manners," *WLM* 66 (May 1958): 22–24.

21. Bernice Baker, "A Day at Arcadia," *WLM* 46 (June 1938): 637.

22. Edgar Krentz, "Arcadia Is People," *WLM* 64 (April 1956): 28.

23. Carl Schalk, "By a Lake, We Come to Know Him"; available from Camp Arcadia, P.O. Box 229, Arcadia, MI 49613.

24. Hilda Jass, "Arcadia," *WLM* 64 (May 1956): 44.

25. Baker, "A Day at Arcadia."

26. See Frank W. Miller, *Camp Arcadia: The First Sixty Years* (Manistee, Mich.: J. B. Publications, 1982). For another "house" history of a Christian camp (there are probably others), see W. B. Freeland and Orrin Manifold, *Epworth Forest: The First Fifty Years* (Winona Lake, Ind.: Light and Life, 1974).

27. See John Strietelmeier, *Valparaiso's First Century* (Valparaiso, Ind.: Valparaiso University Press, 1959); and James W. Albers, *From Centennial to Golden Anniversary: The History of Valparaiso University from 1959–1975* (Valparaiso, Ind.: Valparaiso University Press, 1976). On Lutheran higher education more generally, see Richard W. Solberg, *Lutheran Higher Education in North America* (Minneapolis: Augsburg, 1985).

28. Pahl, *Hopes and Dreams of All,* 158.

29. Walter A. Maier, "Hitler Shows the Way," *WLM* 41 (April 1933): 461; "The Credit Side of the Hitler Ledger," 42 (June 1934): 620.

30. O. P. Kretzmann, "The Pilgrim: Terror in Germany," *Cresset* 2 (January 1939): 15–17.

31. See, e.g., Walter A. Maier, "Keep Clean!" *WLM* 53 (January 1945): 193.

32. "Letters," *WLM* 55 (February 1947): 40; *WLM* 56 (December 1948): 4.

33. Robert Ihde, "Labor Leader," *WLM* 56 (April 1948): 8.

34. Alfred P. Klausler, "Editorial Window," *WLM* 55 (September 1946): 15.

35. Paul G. Hansen, "It's Your Problem," *WLM* 64 (February 1956): 29.

36. Elmer N. Witt, "Life Can Be Sexual—Now!" *Arena One* 1 (June 1967): 7–8.

37. Ruth Erdman, interview with Jon Pahl, October 20, 1992; transcript in Walther League Collection, Concordia Historical Institute, St. Louis.

38. "A Tale of Hospice Work," *Central Illinois District Walther Leaguer* 7 (September 1933): 16.

39. Walther League, *Annual Financial Statement, 1948–1949* (Chicago: Walther League, 1949).

40. O. H. Theiss, "Support from All, Service to All: The Wheat Ridge Foundation," *WLM* 35 (May 1945): 342–43, 362.

41. Ibid.

42. Martin E. Marty, "Our Heritage: The 200th Anniversary of Bach's Death," *WLM* 58 (July 1950): 9–10.

43. "Abound in Love," *WLM* 55 (September 1946): 24.

44. "The Messenger Round Table: What the L.S.V. Schools Have Meant to Me," *WLM* 54 (March 1946): 12.

45. "Our Foreign Mission Builders," *WLM* 64 (April 1955): 63.

46. Linda Gerling, "Here We Stand," *WQ* 33 (April 1962): 15–16.

47. Oswald Hoffman, "Who Is My Neighbor?" *WQ* 32 (April 1961): 53.

48. Elmer N. Witt, "Work Campers Can Be Anyone," *WLM* 70 (December 1961): 21.

49. This is true especially of the new Evangelical Lutheran Church in America, founded in 1988. See Todd W. Nichol, *All These Lutherans: Three Paths toward a New Lutheran Church* (Minneapolis: Augsburg, 1986), for a concise story of this change. Many former members of the Walther League, and especially its leaders, eventually found a home in the ELCA, after the Missouri Synod experienced a conservative takeover in 1974.

50. "Operation Live-In," *WQ* (January 1967): 38:16.

51. Here the parallel between the league and mainline churches is clearest. Having compassionately embraced marginality from a position of strength, the league, like the mainline denominations more broadly, was delivered unto the marginality it sought. For a close case study of where this plot is manifest among a clearly mainline constituency of youth, see Dorothy C. Bass, "Revolutions Quiet and Otherwise: Protestants and Higher Education during the 1960s," in *Caring for the Commonweal: Education for Religious and Public Life* (ed. Parker J. Palmer, Barbara G. Wheeler, and James W. Fowler; Macon, Ga.: Mercer University Press, 1990), 207–26.

52. See Pahl, *Hopes and Dreams of All*, 235.

53. See William L. O'Neill, *Coming Apart: An Informal History of America in the 1960s* (Chicago: Quadrangle, 1971); and Todd Gitlin, *The Sixties: Years of Hope, Days of Rage* (New York: Bantam, 1987).

54. I develop this argument in fuller detail in Jon Pahl, "Accommodation to Violence: The Rise and Demise of the Walther League," *CurTM* 23 (October 1996): 336–46.

55. T. J. Vogel, letter to Edgar Fritz, March 21, 1953, in Walther League Collection, Concordia Historical Institute, St. Louis, box 92, file 16.

56. "Dialog: An *Arena* Feature," *Arena* 72 (November 1963): 8.

57. Ibid.

58. "A Lutheran Looks at the Jews," *Arena* 73 (April 1965): 3.

59. The Lutheran Church–Missouri Synod, *Unpublished Reports and Overtures (Supplement to Convention Workbook: Forty-Sixth Regular Convention, the Lutheran Church–Missouri Synod)* (St. Louis: Concordia Publishing House, 1965), 39–43.

60. "A Christian Mother," letter to Paul A. Schreivogel, May 17, 1965, in Walther League Collection, Concordia Historical Institute, St. Louis. The letter is postmarked Cape Girardeau, Missouri.

61. Edge 1 (November 1967): 1.

62. Online: Wheat Ridge Ministries home page, www.wheatridge.org.

63. Online: Lutheran Volunteer Corps home page, www.lvchome.org.

64. Online: The Lutheran Church–Missouri Synod home page, www .lcms.org. Between 1968 and 1975 the annual synodical expenditure on youth ministry dropped from $330,000 to $185,000. The spirit of pan-Lutheran cooperation in youth ministry fostered by the Walther League continued through the seventies as Lutheran Church–Missouri Synod youth (including myself) participated in "All-Lutheran" youth gatherings at sites around the country and in "servant events" similar to those initiated by the league. In 1980, however, the church began separate biennial youth gatherings. See The Lutheran Church–Missouri Synod, *Jesus Christ Is Lord: Convention Proceedings of the Fifty-First Regular Convention of the Lutheran Church–Missouri Synod* (St. Louis: Concordia Publishing House, 1975), 377.

65. Charles Sauer, "The Walther League: An Interim Report submitted to the Wheat Ridge Foundation Board of Directors and the Walther League Council and Trustees," May 1972, 23. Concordia Historical Institute, Walther League Collection.

66. Margaret Hartmeister, "Memories!" mimeographed report, May 23, 1975. Concordia Historical Institute, Walther League Collection.

NOTES TO CHAPTER 2

1. "Pope Pius XII Addresses Thirty Thousand Young Christian Workers at the International Pilgrimage," reprint from the *Torch*, n.d., Zotti papers (the private papers of Mary Zotti), as cited in Mary Irene Zotti, *A Time of Awakening: The Young Christian Worker Story in the United States, 1938 to 1970* (Chicago: Loyola University Press, 1991), 208. Zotti's work is a fine in-house history, written by a former member and leader in the movement. The popes have been remarkably prolific on the topic of youth. See, for early examples, Raymond B. Fullam, S.J., ed., *The Popes on Youth:*

Principles for Forming and Guiding Youth from Popes Leo XIII to Pius XII (New York: McKay, 1958).

2. Frank Ardito, "YCW—Pilgrimage—Rome—1957," *Apostolate* 5 (Winter 1957): 2–3.

3. Rev. John Hill, "Recollections of a Chaplain," *Apostolate* 9 (Fall 1962): 24–38. For a report on the demise of the same section, see idem, "The Way It Was," *Apostolate* 11 (Summer 1965): 2–9; (Fall 1965): 2–11.

4. For general historical treatments of Catholic Action, see Jay Dolan, *The American Catholic Experience: A History from Colonial Times to the Present* (Garden City, N.Y.: Doubleday, 1985); Aaron I. Abell, *American Catholicism and Social Action: A Search for Social Justice, 1865–1950* (South Bend, Ind.: University of Notre Dame Press, 1963); Debra Campbell, "Reformers and Activists," in *American Catholic Women: A Historical Exploration* (ed. Karen Kennelly, C.S.J; New York: Macmillan, 1989), 152–81; see also "Labor and Lay Movements: Part One," *USCathHist* 9 (Summer 1990): 223–333; and esp. "Labor and Lay Movements: Part Two" (Fall 1990): 335–467.

5. See Michael De La Bedoyere, *The Cardijn Story* (New York: Longmans, Green, 1958). Among Cardijn's writings in translation, see Joseph Cardijn, *Challenge to Action: Addresses of Monsignor Joseph Cardijn* (ed. Eugene Langdale; Chicago: Fides, 1955); and *Laymen into Action* (trans. Anne Heggie; London: Geoffrey Chapman, 1964).

6. Zotti, *A Time of Awakening*, 153.

7. R. Scott Appleby, "Present to the People of God: The Transformation of the Roman Catholic Parish Priesthood," in *Transforming Parish Ministry: The Changing Roles of Catholic Clergy, Laity, and Women in Religion* (ed. Jay P. Dolan et al.; New York: Crossroad, 1990), 27.

8. Robert Handy, *A Christian America: Protestant Hopes and Historical Realities* (New York: Oxford University Press, 1971). See also Nathan O. Hatch, *The Democratization of American Christianity* (New Haven, Conn.: Yale University Press, 1989).

9. See Christopher J. Kaufmann, *Faith and Fraternalism: The History of the Knights of Columbus* (rev. ed.; New York: Simon & Schuster, 1992); and "The Knights of Columbus: Lay Activism from the Origins through the Great Depression," *USCathHist* 9 (Summer 1990): 261–74.

10. Pope Leo XIII, *Rerum Novarum*, in *The Papal Encyclicals, 1878–1903* (5 vols.; ed. Claudia C. Ihm; Raleigh, N.C.: Duke University Press, 1981), 3:241, as cited by Richard Gribble, C.S.C., "*Rerum Novarum* and the San Francisco Labor Movement," *USCathHist* 9 (Summer 1990): 284.

11. The three points are from John A. Zahm, "Leo XIII and the Social Question," *North American Review* 161 (August 1895): 209, as cited by Gribble, "*Rerum Novarum,*" 282.

12. Francis L. Broderick, *Right Reverend New Dealer: John A. Ryan* (New York: Macmillan, 1963).

13. Rodger Van Allen, *The Commonweal and American Catholicism: The Magazine, the Movement, the Meaning* (Philadelphia: Fortress, 1974). The literature on Day is vast. See among others Robert Coles, *Dorothy Day: A Radical Devotion* (Reading, Mass.: Addison-Wesley, 1987).

14. Yves Congar, *Lay People in the Church: A Study for a Theology of the Laity* (trans. Donald Attwater; Westminster, Md.: Newman, 1957). Congar was French, but his work was widely read in the United States.

15. Daniel Callahan, *The Mind of the Catholic Layman* (New York: Scribners, 1963).

16. On John Courtney Murray, see especially his *We Hold These Truths: Reflections on the American Proposition* (New York: Sheed & Ward, 1960); and Robert W. McElroy, *The Search for an American Public Theology: The Contribution of John Courtney Murray* (New York: Paulist, 1989).

17. Patrick Carey, "Lay Catholic Leadership in the United States," *USCathHist* 9 (Summer 1990): 223–47, here 238.

18. Florence Henderson Davis, "Lay Movements in New York City," *USCathHist* 9 (Fall 1990): 408.

19. Andrew M. Greeley, "The Catholics in the World and in America," in *World Religions in America: An Introduction* (ed. Jacob Neusner; Louisville: Westminster John Knox, 1994), 95.

20. An important movement to compare to YCW is Dorothy Day and Peter Maurin's Catholic Worker, which endures to the present. Although it was not intended to be a youth movement and did not follow the "like-to-like" method of service encouraged by Cardijn, the voluntary poverty, community life, and practical focus of the Catholic Worker movement has many parallels to YCW. On Day, see n. 13, above; William D. Miller, *Dorothy Day: A Biography* (San Francisco: Harper & Row, 1982); and Mel Piehl, *Breaking Bread: Dorothy Day and the Catholic Worker Movement* (Philadelphia: Temple University Press, 1982), along with Day's own writings, notably *The Long Loneliness* (San Francisco: Harper, 1952). It is perhaps fair to say that the key feature distinguishing the Catholic Worker from YCW—apart from its age-inclusive character—was intentional radicalism and the refusal to compromise with the state and culture (anarchism).

21. Mary Irene Zotti, "The Young Christian Workers," *USCathHist* 9 (Summer 1990): 387.

22. Cardijn, *Laymen into Action,* 17–22.

23. This summary of the formula follows closely a local Catholic Action publication, Rev. Stephen Anderl and Sr. M. Ruth, *The Technique of the Catholic Action Cell* (LaCrosse, Wisc.: St. Rose Convent, 1946).

24. Louis J. Putz, C.S.C., *The Modern Apostle* (South Bend, Ind.: Fides, 1964), 14–15.

25. Zotti, *A Time of Awakening,* 15.

26. "Minutes, St. Joan of Arc Cell, Meeting of September 22, 1939," Zotti papers, as cited by Zotti, *A Time of Awakening,* 46.

27. "South Bend" (an anoymous YCW member), in "Former Members Look Back," in Zotti, *A Time of Awakening,* 68.

28. Appleby, "Present to the People of God," 7.

29. On the CYO, see Mark B. Sorvillo, "Bishop Bernard Sheil: Hero of the Catholic Left" (Ph.D. diss., University of Chicago Divinity School, 1990).

30. Tony Zivalich, letter to Pat Keegan, May 7, 1948, as cited by Zotti, *A Time of Awakening,* 112.

31. Zotti, *A Time of Awakening,* 112.

32. Ibid., 115.

33. See, e.g., Jeremiah Newman, *What Is Catholic Action: An Introduction to the Lay Apostolate* (Westminster, Md.: Newman, 1958), 23, who argues in typical fashion that the "alarming" growth of communism made Catholic Action necessary.

34. Bob Senser, *Specialized Apostolates in Action* (Chicago: CFM/YCW/YCS, 1959), 5.

35. Louis J. Putz, C.S.C., "YCW—an Apostolate of Faith through Service," notes of Irene Zotti, as cited in Zotti, "Young Christian Workers," 397.

36. Msgr. Reynold Hillenbrand, "About Mixed Groups," Chaplain's Notes (unpublished), n.d., as cited by Zotti, *A Time of Awakening,* 150.

37. Zotti, *A Time of Awakening,* 151.

38. "New York City" (an anonymous YCW member), in "Members from the Sixties Look Back," as cited ibid., 245.

39. Dodie Marino, "YCW in Our Factory," *Apostolate* 2 (Winter 1954): 20–26; "YCW Joins a Picket Line," *Apostolate* 4 (Spring 1957): 10–14.

40. YCW [Women's] Staff, "U.S. Girls' Biggest Problem: Loneliness," *AIM* 2 (March 1958): 4.

41. Bob Olmstead, "Omaha's Young Christian Workers Pinpoint Discrimination in Restaurants," *AIM* 2 (July 1958): 1.

42. Bernard Lyons, "Ain't Gonna Rock 'n' Roll No More," *AIM* 3 (April 1959): 2.

43. Zotti, *A Time of Awakening,* 139.

44. See, e.g., Frank J. McVeigh, "Third of Jobless Are 14–24," *AIM* 2 (March 1958): 1; and "Shoptalk," *AIM* 2 (November 1958): 5.

45. Fr. Keith Kennedy, "YCW: A Workers' Apostolate?" in *Apostolate* 5 (Spring 1958): 15–20.

46. Msgr. Reynold Hillenbrand, "Council Meeting Report," July 1957, as cited by Zotti, *A Time of Awakening,* 140.

47. "Two Reports on YCW City Chaplains," *Apostolate* 9 (Fall 1962): 5–6.

48. See YCM, "A Time to Begin: Introducing YCM," typed master manuscript, Chicago, 1967, in University of Notre Dame Archives, CYCM Collection, Box 20.

49. Zotti, *A Time of Awakening,* 157–59.

50. Ibid., 229–30.

51. Appleby, "Present to the People of God," 38.

52. On World Youth Day, see (along with newspaper reports) U.S. Catholic Conference, *Building the City of God: World Youth Day, 1990—Celebrating Our Heritage* (Washington, D.C.: U.S. Catholic Conference, 1990); and Catholic News Service, *John Paul II Speaks to Youth at World Youth Day* (Washington, D.C.: Catholic News Service, 1994). On more general trends in Catholic work with youth, see Raymond H. Potvin, Dean R. Hoge, and Hart M. Nelsen, *Religion and American Youth: With Emphasis on Catholic Adolescents and Young Adults* (Washington, D.C.: U.S. Catholic Conference, 1976); Maria Harris, *Portrait of Youth Ministry* (New York: Paulist, 1981); E. Nancy McAuley and Moira Mathieson, *Faith without Form: Beliefs of Catholic Youth* (Kansas City, Mo.: Sheed & Ward, 1986); Kieran Sawyer, *The Risk of Faith and Other Youth Ministry Activities* (South Bend, Ind.: Ave Maria, 1988); Patrick McNamara, "Catholic Youth in the Modern Church," in *Religion and the Social Order: Vatican II and U.S. Catholicism* (ed. Helen Rose Ebaugh; Greenwich, Conn.: JAI, 1991), 57–65; and Bert Ghezzi, ed., *Keeping Your Kids Catholic: It May Seem Impossible but It Can Be Done* (Ann Arbor, Mich.: Servant Publications, 1989). Two institutional histories and analyses also discuss Catholic youth in important contexts: John Witney Evans, *The Newman Movement: Roman Catholics in American Higher Education, 1883–1971* (South Bend, Ind.: University of Notre Dame Press, 1980); and Anthony S. Bryk, Valerie E. Lee, and Peter B. Holland, *Catholic Schools and the Common Good* (Cambridge: Harvard University Press, 1993).

53. Debra Campbell, "The Struggle to Serve: From the Lay Apostolate to the Ministry Explosion," in *Transforming Parish Ministry* (ed. Dolan et al.), 251–52, traces the origin and development of this expanded theological reflection.

54. Zotti, *A Time of Awakening*, 285.

NOTES TO CHAPTER 3

1. The field of Evangelical history has blossomed in recent decades. An indispensable guide is Edith W. Blumhofer, *Twentieth-Century Evangelicalism: A Guide to the Sources* (New York: Garland, 1990).

2. "What Happened to Me When I Witnessed," *YFC* 21 (November 1963): 42–43. The success of these witnesses contrasts somewhat markedly, of course, with the original meaning of the term *to witness* (Greek *martyrein*) both in Christian and in Evangelical history, where it meant to die for the faith. This transformation of the term from connoting sacrifice to connoting success is an intriguing tangent in this history. See, on the fascination of young midcentury Evangelicals with martyrdom, Joel Carpenter, ed., *Sacrificial Lives: Young Martyrs and Fundamentalist Idealism* (New York: Garland, 1988).

3. See Timothy L. Smith, *Revivalism and Social Reform: American Protestantism on the Eve of the Civil War* (New York: Harper & Row, 1957); and Donald W. Dayton, *Discovering an Evangelical Heritage* (Grand Rapids, Mich.: Eerdmans, 1976).

4. The classic case for this development is made by Alan Heimert, *Religion and the American Mind: From the Great Awakening to the Revolution* (Cambridge: Harvard University Press, 1966). For a more nuanced view, see Jon Pahl, *Paradox Lost: Free Will and Political Liberty in American Culture, 1630–1760* (Baltimore: Johns Hopkins University Press, 1992).

5. See Whitney R. Cross, *The Burned-Over District* (Ithaca, N.Y.: Cornell University Press, 1950).

6. On Sunday, see Jon Pahl, "Billy Sunday," in *Twentieth-Century Shapers of American Popular Religion* (ed. Charles H. Lippy; New York: Greenwood, 1989), 410–17.

7. See William G. McLoughlin, *Revivals, Awakenings, and Reform: An Essay on Religion and Social Change in America, 1607 to 1977* (Chicago History of American Religion; Chicago: University of Chicago Press, 1978).

8. The best histories of this period are, for fundamentalism, George Marsden's groundbreaking *Fundamentalism and American Culture: The Shaping of Twentieth-Century Evangelicalism, 1870–1925* (New York: Oxford University Press, 1980); and for modernism, William R. Hutchison, *The Modernist Impulse in American Protestantism* (New York: Oxford University Press, 1976). For the broad scope of the period, I am indebted to the brilliant work of Marty, *The Irony of It All.*

9. Donald W. Dayton and Robert K. Johnston, eds., *The Variety of American Evangelicalism* (Knoxville: University of Tennessee Press, 1991).

10. On Lewis, see Jon Pahl, "Sinclair Lewis," in *Twentieth-Century Shapers* (ed. Lippy), 241–46.

11. On this "pre-millennial" strand in Evangelical thought, see Ernest R. Sandeen, *The Roots of Fundamentalism: British and American Millenarianism, 1800–1930* (Chicago: University of Chicago Press, 1970).

12. Virginia Brereton, *Training God's Army: The American Bible School, 1880–1940* (Bloomington: Indiana University Press, 1990).

13. Borgman, "A History," 70. See also Bruce Shelley, "The Rise of Evangelical Youth Movements," *Fides et Historia* 18 (1986): 47–63; and Mark H. Senter III, "The Youth for Christ Movement as an Educational Agency and Its Impact upon Protestant Churches, 1931–1979" (Ph.D. diss.; Loyola University of Chicago, 1993), which appears in another form as *The Coming Revolution in Youth Ministry* (Wheaton, Ill.: Victor, 1992).

14. Shelley, "The Rise of Evangelical Youth Movements," 49. The office moved to Wheaton, Illinois, in 1953, and Denver in 1990.

15. Harold E. Fey, "What about 'Youth for Christ'?" *ChrCent* 20 (June 1945): 729.

16. Ibid.

17. See Peter Partner, *God of Battles: Holy Wars of Christianity and Islam* (Princeton, N.J.: Princeton University Press, 1998); and Karen Armstrong, *Holy War: The Crusades and Their Impact on Today's World* (New York: Doubleday, 1991).

18. Billy Graham, "We Need Revival," in *Revival in Our Time: The Story of the Billy Graham Evangelistic Campaigns* (Wheaton, Ill.: Van Kampen, 1950), as reprinted in *The Early Billy Graham: Sermon and Revival Accounts* (ed. Joel A. Carpenter; Fundamentalism in American Religion, 1880–1950, no. 44; New York: Garland, 1988), 61.

19. Billy Graham, *Calling Youth to Christ* (Grand Rapids, Mich.: Zondervan, 1947), as reprinted in Carpenter, *The Early Billy Graham*, 29.

20. Martin E. Marty, *The New Shape of American Religion* (New York: Harper, 1959), 21–27, as cited by Joel A. Carpenter, "Youth for Christ and the New Evangelicals," in *Religion and the Life of the Nation: American Recoveries* (ed. Rowland A. Sherrill; Urbana: University of Illinois Press, 1990), 140. On Graham more broadly, see Charles H. Lippy, "Billy Graham," in *Twentieth-Century Shapers* (ed. Lippy), 179–86; John Pollock, *Billy Graham, Evangelist to the World: An Authorized Biography of the Decisive Years* (San Francisco: Harper & Row, 1979); and Marshall Frady, *Billy Graham: A Parable of American Righteousness* (Boston: Little-Brown, 1979).

21. In later years, Graham tempered his patriotism considerably. In 1974 at Lausanne, he warned that "to tie the gospel to any political system, secular program, or society is dangerous. The gospel transcends the goals and methods of any political system or society. . . . Our gospel is not America." See Joel Carpenter, "Geared to the Times, but Anchored to the Rock: How Contemporary Techniques and Exuberant Nationalism Helped Create an Evangelical Resurgence," *Christianity Today* 30 (November 8, 1985): 47.

22. Shelley, "The Rise of Evangelical Youth Movements," 49.

23. Carpenter, "Youth for Christ and the New Evangelicals," 135.

24. Ibid.

25. See Carpenter, "Geared to the Times," 44–47; and Shelley, "The Rise of Evangelical Youth Movements," 50. The first documentary film created by YFC, in 1951, bore the illustrative title "Counter Attack." See *YFC* 9 (December 1951): 40.

26. See Anne C. Loveland, *American Evangelicals and the U.S. Military, 1942–1993* (Baton Rouge: Louisiana State University Press, 1996).

27. "How I Study My Bible: A Symposium," *YFC* 8 (January 1951): 27–36.

28. See, e.g., Gary Dausey, "Rendevous—A Plan for Your Daily Appointment with the Lord: Why Do I Goof?" *YFC* 22 (April 1965): 5.

29. James Davison Hunter, *Evangelicalism: The Coming Generation* (Chicago: University of Chicago Press, 1987), 23.

30. "Youth for Christ, International, Inc., Statement of Faith," and "Youth for Christ Policy," *YFC* 9 (December 1951): 4.

31. Borgman, "A History," 68. The history of these organizations is best told by Senter, "The Youth for Christ Movement," and *The Coming Revolution in Youth Ministry.*

32. Jim Rayburn III, *Dance Children, Dance* (Wheaton: Tyndale House, 1984).

33. Shelley, "The Rise of Evangelical Youth Movements," 51.

34. Jack Hamilton, "Are High Schools Pagan?" *YFC* 7 (February 1950): 9–11, 74; idem, "Missionaries Are Made in High School," *YFC* 7 (March 1950): 18.

35. *YFC* 22 (October 1964): 27–42.

36. On the former, see Lawrence N. Jones, "The Intervarsity Christian Fellowship in the U.S." (Ph.D. diss., Yale University, 1961); on the latter, Richard Quebedeaux, *I Found It! The Story of Bill Bright and Campus Crusade* (San Francisco: Harper & Row, 1979).

37. Billy Graham, "I Tasted Revival," *YFC* 7 (January 1950): 11.

38. Torrey Johnson, *Reaching Youth for Christ* (Chicago: Moody, 1944), 35.

39. "YFC Club Camera," *YFC* 18 (June 1960): 27.

40. Lloyd G. Hamill, "God Works in San Francisco," *YFC* 7 (September 1949): 22–24.

41. Dorothy Haskins, "For Girls Only," *YFC* 5 (February 1947): 6, 28.

42. See, on the issue of gender dynamics in Evangelical and fundamentalist Christianity, Betty DeBerg, *Ungodly Women: Gender and the First Wave of American Fundamentalism* (Minneapolis: Fortress, 1990); John Stratton Hawley, ed., *Fundamentalism and Gender* (New York: Oxford University Press, 1994); and Margaret Bendroth, *Fundamentalism and Gender, 1875 to the Present* (New Haven, Conn.: Yale University Press, 1993).

43. Don Jacobs, "For Boys Only," *YFC* 5 (February 1947): 7, 58–59. The athlete as an ideal type for Evangelical males has a long and enduring history. See, e.g., *YFC* 22 (September 1965), an entire issue featuring testimonies by famous athletes; and, for evidence of continuity, *Campus Life* 53 (July/August 1994), which profiled World Series hero Joe Carter.

44. Carpenter, "Youth for Christ and the New Evangelicals," 131.

45. "It Does Happen to Christian Teens," *YFC* 22 (April 1965): 16–17.

46. *YFC* 22 (September 1964): 27–29.

47. The same avoidance of policy issues in favor of individual questions of morality appears in YFC treatments of Vietnam. The question was not whether the conflict was just or not but, rather, "Are You Willing to Go to War?" (indeed, on the cover the title was changed to "When You Go to War," which more accurately conveyed the intent of the author). Conscientious objection was nowhere mentioned in the article, which quoted Romans 13 and other Scripture to conclude, "It would seem, therefore, that it is legitimate for the Christian to hazard his life in the armed forces in the defense of a country such as ours."

Dr. Hudson Armerding, "Are You Willing to Go to War?" *YFC* 21 (February 1964): 29–30.

48. More than one commentator, including some within the Evangelical community, have registered this complaint. See esp. Mark A. Noll, *The Scandal of the Evangelical Mind* (Grand Rapids, Mich.: Eerdmans, 1995).

49. Marsden, *Fundamentalism and American Culture,* 212–23.

50. Carpenter, "Youth for Christ and the New Evangelicals," 131.

51. Mel Larson, *Youth for Christ: Twentieth-Century Wonder* (Grand Rapids, Mich.: Zondervan, 1947), 77.

52. Cliff Barrows, "We Met with the President!" *YFC* 8 (September 1950): 58.

53. Joel Carpenter, "Youth for Christ and the New Evangelicals," 130, 135. There is clearly both a continuity and a discontinuity between this "witness" and the emergence of the New Right in the eighties and nineties. Carpenter writes, "Militant fundamentalists and a host of pentecostal allies, newly politicized, have emerged out of the cultural hinterlands and have refused to go away," reasserting an "older version of the 'Christian America' myth" without "polite veneer." He adds, "The new fundamentalism is adamantly political, and the occasion is not a friendly invitation to participate but the forcible intrusion of resentful, uninvited guests" (p. 142).

54. Joel A. Carpenter, introduction to *The Youth for Christ Movement and Its Pioneers* (ed. Joel A. Carpenter; Fundamentalism in American Religion, 1880–1950, no. 43; New York: Garland, 1988), n.p. [6].

55. The best of the many books on the New Religious Right is Michael Lienesch, *Redeeming America: Piety and Politics in the New Christian Right* (Chapel Hill: University of North Carolina Press, 1993).

56. Betsy LaMar Franzwa, letter to Jon Pahl, December 13, 1994.

57. Bill Dean, interview with Jon Pahl, January 24, 1995, and Youth for Christ, N.W. Indiana, *Report to the People, 1994* (Valparaiso, Ind.: Youth for Christ, N. W. Indiana, 1994), 2.

58. See "So What Is Campus Life," *Campus Life* (October 1972): 51–66 for another period-specific picture of the movement. No longer a YFC publication, the journal was acquired by *Christianity Today* in 1982, but connections with YFC remained close.

59. Youth for Christ, N.W. Indiana, *Report to the People, 1994*, 2. The N.W. Indiana chapter calls its therapeutic ministry the "Family Concern Counseling Center." It was established in 1987.

60. Shelley, "The Rise of Evangelical Youth Movements," 51.

61. "Youth for Christ's National Ministries," n.p., online: www .gospelcom.net/yfc/yfc/Ministries/Ministries.html.

62. Randall Balmer, *Mine Eyes Have Seen the Glory: A Journey into the Evangelical Subculture in America* (New York: Oxford University Press, 1993), 97–98. Also available on video: Gateway Films/Vision Video (Worcester, Penn., 1992).

63. Ibid., 106.

64. Guidelines for successful Evangelical camps abound. See, e.g., Chap Clark, *The Youth Specialties Handbook for Great Camps and Retreats* (El Cajon, Cal.: Youth Specialties, 1990).

65. Tony Campolo, *The Church and the American Teenager: What Works and What Doesn't Work in Youth Ministry* (Grand Rapids, Mich.: Zondervan, 1989), 41.

66. The current mission and purpose statements of YFC would seem to be highly critical of this sort of accommodation. Youth for Christ's mission is "To communicate the life-changing message of Jesus Christ to every young person." Its purpose: "To participate in the Body of Christ in the responsible evangelism of youth, presenting them with the person, work, and teaching of Jesus Christ, discipling them and leading them into the local church." *Report to the People, 1994*, 1. See also "Our Mission," n.p., online: www.gospelcom.net/yfc/yfci/yfc12.html.

67. See esp. Quentin J. Schultze, et al., *Dancing in the Dark: Youth, Popular Culture, and the Electronic Media* (Grand Rapids, Mich.: Eerdmans, 1991). The "pull for souls" in American revivalism has often tended to blur with middle-class showmanship. At early YFC rallies, magicians performed tricks before their young audiences, "gospel whistlers" and "musical saws" took church hymnody to new depths, and a "gospel horse" called MacArthur was called upon to demonstrate proper behavior and doctrine for Christian youth. MacArthur "moved his jaws to show 'how the girls in the choir chew gum' and . . . [tapped] his hoof three times when asked 'how many Persons are in the Trinity.' " Mel Larson, *Young Man on Fire: The Story of Torrey Johnson and Youth for Christ* (Chicago: Youth for Christ, 1945), 41.

68. Youth Specialties, Inc., *The Catalog for Youth Ministry, Spring/Summer, 1999* (El Cajon, Cal.: Youth Specialties, 1999).

69. *Youthworker Update: The Newsletter for Christian Youth Workers.*

70. The same openness is true, in a somewhat less substantive way (the journal is intended for youth rather than youth ministers), in the continuing YFC publication *Campus Life*. See, e.g., Tim Stafford, "Love, and Sex, and the Whole Person," *Campus Life* 56 (July/August 1997): 42–44; this is regular feature column where topics such as "I'm Addicted to Porn," "I'm in Love with My Youth Worker," and others get discussed.

71. Online: Youth Specialties, Inc., home page, www.gospelcom .net/ys.

72. *Youthworker: The Contemporary Journal for Youth Ministry* 11 (Fall 1994): 6.

73. Campolo, *The Church and the American Teenager*, 199.

74. Senter, "The Youth for Christ Movement," 371.

75. Hunter, *Evangelicalism*, 42.

76. *Sojourners* 25 (January/February 1994).

77. In addition to World Vision (www.wvi.org), other important examples of Evangelical social justice agencies are Evangelicals for Social Action, the Shalom Communities, Kairos Associates, and the aptly named Compassion International. See Hunter, *Evangelicalism*, 40–45; and Tony Campolo, *Ideas for Social Action* (ed. Wayne Rice; El Cajon, Cal.: Youth Specialties Press, 1983), who catalogs several dozen, 133–60. Domestically, programs such as Amor Industries (Aiding Mexican Orphans and Refugees), the Mennonite Central Committee, and the Pittsburgh Project involve Evangelical youth in direct social action. See *Youthworker* 11 (Fall 1994): 62.

78. The many works of Robert Wuthnow both explore and attempt to heal this split. See esp. *The Restructuring of American Religion: Society and Faith since World War II* (Princeton, N.J.: Princeton University Press, 1988); *The Struggle for America's Soul: Evangelicals, Liberals, and Secularism* (Grand Rapids, Mich.: Eerdmans, 1989); and *Acts of Compassion: Caring for Others and Helping Ourselves* (Princeton, N.J.: Princeton University Press, 1991).

79. Carpenter, "Youth for Christ and the New Evangelicals," 143. Carpenter is citing Grant Wacker, "Uneasy in Zion: Evangelicalism in Postmodern Society," in *Evangelicalism and Modern America* (ed. George Marsden; Grand Rapids, Mich.: Eerdmans, 1984), 22–24.

80. Carpenter, "Youth for Christ and the New Evangelicals," 143.

NOTES TO CHAPTER 4

1. Maya Angelou, *I Know Why the Caged Bird Sings* (New York: Bantam, 1969), 154–56.

2. Gayraud Wilmore, *Black Religion and Black Radicalism: An Interpretation of the Religious History of Afro-American People* (2d ed.; Maryknoll, N.Y.: Orbis, 1983). See also Peter Paris, *The Social Teaching of the Black Churches* (Philadelphia: Fortress, 1985).

3. "By the Grace of God: History of Bethel A.M.E. Church Baltimore, Maryland," n.p., online: www.bethel1.org, 1.

4. See Howard D. Gregg, *History of the African Methodist Episcopal Church* (Nashville: AMEC, 1980).

5. Clarence E. Walker, *A Rock in a Weary Land: The African Methodist Episcopal Church during the Civil War and Reconstruction* (Baton Rouge: Louisiana State University Press, 1982).

6. C. Eric Lincoln and Lawrence H. Mamiya, *The Black Church in the African American Experience* (Durham, N.C.: Duke University Press, 1990), 332.

7. "By the Grace of God," 2–3.

8. Lawrence H. Mamiya, "A Social History of the Bethel African Methodist Episcopal Church in Baltimore: The House of God and the Struggle for Freedom," in *Portraits of Twelve Religious Communities*, vol. 1 of

American Congregations (2 vols.; ed. James P. Wind and James W. Lewis; Chicago: University of Chicago Press, 1994), 255.

9. "By the Grace of God," 6.

10. The rediscovery of this insight has been a chief feature of the recent generation of scholarship on the African-American church. See, among many, James H. Cone, *God of the Oppressed* (New York: Seabury, 1976); Eugene D. Genovese, *Roll, Jordan, Roll: The World the Slaves Made* (New York: Vintage, 1976); Lawrence W. Levine, *Black Culture and Black Consciousness: Afro-American Folk Thought from Slavery to Freedom* (New York: Oxford University Press, 1977); Albert J. Raboteau, *Slave Religion: The "Invisible Institution" in the Antebellum South* (New York: Oxford University Press, 1978).

11. Mamiya, "A Social History," 257.

12. Lincoln and Mamiya, *The Black Church*, 241.

13. Mamiya, "A Social History," 258–61.

14. On the theme of continuity, see Albert J. Raboteau, "The Black Church: Continuity within Change," in *Altered Landscapes: Christianity in America, 1935–1985* (ed. David W. Lotz; Grand Rapids, Mich.: Eerdmans, 1989), 77–91. On the role of churches in the civil rights movement, see, among many, Aldon D. Morris, *The Origins of the Civil Rights Movement: Black Communities Organizing for Change* (New York: Free Press, 1984); David J. Garrow, *Bearing the Cross: Martin Luther King, Jr., and the Southern Christian Leadership Conference* (New York: Vintage, 1986); Taylor Branch, *Parting the Waters: America in the King Years, 1954–1963* (New York: Simon & Schuster, 1988); and Adam Fairclough, "The Southern Christian Leadership Conference and the Second Reconstruction, 1957–1973," in *Native American Religion and Black Protestantism*, vol. 9 of *Modern American Protestantism and Its World* (14 vols.; ed. Martin E. Marty; Munich: K. G. Sauer, 1993), 188–205.

15. See, among others, Anthony M. Orum, "A Reappraisal of the Social and Political Participation of Negroes," *American Journal of Sociology* 72 (July 1966): 33; and Charles E. Silberman, *Crisis in Black and White* (New York: Random House, 1964).

16. On the ring-shout, a form of liturgical dancing with roots in Africa, see Raboteau, *Slave Religion*. E. Franklin Frazier, *The Negro Church in America* (New York: Schocken, 1963), although a pioneering work, depends upon an integrationist model of African-American history that takes its lead from the white middle classes and thereby falls prey to some of these stereotypes.

17. William R. Myers, *Black and White Styles of Youth Ministry: Two Congregations in America* (New York: Pilgrim, 1991), traces some of this history.

18. See n. 10, above, and Lincoln and Mamiya, *The Black Church*.

19. Lincoln and Mamiya, *The Black Church*, 12–15.

20. Ibid., 309–10.

21. Ibid., 8–9.

22. The figure of 30 percent is more common. See Robert Hill, "The Black Middle Class: Past, Present, and Future," in National Urban League, *The State of Black America, 1986* (New York: National Urban League, 1986): 43–64; and Andrew Billingsley, "Black Families in a Changing Society," in National Urban League, *The State of Black America, 1987* (New York: National Urban League, 1987), 97–111, as cited by Lincoln and Mamiya, *The Black Church,* 267. Current sociological studies do not document a widespread flight by middle-class blacks from the churches. See ibid., 342–43.

23. C. Eric Lincoln, *The Black Church since Frazier* (New York: Schocken, 1974), 127. See also C. Eric Lincoln and Lawrence H. Mamiya, "Black Militant and Separatist Movements," in *The Encyclopedia of the American Religious Experience* (3 vols.; ed. Charles H. Lippy and Peter W. Williams; New York: Scribners, 1988), 2:755–71.

24. On Garvey, see Randall K. Burkett, *Garveyism as a Religious Movement* (Metuchen, N.J.: Scarecrow, 1978); Judith Stein, *The World of Marcus Garvey: Race and Class in Modern Society* (Baton Rouge: Louisiana State University Press, 1986); and Robert A. Hill, ed., *The Marcus Garvey and Universal Negro Improvement Association Papers* (Berkeley: University of California Press, 1983). On the growth of Islam as an alternative to Christianity among African-American youth, see Richard Wormser, *American Islam: Growing Up Muslim in America* (New York: Walker, 1994).

25. On the way systemic violence has targeted youth, see Males, *The Scapegoat Generation.*

26. For one interpretation of Vietnam as the pivotal event in recent U.S. religious history, see Walter T. Davis Jr., *Shattered Dream: America's Search for Its Soul* (Valley Forge, Penn.: Trinity Press International, 1994). For a more focused study of the relationship between religion and violence in the memory of Vietnam, see Jon Pahl, "A National Shrine to Scapegoating? The Vietnam Veterans Memorial, Washington, D.C.," *Contagion* 2 (Summer 1995): 169–93.

27. The most egregious example is California's Proposition 209, which established "color-blind" admissions criteria for state colleges. See the careful deconstruction of the racist effects of this policy in Hugh B. Price, "Color-Blindness Equals Exclusion," February 8, 1999, n.p., online: National Urban League Web site, www.nul.org/tobearch.html. In essence, by using "standardized tests" and "advanced placement course credit" as supposedly color-blind application criteria, Proposition 209 rules out many African-American and Latino students from impoverished school districts where advanced-placement courses are simply not offered because of budgetary constraints.

28. See Mark Roscoe and Reggie Morton, "Disproportionate Minority Confinement," n.p., online: National Criminal Justice Reference Service Web site, www.ncjrs.org/txtfiles/fs-9411.txt., who conclude that

"African-American juveniles comprise a disproportionately higher percentage of juvenile arrests than other races."

29. William Julius Wilson, "Jobless Ghettos: The Impact of the Disappearance of Work in Segregated Neighborhoods," in National Urban League, *The State of Black America, 1998* (New York: National Urban League, 1998).

30. Lincoln and Mamiya, *The Black Church,* 322, citing David Swinton, "The Economic Status of Blacks, 1986," in National Urban League, *The State of Black America, 1987,* 58.

31. Hugh B. Price, "Where Are the Jobs?" March 23, 1998, n.p., online: www.nul.org/tobearch.html.

32. Joyce Ladner, "Teenage Pregnancy: The Implication for Black Americans," in National Urban League, *The State of Black America, 1986,* 68–70, as cited by Lincoln and Mamiya, *The Black Church,* 324.

33. See Linda Darling-Hammond, "New Standards, Old Inequalities: The Current Challenge for African American Education," in National Urban League, *The State of Black America, 1998.*

34. Simons, Finlay, and Yang, *Fact Book,* as cited by Milbrey W. McLaughlin, Merita A. Irby, and Julie Langman, *Urban Sanctuaries: Neighborhood Organizations in the Lives and Futures of Inner-City Youth* (San Francisco: Jossey-Bass, 1994), 11. See also *Crisis* 93 (March 1986), as cited by Bruce R. Hare, "Black Youth at Risk," in National Urban League, *The State of Black America, 1988* (New York: National Urban League, 1988), 84.

35. See "Criminal Offenders Statistics," n.p., online: U.S. Department of Justice Web site, www.ojp.usdoj.gove/bjs/crimoff.htm, "Based on current rates of first incarceration, an estimated 28% of black males will enter State or Federal prison, compared to 16% of Hispanic males, and 4.4% of white males."

36. On this distinction, see Kairos Theologians Group, *The Kairos Document: Challenge to the Church—A Theological Comment on the Political Crisis in South Africa* (rev. 2d ed.; Grand Rapids, Mich.: Eerdmans, 1986), esp. 13.

37. Nathan McCall, *Makes Me Wanna Holler: A Young Black Man in America* (New York: Random House, 1994), 64–65.

38. James H. Cone, *Black Theology and Black Power* (New York: Seabury, 1969).

39. Lincoln and Mamiya, *The Black Church,* 320–33.

40. Myers, *Black and White Styles,* 109.

41. Ibid.

42. John Mbiti, *African Religions and Philosophy* (New York: Praeger, 1969).

43. Myers, *Black and White Styles,* 126.

44. Ibid., 98–99.

45. See Gerald L. Davis, *"I Got the Word in Me and I Can Sing It, You Know": A Study of the Performed African-American Sermon* (Philadelphia: University of Pennsylvania Press, 1985).

46. "[Grace] Church Voluntary Organization Roster," spring 1993.

47. Samuel G. Freedman, *Upon This Rock: The Miracles of a Black Church* (New York: HarperCollins, 1993).

48. Myers, *Black and White Styles,* 145.

49. See also Carol B. Stack, *All Our Kin: Strategies for Survival in a Black Community* (New York: Harper & Row, 1974).

50. The black Baptist churches are documented in Leroy Fitts, *A History of Black Baptists* (Nashville: Broadman, 1985).

51. Freedman, *Upon This Rock,* 9.

52. Ibid., 249–53.

53. Ibid., 256.

54. Ibid., 258.

55. McLaughlin, Irby, and Langman, *Urban Sanctuaries.*

56. Ibid., 89.

57. Ibid., 86.

58. Ibid., 194–200.

59. Ibid., 88.

60. BEST is hardly alone. Parachurch agencies or programs to work with African-American urban youth have mushroomed in recent years. See, e.g., Project IMAGE in Chicago; Black Manhood Training out of the University of Virginia; Project Spirit, sponsored by the Congress of National Black Churches; and many others described by Lincoln and Mamiya, *The Black Church,* 339–40.

61. Teri is one of six composite portraits, drawn from fieldwork, interviews, and relationships with young individuals identified by McLaughlin as "hopefuls," *Urban Sanctuaries,* 26.

62. Ibid., 27.

63. Ibid., 28.

64. Ibid., 29.

65. See "Hospitality," in *Practicing Our Faith* (ed. Bass), 29–42.

66. David DeVaux, interview with Jon Pahl, December 16, 1998.

67. Lincoln and Mamiya, *The Black Church,* 380–81. See also James H. Cone, *The Spirituals and the Blues: An Interpretation* (San Francisco: Harper & Row, 1972); Wyatt Tee Walker, *"Somebody's Calling My Name": Black Sacred Music and Social Change* (Valley Forge, Penn.: Judson, 1979); and Michael W. Harris, *The Rise of Gospel Blues: The Music of Andrew Dorsey in the Urban Church* (New York: Oxford University Press, 1992).

68. Bethel is one of the A.M.E. churches (with A.M.E. Zion and Baptist) to be involved since the seventies in the neo-Pentecostal movement. This movement, drawing on the dramatic growth of the Church of God in Christ in the United States, has transformed many traditionally "decorous" black churches into congregations featuring vibrant, spirit-infused worship. Speaking in tongues is not considered essential for membership in these churches, but it is welcomed as one of many spiritual gifts. See Lincoln and Mamiya, *The Black Church,* 385–88.

69. "Bethel AME Rites of Passage Syllabus," 8.

70. Mamiya, "A Social History," 269.

71. Ibid., 269.

72. DeVaux, interview, 3.

73. "Bethel Ministries," n.p., online: www.bethel1.org/ministries.htm.

74. "Statement of Purpose," n.p., online: www.bethel1.org/admin .htm payne.

NOTES TO CHAPTER 5

1. Kett, *Rites of Passage,* 210, 194, 190, 248.

2. Ibid., 248.

3. Ibid., 243.

4. Ibid., 253. The quote ("devastating but accurate") is from Hollingshead, *Elmtown's Youth,* 149.

5. See Roland Bainton, *Here I Stand: A Life of Martin Luther* (New York: Abingdon-Cokesbury, 1950), which is still the standard narrative biography. Bainton tells how, in an age when priests were not to marry, Luther married Katherine von Bora; how, long after being excommunicated, Luther continued to give and receive Holy Communion; and how, by the time of his death in 1546, twenty years after the pope had demanded his silence, Luther had written and delivered hundreds of essays, sermons, treatises, and disputations.

6. See chapter 1, 23.

7. See chapter 1, 21.

8. See chapter 1, 26–28.

9. See chapter 1, 29–34.

10. Thomas Aquinas, *Summa Theologiae: A Concise Translation* (ed. Timothy McDermott; Westminster, Md.: Christian Classics, 1989).

11. Ibid., 303.

12. Timothy McDermott, "What the *Summa* Is About," ibid., xxiii.

13. Thomas Aquinas, *Summa Theologiae* 1a, 2, 3 (trans. Timothy McDermott; New York: McGraw-Hill, 1964), 2:13, 15, as cited by William C. Placher, *A History of Christian Theology: An Introduction* (Philadelphia: Westminster, 1983), 154.

14. See chapter 2, 39.

15. See chapter 2, 46–54.

16. John Calvin, Sermon 103 on Job, 522–253; cf. *The Institutes of the Christian Religion,* II, ii, 16, as cited by William G. Bouwsma, *John Calvin: A Sixteenth Century Portrait* (New York: Oxford University Press, 1988), 99.

17. John Calvin, *Institutes of the Christian Religion* (ed. J. T. McNeill; trans. Ford Lewis Battles; Library of Christian Classics; Philadelphia: Westminster, 1960).

18. John Calvin, Sermon 50 on Job, 627, ibid., 161.

19. John Calvin, *Traité des scandales* [*Concerning Scandals*], 157, 163–64, 182–83, as cited by Bouwsma, *John Calvin*, 68.

20. John Calvin, Sermon 45 on Deuteronomy, 426–427, as cited by Bouwsma, *John Calvin*, 192.

21. John Calvin, Sermon 30 on Deuteronomy 238, as cited by Bouwsma, *John Calvin*, 192.

22. Calvin, *Institutes*, IV, xx, 2, as cited by Bouwsma, *John Calvin*, 213.

23. The long debate about the economic impact of Protestantism deserves noting. See, most significantly, Max Weber, *The Protestant Ethic and the Spirit of Capitalism* (New York: Scribners, 1958). Weber's argument, that out of the "anxiety" created by Calvin's emphasis on God came a search by humans to prove their "election" through economic activity, has been remarkably provocative and appears confirmed by much of recent history.

24. George Hunston Williams, *The Radical Reformation* (Philadelphia: Westminster, 1962).

25. See Joseph Haroutunian, *Piety versus Moralism: The Passing of the New England Theology* (New York: Holt, 1932).

26. On Finney, see Keith A. Hardacre, *Charles Grandison Finney* (Cambridge: Harvard University Press, 1988); and David L. Weddle, *The Law as Gospel: Revival and Reform in the Theology of Charles G. Finney* (Studies in Evangelicalism 6; Metuchen, N.J.: Scarecrow, 1985).

27. William G. McLoughlin Jr., *Modern Revivalism: Charles Grandison Finney to Billy Graham* (New York: Ronald, 1959).

28. On this typology, see H. Richard Niebuhr, *Christ and Culture* (New York: Harper & Row, 1951).

29. Raboteau, *Slave Religion*, 92.

30. James H. Cone, *A Black Theology of Liberation: Twentieth Anniversary Edition* (Maryknoll, N.Y.: Orbis, 1990).

31. See chapter 4, 81–82.

32. Theophus Smith, *Conjuring Culture: Biblical Formations of Black America* (New York: Oxford University Press, 1994), 4–6. Conversion provides another example. African-American conversions may be as much akin to African traditions of spirit possession as to Evangelical "second birth." In white churches, conversion is often defensive—away from sin and "the world." In African-American communities, conversion often impels a recipient of the experience into action on behalf of his or her community. See, for a collection of early African-American conversion narratives, Clifton H. Johnson, ed., *God Struck Me Dead* (Philadelphia: Pilgrim, 1969).

33. Ibid., 58–59.

34. See Ferenc Morton Szasz, *The Divided Mind of Protestant America, 1880–1930* (University, Ala.: University of Alabama Press, 1982).

35. Martin E. Marty, "Religion: A Private Affair, in Public Affairs," *Religion and American Culture* 3 (Summer 1993): 116.

36. The dilemma is complex psychologically and socially. Psychologically, the issue is perhaps the distinction between narcissistic and transcendent modes of faith; socially, what might be called vernacular and national faiths. See, on the former, Christopher Lasch, *The Culture of Narcissism: American Life in an Age of Diminishing Expectations* (New York: Norton, 1978); and Tony Campolo, *The Church and the American Teenager* (Grand Rapids, Mich.: Zondervan, 1989), 203. For a discussion of civil religion, see, among many others, Donald G. Jones and Russell E. Richey, *American Civil Religion* (New York: Harper & Row, 1974); and John F. Wilson, *Public Religion in American Culture* (Princeton, N.J.: Princeton University Press, 1979).

37. See Walter Capps, ed., *The Vietnam Reader* (New York: Routledge, 1990).

38. In my own teaching and youth ministry, I have been informed by the work of Sallie McFague, notably *Models of God: Theology for an Ecological, Nuclear Age* (Philadelphia: Fortress, 1987). The book is hardly suitable for a youth group, as it is laden with academic jargon, but the ideas McFague conveys translate very well to contemporary youth.

39. On the long history of this question in Christian theology, see the badly titled survey of Harry J. McSorley, *Luther, Right or Wrong? An Ecumenical-Theological Study of Luther's Major Work, The Bondage of the Will* (New York: Newman, 1969). McSorley's work (somewhat tendentiously) uses Luther's text as a historical pivot, but it remains the single best survey of the long Christian debate over free will and voluntarism. On the recurrent importance of this theme in American religious history, see McLoughlin, *Revivals, Awakenings, and Reform.* For a close study of the formation of early but enduring patterns connected with this question, see Pahl, *Paradox Lost.* Finally, two sociological works draw attention to this theme. See Warner, "Work in Progress," 1044–93, which argues for a rich compatibility between voluntarism and religious life in U.S. culture; and John Modell, *Into One's Own: From Youth to Adulthood in the United States, 1920–1975* (Berkeley: University of California Press, 1989), where the increasing importance of voluntarism in the lives of youth in America is the predominant theme.

40. Many mainline youth ministers are aware of the problem. See, e.g., the recent work by Dean and Foster, *The Godbearing Life,* who recognize the need for programs in mainline churches but urge local youth ministers primarily to develop the art of "soul tending" as a path of ministry. Programming becomes less important than relating to youth as a representative of Christ's compassion and practices.

41. This trend was noted in the mideighties by Wade Clark Roof and William McKinney, *American Mainline Religion: Its Changing Shape and Future* (New Brunswick, N.J.: Rutgers University Press, 1987).

42. Modell, *Into One's Own,* 14, 331.

43. William R. Myers, ed., *Becoming and Belonging: A Practical Design for Confirmation* (Cleveland: United Church, 1993), 9.

44. See Wade Clark Roof, *A Generation of Seekers: The Spiritual Journeys of the Baby Boom Generation* (San Francisco: Harper & Row, 1993); and William Mahedy and Janet Bernardi, *A Generation Alone: Xers Making a Place in the World* (Downers Grove, Ill.: InterVarsity Press, 1994).

45. As sociologist Robert Bellah concluded, "Religion is one of the most important of the many ways in which Americans 'get involved' in the life of their community and society." See Robert Bellah et al., *Habits of the Heart: Individualism and Commitment in American Life* (New York: Harper & Row, 1985), 219.

46. These phrases are Max Weber's. See Graham Murdock, "The Re-enchantment of the World: Religion and the Transformations of Modernity," in *Rethinking Media, Religion, and Culture* (ed. Stewart M. Hoover and Knut Lundby; Thousand Oaks, Cal.: Sage, 1997), 85–101.

47. See Kathleen Stassen Berger and Ross A. Thompson, *The Developing Person: Through Childhood and Adolescence* (4th ed.; Dallas: Worth, 1996).

NOTES TO CHAPTER 6

1. This is changing. See the often brilliant essays collected in Levi and Schmitt, eds., *A History of Young People in the West*. On America, see Austin and Willard, *Generations of Youth*, along with Modell, *Into One's Own,* and Grace Palladino, *Teenagers: An American History* (New York: Basic Books, 1996).

2. Shils, *Tradition,* 8.

3. Ibid., 213–61.

4. See ch. 5.

5. Borgman, "A History," 71.

6. Peter C. Scales et al., *The Attitudes and Needs of Religious Youth Workers: Perspectives from the Field* (Minneapolis: Search Institute, 1995), 13, as cited by Dean and Foster, *The Godbearing Life.*

7. David Ng, "Rethinking Youth Ministry," in *Rethinking Christian Education: Explorations in Theory and Practice* (ed. David S. Sculler; St. Louis: Chalice, 1993), 88.

8. Ibid.

9. Dean and Foster, *The Godbearing Life,* 25.

10. John Coleman and Gregory Baum, eds., *Youth without a Future?* (Concilium 181; Edinburgh: T. & T. Clark, 1985).

11. See Brereton, *Training God's Army;* Pahl, *Hopes and Dreams of All.*

12. The best-studied organizations are the YMCA and the YWCA. See Nina Mjagkij and Margaret Spratt, eds., *Men and Women Adrift: The YMCA and YWCA in the City* (New York: New York University Press, 1997).

13. Tom Engelhardt, *The End of Victory Culture: Cold War America and the Disillusioning of a Generation* (Amherst: University of Massachusetts Press, 1995), 6.

14. "Patricia E. Munk, Pelham Manor, NY, to H. V. Kaltenborn, August 9, 1945, Kaltenborn Papers," as cited by Paul E. Boyer, *By the Bomb's Early Light: American Thought and Culture at the Dawn of the Atomic Age* (New York: Pantheon, 1985), 16.

15. Dwight D. Eisenhower, *Public Papers of the Presidents of the United States: Dwight D. Eisenhower, 1960–1961* (Washington, D.C.: Government Printing Office, 1961), 1036–40, as excerpted in *A History of Our Time: Readings on Postwar America* (William H. Chafe and Harvard Sitkoff; 3d ed.; New York: Oxford University Press, 1991), 108.

16. *Congressional Record*, 82d Cong., 1st sess., June 14, 1951, 6602, as cited by Richard Hofstadter, "The Paranoid Style in American Politics," in *The Paranoid Style in American Politics and Other Essays* (New York: Knopf, 1965), 7–8.

17. Joseph McCarthy, "Speech at Wheeling, West Virginia," *Congressional Record*, 81st Cong., 2d session, p. 1954, February 20, 1950, as cited in *A History of Our Time* (ed. Chafe and Sitkoff), 75.

18. Davis, *Shattered Dream*, 7.

19. Engelhardt, *The End of Victory Culture*, 193.

20. Davis, *Shattered Dream*, 12.

21. See, among others, Irwin Unger, *The Movement: A History of the American New Left, 1959–1972* (New York: Harper & Row, 1974); and the memoir of SDS member Todd Gitlin, *The Sixties*.

22. See, e.g., Clyde Taylor, ed., *Vietnam and Black America: An Anthology of Protest and Resistance* (New York: Anchor/Doubleday, 1973).

23. An excellent collection of primary sources from the period is Marvin E. Gettleman et al., eds., *Vietnam and America: A Documented History* (New York: Grove Weidenfeld, 1985).

24. See, among many others, Myra MacPherson, *Long Time Passing: Vietnam and the Haunted Generation* (New York: Doubleday, 1984). For perhaps the most widely read reflection on the attempts to develop a new version of Christianity attuned to the post-Vietnam realities, see Bellah et al., *Habits of the Heart*.

25. Zotti, *A Time of Awakening*, 270–71.

26. See William E. Leuchtenberg, *The FDR Years: On Roosevelt and His Legacy* (New York: Columbia University Press, 1995), 255.

27. See J. A. Salmond, *The Civilian Conservation Corps, 1933–42* (Durham, N.C.: Duke University Press, 1967).

28. Alvin Klatt, "Conservation of Youth in C.C.C. Work," *WLM* 42 (May 1933): 73.

29. Leuchtenberg, *The FDR Years*, 255.

30. Elaine Tyler May, "Cold War: Warm Hearth, Politics, and the Family in Postwar America," in *The Rise and Fall of the New Deal Order,*

1930–1980 (ed. Steve Fraser and Gary Gerstle; Princeton, N.J.: Princeton University Press, 1989), 157–58.

31. See the provocative argument of Peter Gardella, *Domestic Religion: Work, Food, Sex, and Other Commitments* (Cleveland: Pilgrim, 1998).

32. William H. Chafe, *America since 1945* (New American History Series; Washington, D.C.: American Historical Association, 1990), 13.

33. Ronald W. Reagan, "The Second American Revolution," in *A History of Our Time* (ed. Chafe and Sitkoff), 445–50.

34. Jeffrey E. Mirel, "Twentieth-Century America, Adolescence in," in *The Encyclopedia of Adolescence* (2 vols.; ed. Richard M. Lerner, Anne C. Petersen, and Jeanne Brooks-Gunn; New York: Garland, 1991), 2:1153–67.

35. Although they were attempts by the churches to counter the "secularization" of public schools, parochial schools complicated youth ministry by removing the locus of the programs from local congregations or youth ministry organizations. See James C. Carper and Thomas C. Hunt, *Religious Schooling in America* (Birmingham, Ala.: Religious Education Press, 1984); and Bryk, Lee, and Holland, *Catholic Schools.*

36. Pahl, *Hopes and Dreams of All*, 226.

37. Zotti, *A Time of Awakening*, 238.

38. Pahl, *Hopes and Dreams of All*, 219.

39. See Potvin, Hoge, and Nelsen, *Religion and American Youth.*

40. See Evans, *The Newman Movement.*

41. See John Modell, *Into One's Own.*

42. See David L. Lewis and Laurence Goldstein, eds., *The Automobile and American Culture* (Ann Arbor, Mich.: University of Michigan Press, 1983).

43. See Palladino, *Teenagers*, 101.

44. Beth L. Bailey, *From Front Porch to Back Seat: Courtship in Twentieth-Century America* (Baltimore: Johns Hopkins University Press, 1988).

45. See, e.g., the 1999 summer camp curriculum produced by the National Council of Churches, entitled "God in Our Midst." The ecologically centered materials link nature with Christian practices throughout.

46. The turn to violence by youth, and the attention given to such episodes by the media, is similar to a role played in the past by ethnic groups in America in relationship to national culture. See John Bodnar, *Remaking America: Public Memory, Commemoration, and Patriotism in the Twentieth Century* (Princeton, N.J.: Princeton University Press, 1992). Bodnar's distinction between "official" (national) and "vernacular" (subcultural) expressions of memory holds true also for the educational and formative practices of churches, and nowhere more than with youth.

47. Mahedy and Bernardi, *A Generation Alone.*

NOTES TO CHAPTER 7

1. Shils, *Tradition*, 213–15.

2. Ibid., 228.

3. Ibid., 230.

4. This claim is no doubt controversial but is gaining support from a new paradigm for the study of American religions. See Warner, "Work in Progress," 1044–93.

5. The standard history, in need of updating, remains Ruth Rouse and Stephen Charles Neill, eds., *A History of the Ecumenical Movement* (2d ed.; 2 vols; Philadelphia: Westminster, 1967–[1970]).

6. Online: World Council of Churches home page, wcc-coe.org.

7. Online: National Council of Churches of Christ home page, ncccusa.org.

8. H. George Anderson, "Ecumenical Movements," in *Altered Landscapes* (ed. Lotz), 92–105.

9. Online: National Association of Evangelicals home page, www.nae .net.

10. See the sketch by Nichol, *All These Lutherans.*

11. See, among many other sources of such statistics, Daniel G. Reed et al., eds., *Dictionary of Christianity in America* (Downers Grove, Ill.: Intervarsity, 1990).

12. See, e.g., the Lutheran-Episcopal dialogue, William A. Norgren and William G. Rusch, eds., *"Toward Full Communion" and "Concordat of Agreement": Lutheran-Episcopal Dialogue, Series III* (Minneapolis: Augsburg, 1991). The agreement was ratified by Episcopalians on a first vote, but narrowly defeated among Lutherans. A slightly changed new text, "Called to Common Mission," was ratified by Lutherans in 1999. See "ELCA Assembly Approves Full Communion with Episcopal Church," online: listserv.elca.org/scripts/wa.exe?AZ:ind9908&L=elcanews&P= R4075.

13. Online: Evangelical Lutheran Church in America home page, www/elca.org. A "Joint Statement on Justification" was signed by the two groups in 1999. See "Lutherans, Roman Catholics Overcome Historic Condemnations," online: listserv.elca.org/scripts/wa.exe?AZ=ind 9911&L-elcanews&P=R612.

14. The annual CROP WALKS are sponsored by Church World Service, a relief agency under the auspices of the National Council of Churches. See online: www.churchworldservice.org.

15. Martin E. Marty, *Church Unity and Church Mission* (Grand Rapids, Mich.: Eerdmans, 1964), 47, 21.

16. See Norman E. Thomas, ed., *Classic Texts in Mission and World Christianity* (Maryknoll, N.Y.: Orbis, 1995).

17. Rodger C. Bassham, *Mission Theology: 1948–1975* (Pasadena: William Carey Library, 1979), 21–25, as cited by William R. Hutchison, "Americans in World Missions: Revision and Realignment," in *Altered Landscapes* (ed. Lotz), 159.

18. See esp. the "Wheaton Declaration," in *The Church's Worldwide Mission* (ed. Harold Lindsell; Waco, Tex.: Word, 1966), 223–30.

19. Hutchison, "Americans in World Missions," 155–69.

20. Ibid., 170.

21. The most notable were perhaps the scholars of the Jesus Seminar. See online: Jesus Seminar home page, religion.rutgers.edu/jseminar/ jsem_b .html.

22. The K–12 Project of the American Academy of Religion seeks to infuse teaching about religions into public schools; online: American Academy of Religion home page, www.aarweb.org.

23. See Ernest S. Frerichs, ed., *The Bible and Bibles in America* (Atlanta: Scholars Press, 1988).

24. See, e.g., Kenneth Hagen et al., eds., *The Bible in the Churches: How Different Christians Interpret the Scriptures* (New York: Paulist, 1985).

25. See Mark A. Noll, *Between Faith and Criticism: Evangelicals, Scholarship, and the Bible in America* (San Francisco: Harper & Row, 1986).

26. See, e.g., online: Bible Gateway home page, bible.gospelcom .net/bible.

27. See, e.g., the dialogue between Lutheran and Catholic liturgists, Romey P. Marshall and Michael J. Taylor, S.J., *Liturgy and Christian Unity* (Englewood Cliffs, N.J.: Prentice-Hall, 1965). The book's first sentences read, "Ten years ago a Catholic-Protestant dialogue such as this book would have been unlikely. Twenty-five years ago, it would have been unthinkable" (p. iii).

28. James F. White, "Public Worship in Protestantism," in *Altered Landscapes* (ed. Lotz), 116.

29. Ibid., 114.

30. Perhaps the most notable exception to this trend is in Evangelical megachurches, where performance prevails over participation. Even this trend, however, is designed to meet people's desires and to invite them into the broader life of the community. User-friendly worship thus takes many forms. See Crystal Kirgiss, "The Changing Face of Christian Music . . . and What It Means for Youth Ministry," *Youthworker* (March/April 1997): 20–25.

31. See Wuthnow, *The Struggle for America's Soul,* 41, who argues,

> The issues that have drawn religious groups into the public sphere in recent years are bewilderingly diverse. Nuclear arms negotiations, the sale of infant formula to mothers in the Third World, aid to Contra rebels in Nicaragua, an Equal Rights Amendment to the Constitution, military and economic policy in the Middle East, prayer in public schools, abortion, nominations to the Supreme Court, and a host of other issues have all been the subject of intense discussion, and often activism as well, by religious groups.

The diversity, however, hides the common thread of activism and public engagement.

32. Leonard I. Sweet, "The Modernization of Protestant Religion in America," in *Altered Landscapes* (ed. Lotz), 32–34.

33. See, e.g., online: National Conference of Catholic Bishops home page, www.nccbuscc.org.

34. Ralph Reed, *Active Faith: How Christians Are Changing the Soul of American Politics* (New York: Free Press, 1996).

35. Online: Habitat for Humanity home page, www.habitat.org.

36. See Millard Fuller, *The Theology of the Hammer* (Macon, Ga.: Smyth & Helwys, 1994), 7.

37. See Peter J. Paris, "The Religious World of African Americans," in *World Religions in America* (ed. Neusner), 69–91.

38. See Sidney E. Mead, *The Lively Experiment: The Shaping of Christianity in America* (New York: Harper & Row, 1963). See also Jerald C. Brauer, ed., *The Lively Experiment Continued: Essays in Honor of Sidney E. Mead* (Macon, Ga.: Mercer University Press, 1987).

39. R. Laurence Moore, *Selling God: American Religion in the Marketplace of Culture* (New York: Oxford University Press, 1994).

40. Philip Rieff, *The Triumph of the Therapeutic* (New York: Harper & Row, 1966); Lasch, *The Culture of Narcissism*.

41. William C. Placher, *The Domestication of Transcendence: How Modern Thinking about God Went Wrong* (Louisville: Westminster John Knox, 1996).

42. Robert N. Bellah et al., *The Good Society* (New York: Alfred A. Knopf, 1991), 43.

43. Bellah et al., *Habits of the Heart,* vii.

44. Robert S. Ellwood, *The Fifties Spiritual Marketplace: American Religion in a Decade of Conflict* (New Brunswick, N.J.: Rutgers University Press, 1997).

45. Warner, "Work in Progress," 1070.

46. Leigh Eric Schmidt, *Consumer Rites: The Buying and Selling of American Holidays* (Princeton, N.J.: Princeton University Press, 1995), 9.

47. See Martin E. Marty, "The Diffusion of Religion," in "Religion in America since Mid-Century," *Daedalus* 3 (Winter 1982): 154–57.

48. Philip E. Hammond, *Religion and Personal Autonomy: The Third Disestablishment in America* (Columbia: University of South Carolina Press, 1992), 11.

49. Barbara MacHaffie, *Herstory: Women in Christian Tradition* (Philadelphia: Fortress, 1986), 143.

50. *Concerning the Ordination of Women* (Geneva: World Council of Churches, 1964), 5–6, as cited in Rosemary Skinner Keller and Rosemary Radford Ruether, eds., *In Our Own Voices: Four Centuries of American Women's Religious Writing* (San Francisco: HarperCollins, 1995), 333.

51. MacHaffie, *Herstory,* remains the best overview. See, on America, Susan Hill Lindley, *"You Have Stept out of Your Place": A History of Women and Religion in America* (Louisville: Westminster John Knox, 1996).

52. See, e.g., the staff and membership of the National Federation of Catholic Youth Ministry, Inc., where women are well represented. Online: NFCYM home page, nfcym.org.

53. Gabriel Fackre, "Theology: Ephemeral, Conjunctural, and Perennial," in *Altered Landscapes* (ed. Lotz), 248. See Reinhold Niebuhr, *Moral Man and Immoral Society* (New York: Scribners, 1932).

54. Fackre, "Theology," 255. See Paul Tillich, *Systematic Theology* (3 vols.; Chicago: University of Chicago Press, 1951–1963). On "secular theology," see esp. Harvey Cox, *The Secular City* (New York: Macmillan, 1965).

55. Fackre, "Theology," 254–57.

56. Gustavo Gutierrez, *A Theology of Liberation* (Maryknoll, N.Y.: Orbis, 1971).

57. Rosemary Radford Ruether, *Sexism and God-Talk: Toward a Feminist Theology* (Boston: Beacon, 1983); Renita J. Weems, *Just a Sister Away: A Womanist View of Women's Relationships in the Bible* (San Diego: Luna Media, 1988); McFague, *Models of God*. See generally Donald Musser and Joseph Price, eds., *The New Handbook of Christian Theology* (Nashville: Abingdon, 1992); and Keller and Ruether, eds., *In Our Own Voices*, which collects countless examples.

58. Fackre, "Theology," 247, 266.

59. Ahlstrom, *A Religious History,* 965–1097.

NOTES TO CHAPTER 8

1. Joe Austin and Michael Nevin Willard, "Introduction: *Angels of History, Demons of Culture,"* in *Generations of Youth* (ed. Austin and Willard), 9, 7.

2. See Bodnar, *Remaking America*, esp. ch. 8, 206–44.

3. The percentage of high school seniors who report weekly religious attendance has declined from 41 percent in 1976 to 32 percent in 1995. Eighth-graders are more likely to attend weekly, at 42 percent in 1995. Roughly 30 percent of all youth, grades eight to twelve, report that religion plays "a very important role" in their lives. See "Religious Attendance and Religiosity," in U.S. Department of Health and Human Services, *Trends in the Well-Being*, SD 1.3, 1; online: aspe.os.dhhs.gov/hsp/97trends.

4. Robert Coles and Geoffrey Stokes, *Sex and the American Teenager* (New York: Harper & Row, 1985), 5, as cited by Palladino, *Teenagers,* 251.

5. Robert Coles, "Adolescence," *Sojourners* 17 (April 1998): 17–19.

6. David Leavett, "The New Lost Generation," *Esquire,* as cited by Neil Howe and Bill Strauss, *13th Gen: Abort, Retry, Ignore, Fail?* (New York: Vintage, 1993), 128.

7. See Arnold van Gennep, *Rites of Passage* (Chicago: University of Chicago Press, 1961); Turner, *The Ritual Process;* and Louise Carus Mahdi, Nancy Geyer Christopher, and Michael Meade, eds., *Crossroads: The Quest for Contemporary Rites of Passage* (Chicago: Open Court, 1996).

8. "Sexually Experienced Teens," in U.S. Department of Health and Human Services, *Trends in the Well-Being,* SD 4.1, 2–3; online: aspe. os.dhhs.gov/hsp/97trends.

9. Bailey, *From Front Porch to Back Seat,* 142.

10. Ibid., 142–43.

11. See "Adolescence and Abstinence," n.p., online: Sexuality Information and Education Council of the United States (SIECUS) home page, www.siecus.org.

12. James LeFanu, "Wrong Lesson for Young Lovers, " *Human Life Review* (Fall 1995): 93–94.

13. Nancy Gibbs, "How Should We Teach Our Children about Sex?" *Time* (May 24, 1993): 60–66.

14. Jill Smolowe, "Sex with a Scorecard," *Time* (April 5, 1993): 41.

15. Pipher, *Reviving Ophelia,* 70.

16. Ibid., 207.

17. See pp. 28–29 above, and pp. 163–65 below.

18. See *Youthworker: The Contemporary Journal for Youth Ministry* 11 (Fall 1994).

19. Much alarm has been expressed over the "epidemic" of teenage pregnancy. In fact, adult and teen birth rates have shown identical trends over the past fifty years. See Males, *The Scapegoat Generation.*

20. "High School Senior Survey," in *The Encyclopedia of Drugs and Alcohol* (3 vols; ed. Jerome H. Jaffee; New York: Macmillan, 1995), 2:548–58.

21. Another survey, however, reported that among younger children, in grades eight and ten, marijuana use climbed significantly between 1992 and 1996. See "Drug Use among Youth," in U.S. Department of Health and Human Services, *Trends in the Well-Being,* SD3.5, 2; online: aspe. os.dhhs.gov/hsp/97trends.

22. "High School Senior Survey."

23. "Binge Drinking among Youth," in U.S. Department of Health and Human Services, *Trends in the Well-Being*, SD 3.3, 1; online: aspe.os .dhhs.gov/hsp/97trends.

24. Roy W. Pickens and Dace S. Svikis, "Vulnerability as Cause of Substance Abuse: An Overview," in *Encyclopedia of Drugs and Alcohol* (ed. Jaffee), 3:1246–52.

25. Marvin Zuckerman, "Vulnerability as Cause of Substance Abuse: Sensation-Seeking," ibid., 3:1260–61.

26. Turner, *The Ritual Process.*

27. Terry Williams, *Crackhouse: Notes from the End of the Line* (Reading, Mass.: Addison-Wesley, 1992), 41.

28. Ibid., 25.

29. Miriam Dror and Flynn Johnson, "Higher Education and Rites of Passage in America," in *Crossroads* (ed. Mahdi, Christopher, and Meade), 402–3.

30. See, e.g., Peter D. Arnott, *An Introduction to the Greek Theatre* (Bloomington: Indiana University Press, 1963); and Oscar G. Brockett, ed., *History of the Theatre* (3d ed.; Boston: Allyn & Bacon, 1977).

31. See Murdock, "The Re-enchantment of the World," and Schultze, *Dancing in the Dark.*

32. See David M. Considine, *The Cinema of Adolescence* (Jefferson, N.C.: McFarland, 1985); and Margaret R. Miles, *Seeing and Believing: Religion and Values in the Movies* (Boston: Beacon, 1996).

33. Roger Ebert, review of *Friday the 13th, Part II,* n.p., *Cinemania '95* (Microsoft CD-ROM, 1995).

34. It is a widely publicized fact that Generation X or the "13th Gen" is the first to face an economic future less prosperous than their parents. See Ryan Moore, "'And Tomorrow Is Just Another Crazy Scam': Postmodernity, Youth, and the Downward Mobility of the Middle Class," in *Generations of Youth* (ed. Austin and Willard), 253–71.

35. Vera Dika, *Games of Terror: Halloween, Friday the 13th, and the Films of the Stalker Cycle* (Rutherford, N.J.: Fairleigh Dickinson, 1990).

36. Rap music is particularly illustrative here. See Robert Walser, "Clamor and Community in the Music of Public Enemy," in *Generations of Youth* (ed. Austin and Willard), 293–310; and George Lipsitz, "The Hip Hop Hearings: Censorship, Social Memory, and Intergenerational Tensions among African Americans," ibid., 395–411.

37. Ans Joachim van der Bent, "Youth in the World Council of Churches," in *Youth without a Future?* (ed. Coleman and Baum), 98.

38. Ibid., 99–101.

39. Philip A. Potter, "Youth and the Ecumenical Movement," *Youth Newsletter* 7 (September 1983): 5, as cited by van der Bent, "Youth in the World Council of Churches," 104.

40. Zotti, *A Time of Awakening,* 163.

41. On black Lutherans, e.g., see Jeff G. Johnson, *Black Christians: The Untold Lutheran Story* (St. Louis: Concordia, 1991). More broadly, see Judith Weisenfeld and Richard Newman, eds., *This Far by Faith: Readings in African-American Women's Religious Biography* (New York: Routledge, 1996).

42. "Youth in God's World," in *Workbook for Assembly Committees* (Geneva: Youth Department, World Council of Churches, 1968), published for the assembly at Uppsala, Sweden, 4–19 July 1968, and as cited by van der Bent, "Youth in the World Council of Churches," 100.

43. Van der Bent, "Youth in the World Council of Churches," 105. See also Ans Joachim van der Bent, *From Generation to Generation: The Story of Youth in the World Council of Churches* (Geneva: World Council of Churches, 1986).

44. See online: Peace Corps home page, www.peacecorps.gov; and Americorps home page, www.americorps.org.

45. See online: Lutheran Volunteer Corps home page, www. lvchome .org; Jesuit Volunteer Corps home page, www. JesuitVolunteers.org;

Habitat for Humanity home page, www.habitat.org; and World Vision home page, www.worldvision.org.

46. See, e.g., a study of how this process occurred in the YWCA, Raymond A. Mohl, "Cultural Pluralism in Immigrant Education: The YWCA's International Institutes, 1910–1940," in *Men and Women Adrift* (ed. Mjagkij and Spratt), 111–37; and the more tangential, but congruent, study by Clifford Putney, "From Character to Body Building: The YMCA and the Suburban Metropolis, 1950–1980," ibid., 231–49.

47. See the poignant and personal memoir of James Carroll, *An American Requiem* (Boston: Houghton-Mifflin, 1996); and, more broadly, Unger, *The Movement.*

48. See Warner, "Work in Progress"; Jon Butler, *Awash in a Sea of Faith: Christianizing the American People* (New Haven, Conn.: Yale University Press, 1993); and Hatch, *The Democratization of American Christianity.*

49. Online: Valparaiso University home page, www.valpo.edu; Loyola University of Chicago home page, www.luc.edu; University of Notre Dame home page, www3.nd.edu; Wheaton College home page, www .wheaton.edu; Calvin College home page, www. calvin.edu; Spelman College home page, www.spelman.edu; Morehouse College home page, www.morehouse.edu.

50. See, among many others, Ernest L. Boyer, *College: The Undergraduate Experience in America* (New York: Harper & Row, 1987).

51. Beth L. Bailey, "From Panty Raids to Revolution: Youth and Authority, 1950–1970," in *Generations of Youth* (ed. Austin and Willard), 199.

52. See Kenneth Keniston, *Young Radicals: Notes on Committed Youth* (New York: Harcourt, Brace & World, 1968).

53. Dror and Johnson, "Higher Education and Rites of Passage," 403–4.

54. Campolo, *The Church and the American Teenager,* 85–86.

55. *Youthworker Update* 8 (September 1993): 3.

56. See Dean and Foster, *The Godbearing Life,* who explicitly encourage an incarnational approach to youth ministry.

57. On this central theme in contemporary, and especially feminist, theology, see Grace Jantzen, *God's World, God's Body* (Philadelphia: Westminster, 1984); Lora Gross, "The Embodied Church," in *Women Ministers* (ed. Judith L. Weidman; San Francisco: Harper & Row, 1981), 135–58, and James B. Nelson, *Embodiment: An Approach to Sexuality and Christian Theology* (Minneapolis: Augsburg, 1978), among many others.

58. See the diatribe by Robert J. Higgs, *God in the Stadium: Sports and Religion in America* (Lexington: University of Kentucky Press, 1995), for a blast at the "heresy" of "sportianity" in America. Higgs pays little attention to the experience of athletes themselves. For an insider's view on the interface between religion and sports, see Phil Jackson, *Sacred Hoops: Spiritual Lessons of a Hardwood Warrior* (New York: Hyperion, 1995); and the youth

organization known as the Fellowship of Christian Athletes, founded in 1954. Online: FCA home page, www.fca.org.

59. The pope's CD, *Abba Pater,* can be sampled online: www.abbapater .com.

60. Dave Urbanski, "Music in Ministry," *Youthworker* (March/April 1997): 1.

61. Catherine Albanese, *Nature Religion in America: From the Algonkian Indians to the New Age* (Chicago: University of Chicago Press, 1990).

62. Shelley, "The Rise of Evangelical Youth Movements," 55.

63. Vincent Harding, *Hope and History: Why We Must Share the Story of the Movement* (Maryknoll, N.Y.: Orbis, 1990).

64. Vincent Harding, "Wrestling toward the Dawn: The Afro-American Freedom Movement and the Changing Constitution," in *Native American Religion,* vol. 9 of *Modern American Protestantism* (ed. Marty), 268–69.

NOTES TO EPILOGUE

1. David Bakan, "Adolescence in America: From Idea to Social Fact," in *Studies in Adolescence* (ed. Robert E. Grinder; New York: Macmillan, 1975), 4.

2. Douglas, *Purity and Danger,* 15.

3. Ibid., 193.

4. Ibid.

5. David Tracy, *Blessed Rage for Order: The New Pluralism in Theology* (New York: Seabury, 1978).

6. See Dean and Foster, *The Godbearing Life,* for more detailed suggestions of how this approach will change youth ministry in the new millennium.

7. This is the inevitable conclusion after reading Graff, *Conflicting Paths.* Graff's wonderfully researched history is linked by only the thinnest interpretive structure; it borders upon an annotated bibliography. His last chapter, covering the period of this book, appropriately ends with a question mark: "The Disappearance of Childhood in Our Own Time?"

8. See p. 151 above, and Turner, *The Ritual Process.*

9. This is the central point of Mahedy and Bernardi, *A Generation Alone.*

10. The example, in the Church of Jesus Christ–Latter Day Saints, of a two-year "voluntary but normative" mission experience for youth is worth close study.

11. See Bass, ed., *Practicing Our Faith,* for twelve of them.

12. See esp. Peter C. Scales and Nancy Leffert, *Developmental Assets: A Synthesis of the Scientific Research on Adolescent Development* (Minneapolis: Search Institute, 1999); and online: Search Institute home page, www .search-institute.org.

13. Eugene C. Roehlkepartain and Peter L. Benson, *Youth in Protestant Churches* (Minneapolis: Search Institute, 1993), 14.

14. For Catholic and mainline adolescents, the rite of Confirmation is crucial here. See, among many other attempts to infuse this rite with new meaning, William O. Roberts Jr., "Christianity's Lost Rite: Initiation to Adulthood," *Christian Ministry* 14 (May 1983): 24–28, who offers another adaptation of Turner's categories to the Christian message; Richard Robert Osmer, "Restructuring Confirmation," *ThTo* (April 1992): 46–67; and Myers, ed., *Becoming and Belonging*. The Roman Catholic Rite of Christian Initiation for Adults (RCIA) is a challenging and formative practice, recently designed and refined. See *Catechism of the Catholic Church* (New York: Doubleday, 1994). Churches without a specific rite of Confirmation may baptize adolescents, and this rite of passage can be a meaningful one for many youth. Given the routinized character of most of these rites, however, experimentation with novel forms is in order.

15. Roehlkepartain and Benson, *Youth in Protestant Churches,* 15.

16. We do this routinely at the congregation where I serve as youth minister, First Christian Church/Disciples of Christ in Valparaiso. For instance, a high-school junior, Heather Hahn, currently serves as a very capable chair of the World Outreach Committee.

17. See, on this possibility, the engaging work by Harvard's Diana L. Eck (whose adolescent experience included participation in youth ministry), *Encountering God: A Spiritual Journey from Bozeman to Banares* (Boston: Beacon, 1993).

18. René Girard, *Violence and the Sacred; The Scapegoat* (trans. Yvonne Freccero; Baltimore: Johns Hopkins University Press, 1986); *Things Hidden since the Foundation of the World* (trans. Stephen Bann and Michael Metteer; Stanford, Cal.: Stanford University Press, 1987).

19. Males, *Scapegoat Generation.*

20. See the "Columbine High School Memorial Proclamation," created by the Fellowship of Christian Athletes in the wake of the Littleton tragedy. The proclamation "denounces violence, racism, hatred and persecution of all kinds, and commits Christian student-athletes to treat fellow students with dignity and respect." See online: Fellowship of Christian Athletes home page, www.gospelcom.net/fca/proclamation1.shtml.

21. See Pope John Paul II, "Nothing Is Resolved by Violence" (address to European parliamentarians, March 29, 1999), n.p., online: www.cin.org/pope.html.

Select Bibliography of Secondary Works Cited and Home Pages

PRIMARY SOURCES ARE CITED IN THE NOTES

PUBLICATIONS

Abell, Aaron I. *American Catholicism and Social Action: A Search for Social Justice, 1865–1950*. South Bend, Ind.: University of Notre Dame Press, 1963.

Ahlstrom, Sidney E. *A Religious History of the American People*. New Haven, Conn.: Yale University Press, 1974.

Albers, James W. *From Centennial to Golden Anniversary: The History of Valparaiso University from 1959–1975*. Valparaiso, Ind.: Valparaiso University Press, 1976.

Appleby, R. Scott. "Present to the People of God: The Transformation of the Roman Catholic Parish Priesthood," 1–108. In *Transforming Parish Ministry: The Changing Roles of Catholic Clergy, Laity, and Women in Religion*. Ed. Jay P. Dolan et al. New York: Crossroad, 1990.

Austin, Joe, and Michael Nevin Willard, eds. *Generations of Youth: Youth Cultures and History in Twentieth-Century America*. New York: New York University Press, 1998.

Bailey, Beth L. *From Front Porch to Back Seat: Courtship in Twentieth-Century America*. Baltimore: Johns Hopkins University Press, 1988.

Balmer, Randall. *Mine Eyes Have Seen the Glory: A Journey into the Evangelical Subculture in America.* New York: Oxford University Press, 1993.

Bass, Dorothy C. "Revolutions Quiet and Otherwise: Protestants and Higher Education during the 1960s." Pages 207–26 in *Caring for the Commonweal: Education for Religious and Public Life,* ed. Parker J. Palmer, Barbara G. Wheeler, and James W. Fowler. Macon, Ga.: Mercer University Press, 1990.

————., ed. *Practicing Our Faith: A Way of Life for a Searching People.* San Francisco: Jossey-Bass, 1997.

Bedoyere, Michael De La. *The Cardijn Story.* New York: Longmans, Green, 1958.

Bellah, Robert Neelly, et al. *Habits of the Heart: Individualism and Commitment in American Life.* New York: Harper & Row, 1985.

Bendroth, Margaret. *Fundamentalism and Gender: 1875 to the Present.* New Haven, Conn.: Yale University Press, 1993.

Benson, Peter L. *The Troubled Journey: A Portrait of 6th–12th Grade Youth.* Minneapolis: Search Institute, 1993.

Berger, Kathleen Stassen, and Ross A. Thompson. *The Developing Person: Through Childhood and Adolescence.* 4th ed. Dallas: Worth, 1996.

Blumhofer, Edith W. *Twentieth-Century Evangelicalism: A Guide to the Sources.* New York: Garland, 1990.

Bodnar, John. *Remaking America: Public Memory, Commemoration, and Patriotism in the Twentieth Century.* Princeton, N.J.: Princeton University Press, 1992.

Borg, Marcus. *Meeting Jesus Again for the First Time.* San Francisco: HarperSanFrancisco, 1994.

Borgman, Dean. "A History of American Youth Ministry," 61–74. In *The Complete Book of Youth Ministry.* Ed. Warren S. Benson and Mark H. Senter III. Chicago: Moody, 1987.

Boyer, Ernest L. *College: The Undergraduate Experience in America.* New York: Harper & Row, 1987.

Boyer, Paul E. *By the Bomb's Early Light: American Thought and Culture at the Dawn of the Atomic Age.* New York: Pantheon, 1985.

Branch, Taylor. *Parting the Waters: America in the King Years, 1954–1963.* New York: Simon & Schuster, 1988.

Brauer, Jerald C., ed. *The Lively Experiment Continued: Essays in Honor of Sydney E. Mead.* Macon, Ga.: Mercer University Press, 1987.

Brereton, Virginia. *Training God's Army: The American Bible School, 1880–1940.* Bloomington: Indiana University Press, 1990.

Brewer, Annie M., ed. *Youth-Serving Organizations Directory.* Detroit: Gale, 1980.

Broderick, Francis L. *Right Reverend New Dealer: John A. Ryan.* New York: Macmillan, 1963.

Brown, Robert McAfee. *Religion and Violence.* Philadelphia: Westminster, 1987.

Bryk, Anthony S., Valerie E. Lee, and Peter B. Holland. *Catholic Schools and the Common Good.* Cambridge: Harvard University Press, 1993.

Butler, Jon. *Awash in a Sea of Faith: Christianizing the American People.* New Haven, Conn.: Yale University Press, 1993.

Callahan, Daniel. *The Mind of the Catholic Layman.* New York: Scribners, 1963.

Campbell, Debra. "Reformers and Activists." Pages 1542–81 in *American Catholic Women: A Historical Exploration.* Ed. Karen Kennelly, C.S.J. New York: Macmillan, 1989.

Campolo, Tony. *The Church and the American Teenager: What Works and What Doesn't Work in Youth Ministry.* Grand Rapids, Mich.: Zondervan, 1989.

Cardijn, Joseph. *Challenge to Action: Addresses of Monsignor Joseph Cardijn.* Ed. Eugene Langdale. Chicago: Fides, 1955.

———. *Laymen into Action.* Trans. Anne Heggie. London: Geoffrey Chapman, 1964.

Carey, Patrick. "Lay Catholic Leadership in the United States." *U.S. Catholic Historian* 9 (Summer 1990): 223–47.

Carpenter, Joel A. "Geared to the Times, but Anchored to the Rock: How Contemporary Techniques and Exuberant Nationalism Helped Create an Evangelical Resurgence." *Christianity Today* 30 (November 8, 1985): 44–47.

———. "Youth for Christ and the New Evangelicals." Pages 128–51 in *Religion and the Life of the Nation: American Recoveries.* Ed. Rowland A. Sherrill. Urbana: University of Illinois Press, 1990.

———., ed. *Sacrificial Lives: Young Martyrs and Fundamentalist Idealism.* New York: Garland, 1988.

Chafe, William H. *America since 1945.* New American History Series. Washington, D.C.: American Historical Association, 1990.

Chafe, William H., and Harvard Sitkoff. *A History of Our Time: Readings on Postwar America.* 3d ed. New York: Oxford University Press, 1991.

Clark, Chap. *The Youth Specialties Handbook for Great Camps and Retreats.* El Cajon, Cal.: Youth Specialties, 1990.

Coleman, John, and Gregory Baum, eds. *Youth without a Future?* Concilium 181. Edinburgh: T. & T. Clark, 1985.

Coles, Robert. *Dorothy Day: A Radical Devotion.* Reading, Mass.: Addison-Wesley, 1987.

Coles, Robert, and Geoffrey Stokes. *Sex and the American Teenager.* New York: Harper & Row, 1985.

Cone, James H. *Black Theology and Black Power.* New York: Seabury, 1969.

————. *A Black Theology of Liberation: Twentieth Anniversary Edition.* Maryknoll, N.Y.: Orbis, 1990.

————. *God of the Oppressed.* New York: Seabury, 1976.

————. *The Spirituals and the Blues: An Interpretation.* San Francisco: Harper & Row, 1972.

Congar, Yves. *Lay People in the Church: A Study for a Theology of the Laity.* Trans. Donald Attwater. Westminster, Md.: Newman, 1957.

Considine, David M. *The Cinema of Adolescence.* Jefferson, N.C.: McFarland, 1985.

Cross, Whitney R. *The Burned-Over District.* Ithaca, N.Y.: Cornell University Press, 1950.

Davis, Florence Henderson. "Lay Movements in New York City." *U.S. Catholic Historian* 9 (Fall 1990): 408–18.

Davis, Gerald L. *"I Got the Word in Me and I Can Sing It, You Know": A Study of the Performed African-American Sermon.* Philadelphia: University of Pennsylvania Press, 1985.

Dayton, Donald W. *Discovering an Evangelical Heritage.* Grand Rapids, Mich.: Eerdmans, 1976.

Dayton, Donald W., and Robert K. Johnston, eds. *The Variety of American Evangelicalism.* Knoxville: University of Tennessee Press, 1991.

Dean, Kenda Creasy, and Ron Foster. *The Godbearing Life: The Art of Soul Tending for Youth Ministry.* Nashville: Upper Room, 1998.

DeBerg, Betty. *Ungodly Women: Gender and the First Wave of American Fundamentalism.* Minneapolis: Fortress, 1990.

Dolan, Jay. *The American Catholic Experience: A History from Colonial Times to the Present.* Garden City, N.Y.: Doubleday, 1985.

Douglas, Mary. *Purity and Danger: An Analysis of Concepts of Pollution and Taboo.* New York: Penguin, 1966.

Ellwood, Robert S. *The Fifties Spiritual Marketplace: American Religion in a Decade of Conflict.* New Brunswick, N.J.: Rutgers University Press, 1997.

Engelhardt, Tom. *The End of Victory Culture: Cold War America and the Disillusioning of a Generation.* Amherst: University of Massachusetts Press, 1995.

Erickson, Judith B. *Directory of American Youth Organizations.* Boys Town, Neb.: Boys' Home, 1983

Evans, John Witney. *The Newman Movement: Roman Catholics in American Higher Education, 1883–1971.* South Bend, Ind.: University of Notre Dame Press, 1980.

Fairclough, Adam. "The Southern Christian Leadership Conference and the Second Reconstruction, 1957–1973." Pages 188–205 in *Native American Religion and Black Protestantism.* Vol. 9 of *Modern American Protestantism and Its World.* Ed. Martin E. Marty. Munich: K. G. Sauer, 1993.

Fey, Harold E., ed. *A History of the Ecumenical Movement.* 2d ed. Geneva: World Council of Churches, 1986.

Fitts, Leroy. *A History of Black Baptists.* Nashville: Broadman, 1985.

Frazier, E. Franklin. *The Negro Church in America.* New York: Schocken, 1963.

Freedman, Samuel G. *Upon This Rock: The Miracles of a Black Church.* New York: HarperCollins, 1993.

Frerichs, Ernest S., ed. *The Bible and Bibles in America.* Atlanta: Scholars Press, 1988.

Fullam, Raymond B., S.J., ed. *The Popes on Youth: Principles for Forming and Guiding Youth from Popes Leo XIII to Pius XII.* New York: McKay, 1958.

Fuller, Millard. *The Theology of the Hammer.* Macon, Ga.: Smyth & Helwys, 1994.

Gallup, George. *Scared: Growing Up in America.* Princeton, N.J.: Gallup Organization, 1995.

Gardella, Peter. *Domestic Religion: Work, Food, Sex, and Other Commitments.* Cleveland: Pilgrim, 1998.

Garrow, David J. *Bearing the Cross: Martin Luther King, Jr., and the Southern Christian Leadership Conference.* New York: Vintage, 1986.

Gennep, Arnold van. *Rites of Passage.* Chicago: University of Chicago Press, 1961.

Genovese, Eugene D. *Roll, Jordan, Roll: The World the Slaves Made.* New York: Vintage, 1976.

Gettleman, Marvin E., et al., eds. *Vietnam and America: A Documented History.* New York: Grove Weidenfeld, 1985.

Ghezzi, Bert, ed. *Keeping Your Kids Catholic: It May Seem Impossible but It Can Be Done.* Ann Arbor, Mich.: Servant, 1989.

Gillespie, Franklin B. "Youth Programs of the United Presbyterian Church: An Historical Overview." *Journal of Presbyterian History* 59 (Fall 1981): 309–82.

Girard, René. *The Scapegoat.* Trans. Yvonne Freccero. Baltimore: Johns Hopkins University Press, 1986.

———. *Things Hidden since the Foundation of the World.* Trans. Stephen Bann and Michael Metteer. Stanford, Cal.: Stanford University Press, 1987.

———. *Violence and the Sacred.* Trans. Patrick Gregory. Baltimore: Johns Hopkins University Press, 1977.

Gitlin, Todd. *The Sixties: Years of Hope, Days of Rage.* New York: Bantam, 1987.

Graff, Harvey J. *Conflicting Paths: Growing Up in America.* Cambridge: Harvard University Press, 1995.

Greeley, Andrew M. "The Catholics in the World and in America," 93–110. In *World Religions in America: An Introduction.* Ed. Jacob Neusner. Louisville: Westminster John Knox, 1994.

Gregg, Howard D. *History of the African Methodist Episcopal Church.* Nashville: AMEC, 1980.

Hammond, Philip E. *Religion and Personal Autonomy: The Third Disestablishment in America.* Columbia: University of South Carolina Press, 1992.

Handy, Robert. *A Christian America: Protestant Hopes and Historical Realities.* New York: Oxford University Press, 1971.

Harding, Vincent. *Hope and History: Why We Must Share the Story of the Movement.* Maryknoll, N.Y.: Orbis, 1990.

Harris, Maria. *Portrait of Youth Ministry.* New York: Paulist, 1981.

Harris, Michael W. *The Rise of Gospel Blues: The Music of Andrew Dorsey in the Urban Church.* New York: Oxford University Press, 1992.

Harvey, Van A. *The Historian and the Believer: The Morality of Historical Knowledge and Christian Belief.* New York: Macmillan, 1966.

Hatch, Nathan O. *The Democratization of American Christianity.* New Haven, Conn.: Yale University Press, 1989.

Hawley, John Stratton, ed. *Fundamentalism and Gender.* New York: Oxford University Press, 1994.

Heimert, Alan. *Religion and the American Mind: From the Great Awakening to the Revolution.* Cambridge: Harvard University Press, 1966.

Hofstadter, Richard. "The Paranoid Style in American Politics," 3–40. In *The Paranoid Style in American Politics and Other Essays.* New York: Knopf, 1965.

Hollingshead, August de B. *Elmtown's Youth: The Impact of Social Class on Adolescents*. New York: Wiley, 1949.

Hunter, James Davison. *Culture Wars: The Struggle to Define America*. New York: HarperCollins, 1991.

———. *Evangelicalism: The Coming Generation*. Chicago: University of Chicago Press, 1987.

Hutchison, William R. *The Modernist Impulse in American Protestantism*. New York: Oxford University Press, 1976.

Indiana University Center for Adolescence Studies. *Adolescence Directory On-Line*. http://education.indiana.edu/cas/adol/adol.html.

Jones, Donald G., and Russell E. Richey. *American Civil Religion*. New York: Harper & Row, 1974.

Kaufmann, Christopher J. *Faith and Fraternalism: The History of the Knights of Columbus*. Rev. ed. New York: Simon & Schuster, 1992.

Kett, Joseph. *Rites of Passage: Adolescence in America, 1790 to the Present*. New York: Basic Books, 1977.

"Labor and Lay Movements: Part One." *U.S. Catholic Historian* 9 (Summer 1990): 223–333.

"Labor and Lay Movements: Part Two." *U.S. Catholic Historian* 9 (Fall 1990): 335–467.

Lasch, Christopher. *The Culture of Narcissism: American Life in an Age of Diminishing Expectations*. New York: Norton, 1978.

Leuchtenberg, William E. *The FDR Years: On Roosevelt and His Legacy*. New York: Columbia University Press, 1995.

Levi, Giovanni, and Jean-Claude Schmitt, eds. *A History of Young People in the West*. Vol. 1, *Ancient and Medieval Rites of Passage*; trans. Camille Naish. Vol. 2, *Stormy Evolution to Modern Times*; trans. Canol Volk. Cambridge: Harvard University Press, 1997.

Levine, Lawrence W. *Black Culture and Black Consciousness: Afro-American Folk Thought from Slavery to Freedom*. New York: Oxford University Press, 1977.

Lewis, David L., and Laurence Goldstein, eds. *The Automobile and American Culture*. Ann Arbor, Mich.: University of Michigan Press, 1983.

Lienesch, Michael. *Redeeming America: Piety and Politics in the New Christian Right*. Chapel Hill: University of North Carolina Press, 1993.

Lincoln, C. Eric, and Lawrence H. Mamiya. *The Black Church in the African American Experience*. Durham, N.C.: Duke University Press, 1990.

Lindley, Susan Hill. *"You Have Stept out of Your Place"*: *A History of Women and Religion in America.* Louisville: Westminster John Knox, 1996.

Loveland, Anne C. *American Evangelicals and the U.S. Military, 1942–1993.* Baton Rouge: Louisiana State University Press, 1996.

Loy, David R. "The Religion of the Market." *Journal of the American Academy of Religion* 65 (Winter 1996): 275–90.

MacHaffie, Barbara. *Herstory: Women in Christian Tradition.* Philadelphia: Fortress, 1986.

MacPherson, Myra. *Long Time Passing: Vietnam and the Haunted Generation.* New York: Doubleday, 1984.

Mahdi, Louise Carus, Nancy Geyer Christopher, and Michael Meade, eds. *Crossroads: The Quest for Contemporary Rites of Passage.* Chicago: Open Court, 1996.

Mahedy, William, and Janet Bernardi. *A Generation Alone: Xers Making a Place in the World.* Downers Grove, Ill.: InterVarsity Press, 1994.

Males, Mike R. *The Scapegoat Generation: America's War on Adolescents.* Monroe, Me.: Common Courage, 1996.

Mamiya, Lawrence H. "A Social History of the Bethel African Methodist Episcopal Church in Baltimore: The House of God and the Struggle for Freedom," 221–292. In *Portraits of Twelve Religious Communities,* vol. 1 of *American Congregations.* 2 vols. Ed. James P. Wind and James W. Lewis. Chicago: University of Chicago Press, 1994.

Marsden, George. *Fundamentalism and American Culture: The Shaping of Twentieth-Century Evangelicalism, 1870–1925.* New York: Oxford University Press, 1980.

Marty, Martin E. *Modern American Religion.* 3 vols. Chicago: University of Chicago Press, 1986–1996.

————. "Religion: A Private Affair, in Public Affairs." *Religion and American Culture* 3 (Summer 1993): 111–26.

May, Elaine Tyler. "Cold War: Warm Hearth, Politics, and the Family in Postwar America," 153–84. In *The Rise and Fall of the New Deal Order, 1930–1980.* Ed. Steve Fraser and Gary Gerstle. Princeton, N.J.: Princeton University Press, 1989.

McAuley, E. Nancy, and Moira Mathieson. *Faith without Form: Beliefs of Catholic Youth.* Kansas City, Mo.: Sheed & Ward, 1986.

McCall, Nathan. *Makes Me Wanna Holler: A Young Black Man in America.* New York: Random House, 1994.

McElroy, Robert W. *The Search for an American Public Theology: The Contribution of John Courtney Murray.* New York: Paulist, 1989.

McLaughlin, Milbrey W., Merita A. Irby, and Julie Langman. *Urban Sanctuaries: Neighborhood Organizations in the Lives and Futures of Inner-City Youth.* San Francisco: Jossey-Bass, 1994.

McLoughlin, William G. *Revivals, Awakenings, and Reform: An Essay on Religion and Social Change in America, 1607 to 1977.* Chicago History of American Religion. Chicago: University of Chicago Press, 1978.

McNamara, Patrick. "Catholic Youth in the Modern Church." Pages 57–65 in *Religion and the Social Order: Vatican II and U.S. Catholicism.* Ed. Helen Rose Ebaugh. Greenwich, Conn.: JAI, 1991.

Mead, Sidney E. *The Lively Experiment: The Shaping of Christianity in America.* New York: Harper & Row, 1963.

Miller, William D. *Dorothy Day: A Biography.* San Francisco: Harper & Row, 1982.

Mirel, Jeffrey E. "Twentieth-Century America, Adolescence in." Pages 1153–67 in vol. 2 of *The Encyclopedia of Adolescence.* 2 vols. Ed. Richard M. Lerner, Anne C. Petersen, and Jeanne Brooks-Gunn. New York: Garland, 1991.

Mjagkij, Nina, and Margaret Spratt, eds. *Men and Women Adrift: The YMCA and YWCA in the City.* New York: New York University Press, 1997.

Modell, John. *Into One's Own: From Youth to Adulthood in the United States, 1920–1975.* Berkeley: University of California Press, 1989.

Moore, R. Laurence. *Selling God: American Religion in the Market-place of Culture.* New York: Oxford University Press, 1994.

Morris, Aldon D. *The Origins of the Civil Rights Movement: Black Communities Organizing for Change.* New York: Free Press, 1984.

Murdock, Graham. "The Re-enchantment of the World: Religion and the Transformations of Modernity." Pages 85–101 in *Rethinking Media, Religion, and Culture.* Ed. Stewart M. Hoover and Knut Lundby. Thousand Oaks, Cal.: Sage, 1997.

Murray, John Courtney. *We Hold These Truths: Reflections on the American Proposition.* New York: Sheed & Ward, 1960.

Myers, William R. *Black and White Styles of Youth Ministry: Two Congregations in America.* New York: Pilgrim, 1991.

———. "Youth between Culture and Church." *Theology Today* 47 (January 1991): 400–409.

————., ed., *Becoming and Belonging: A Practical Design for Confirmation.* Cleveland: United Church, 1993.

National Council for Research on Women. *The Girls Report: What We Know and Need to Know about Growing Up Female.* Washington, D.C.: National Council for Research on Women, 1998.

Nelson, E. Clifford, et al., eds. *The Lutherans in North America.* Philadelphia: Fortress, 1980.

Ng, David. "Rethinking Youth Ministry," 85–98. In *Rethinking Christian Education: Explorations in Theory and Practice.* Ed. David S. Sculler. St. Louis: Chalice, 1993.

Nichol, Todd W. *All These Lutherans: Three Paths toward a New Lutheran Church.* Minneapolis: Augsburg, 1986.

Noll, Mark A. *Between Faith and Criticism: Evangelicals, Scholarship, and the Bible in America.* San Francisco: Harper & Row, 1986.

————. *The Scandal of the Evangelical Mind.* Grand Rapids, Mich.: Eerdmans, 1995.

O'Neill, William L. *Coming Apart: An Informal History of America in the 1960s.* Chicago: Quadrangle, 1971.

Pahl, Jon. *Hopes and Dreams of All: The International Walther League and Lutheran Youth in American Culture, 1893–1993.* Chicago: Wheat Ridge Ministries, 1993.

Palladino, Grace. *Teenagers: An American History.* New York: Basic Books, 1996.

Paris, Peter. *The Social Teaching of the Black Churches.* Philadelphia: Fortress, 1985.

Piehl, Mel. *Breaking Bread: Dorothy Day and the Catholic Worker Movement.* Philadelphia: Temple University Press, 1982.

Pipher, Mary. *Reviving Ophelia: Saving the Selves of Adolescent Girls.* New York: Putnam, 1994.

Placher, William C. *The Domestication of Transcendence: How Modern Thinking about God Went Wrong.* Louisville: Westminster John Knox, 1996.

————. *A History of Christian Theology: An Introduction.* Philadelphia: Westminster, 1983.

Potvin, Raymond H., Dean R. Hoge, and Hart M. Nelsen. *Religion and American Youth: With Emphasis on Catholic Adolescents and Young Adults.* Washington, D.C.: U.S. Catholic Conference, 1976.

Raboteau, Albert J. "The Black Church: Continuity within Change." Pages 77–91 in *Altered Landscapes: Christianity in America, 1935–1985.* Ed. David W. Lotz. Grand Rapids, Mich.: Eerdmans, 1989.

————. *Slave Religion: The "Invisible Institution" in the Antebellum South.* New York: Oxford University Press, 1978.

Reed, Ralph. *Active Faith: How Christians Are Changing the Soul of American Politics.* New York: Free Press, 1996.

Roehlkepartain, Eugene C., and Peter L. Benson. *Youth in Protestant Churches.* Minneapolis: Search Institute, 1993.

Roof, Wade Clark. *A Generation of Seekers: The Spiritual Journeys of the Baby Boom Generation.* San Francisco: Harper & Row, 1993.

Roof, Wade Clark, and William McKinney. *American Mainline Religion: Its Changing Shape and Future.* New Brunswick, N.J.: Rutgers University Press, 1987.

Rouse, Ruth, and Stephen Charles Neill, eds. *A History of the Ecumenical Movement.* 2d ed.; 2 vols. Philadelphia: Westminster, 1967–1970.

Salmond, J. A. *The Civilian Conservation Corps, 1933–42.* Durham, N.C.: Duke University Press, 1967.

Sandeen, Ernest R. *The Roots of Fundamentalism: British and American Millenarianism, 1800–1930.* Chicago: University of Chicago Press, 1970.

Sawyer, Kieran. *The Risk of Faith and Other Youth Ministry Activities.* South Bend, Ind.: Ave Maria, 1988.

Scales, Peter C., et al. *The Attitudes and Needs of Religious Youth Workers: Perspectives from the Field.* Minneapolis: Search Institute, 1995.

Scales, Peter C., and Nancy Leffert. *Developmental Assets: A Synthesis of the Scientific Research on Adolescent Development.* Minneapolis: Search Institute, 1999.

Schultze, Quentin J., et al. *Dancing in the Dark: Youth, Popular Culture, and the Electronic Media.* Grand Rapids, Mich.: Eerdmans, 1991.

Schmidt, Leigh Eric. *Consumer Rites: The Buying and Selling of American Holidays.* Princeton, N.J.: Princeton University Press, 1995.

Senter, Mark H. III. *The Coming Revolution in Youth Ministry.* Wheaton, Ill.: Victor, 1992.

Shelley, Bruce. "The Rise of Evangelical Youth Movements." *Fides et Historia* 18 (1986): 47–63.

Shils, Edward. *Tradition.* Chicago: University of Chicago Press, 1981.

Simons, Janet M., Belva Finlay, and Alice Yang. *The Adolescent and Young Adult Fact Book.* Washington, D.C.: Children's Defense Fund, 1991.

Smith, J. Warren. "Youth Ministry in American Methodism's Mission." *Methodist History* 19 (June 1981): 224–30.

Smith, Theophus. *Conjuring Culture: Biblical Formations of Black America.* New York: Oxford University Press, 1994.

Smith, Timothy L. *Revivalism and Social Reform: American Protestantism on the Eve of the Civil War.* New York: Harper & Row, 1957.

Solberg, Richard W. *Lutheran Higher Education in North America.* Minneapolis: Augsburg, 1985.

Stack, Carol B. *All Our Kin: Strategies for Survival in a Black Community.* New York: Harper & Row, 1974.

Strietelmeier, John. *Valparaiso's First Century.* Valparaiso, Ind.: Valparaiso University Press, 1959.

Szasz, Ferenc Morton. *The Divided Mind of Protestant America, 1880–1930.* University, Ala.: University of Alabama Press, 1982.

Tracy, David. *Blessed Rage for Order: The New Pluralism in Theology.* New York: Seabury, 1978.

Turner, Victor. *The Ritual Process: Structure and Anti-structure.* Ithaca, N.Y.: Cornell University Press, 1969.

Unger, Irwin. *The Movement: A History of the American New Left, 1959–1972.* New York: Harper & Row, 1974.

U.S. Department of Health and Human Services. "Related Projects: Youth Serving and Youth Advocacy Organizations." No pages. Online: http://www.acf.dhhs.gov/programs/fysb/ ysyalink.htm.

———. *Trends in the Well-Being of America's Children and Youth.* Washington, D. C.: Office of the Assistant Secretary for Planning and Evaluation, Department of Health and Human Services, 1997. Online: http://aspe.os.dhhs.gov/hsp/ 97trends.

Walker, Clarence E. *The Rock in a Weary Land: The African Methodist Episcopal Church during the Civil War and Reconstruction.* Baton Rouge: Louisiana State University Press, 1982.

Walker, Wyatt Tee. *"Somebody's Calling My Name": Black Sacred Music and Social Change.* Valley Forge, Penn.: Judson, 1979.

Warner, R. Stephen. "Work in Progress toward a New Paradigm for the Sociological Study of Religion in the United States." *American Journal of Sociology* 98 (March 1993): 1044–93.

Weisenfeld, Judith, and Richard Newman, eds. *This Far by Faith: Readings in African-American Women's Religious Biography.* New York: Routledge, 1996.

Wilmore, Gayraud. *Black Religion and Black Radicalism: An Interpretation of the Religious History of Afro-American People.* 2d ed. Maryknoll, N.Y.: Orbis, 1983.

Wilson, John F. *Public Religion in American Culture.* Princeton, N.J.: Princeton University Press, 1979.

Wormser, Richard. *American Islam: Growing Up Muslim in America.* New York: Walker, 1994.

Wuthnow, Robert. *Acts of Compassion: Caring for Others and Helping Ourselves.* Princeton, N.J.: Princeton University Press, 1991.

———. *The Restructuring of American Religion: Society and Faith since World War II.* Princeton, N.J.: Princeton University Press, 1988.

———. *The Struggle for America's Soul: Evangelicals, Liberals, and Secularism.* Grand Rapids, Mich.: Eerdmans, 1989.

Zotti, Mary Irene. *A Time of Awakening: The Young Christian Worker Story in the United States, 1938 to 1970.* Chicago: Loyola University Press, 1991.

———. "The Young Christian Workers." *U.S. Catholic Historian* 9 (Summer 1990): 387–400.

HOME PAGES

American Academy of Religion: http://www.aarweb.org
Americorps: http://www.americorps.gov
Bethel African Methodist Episcopal Church: http://www.bethel1.org
Calvin College: http://www.calvin.edu
CROP WALK: http://www.churchworldservice.org
Evangelical Lutheran Church in America: http://www/elca.org
Fellowship of Christian Athletes: http://www.fca.org
Habitat for Humanity: http://www.habitat.org
Jesuit Volunteer Corps: http://www.JesuitVolunteers.org
Loyola University of Chicago: http://www.luc.edu
The Lutheran Church–Missouri Synod: http://www.lcms.org
Lutheran Volunteer Corps: http://www.lvchome.org
Morehouse College: http://www.morehouse.edu
National Association of Evangelicals: http://www.nae.net
National Conference of Catholic Bishops: http://www.nccbuscc.org
National Council of Churches of Christ: http://ncccusa.org
National Federation of Catholic Youth Ministry, Inc.: http://www.nfcym.org

Peace Corps: http://www.peacecorps.gov
Search Institute: http://www.search-institute.org
Sexuality Information and Education Council of the United States:
    http://www.siecus.org
Spelman College: http://www.spelman.edu
University of Notre Dame: http://www3.nd.edu
Valparaiso University: http://www.valpo.edu
Wheaton College: http://www.wheaton.edu
Wheat Ridge Ministries: http://www.wheatridge.org
World Council of Churches: http://wcc-coe.org
World Vision: http://www.wvi.org
Youth for Christ: http://www.gospelcom.net/yfc
Youth Specialties: http://www.gospelcom.net/ys

Subject Index